...tional Praise for
...s for Your Small Business

"Owning *201 Great Ideas for Your Small Business* is like having a team of consultants sitting in your office. This book not only educates and inspires, but the ideas will help you save time and money as well."

—Rieva Lesonsky, CEO, GrowBiz Media/SmallBizDaily.com,
Former Editorial Director *Entrepreneur* magazine

201
GREAT IDEAS

for Your

SMALL
BUSINESS

Since 1996, Bloomberg Press has published books for financial professionals, as well as books of general interest in investing, economics, current affairs, and policy affecting investors and business people. Titles are written by well-known practitioners, BLOOMBERG NEWS® reporters and columnists, and other leading authorities and journalists. Bloomberg Press books have been translated into more than 20 languages.

For a list of available titles, please visit our web site at www.wiley.com/go/bloombergpress.

201

GREAT IDEAS

for Your

SMALL

BUSINESS

Third Edition

JANE APPLEGATE

BLOOMBERG PRESS
An Imprint of
WILEY

Published by John Wiley & Sons, Inc., Hoboken, New Jersey.

Published simultaneously in Canada.

For general information on our other products and services or for technical support, please contact our Customer Care Department within the United States at (800) 762-2974, outside the United States at (317) 572-3993 or fax (317) 572-4002.

Wiley also publishes its books in a variety of electronic formats. Some content that appears in print may not be available in electronic books. For more information about Wiley products, visit our web site at www.wiley.com.

Library of Congress Cataloging-in-Publication Data:

Applegate, Jane.
    201 great ideas for your small business / Jane Applegate. — 3rd ed.
      p.   cm. — (Bloomberg series)
    Includes bibliographical references and index.
    ISBN 978-0-470-91966-8 (pbk.); 978-1-118-06769-7 (ebk); 978-1-118-086770-3 (ebk); 978-1-118-06771—0 (ebk)
    1. Small business—Management. I. Title. II. Title: Two hundred one great ideas for your small business. III. Title: Two hundred and one great ideas for your small business.
    HD62.7.A64   2011
    658.02'2—dc22

                                  2010053517

Printed in the United States of America

10 9 8 7 6 5 4 3 2 1

I DEDICATE THIS THIRD EDITION OF 201 GREAT IDEAS
to Joe, my dearest husband,
whose love and wit keep me smiling,
and to our wonderful kids, Jeanne and Evan Applegate,
who light up our lives.

Contents

· ·

Technology and Telecommunications   91

Develop and Launch New
Products and Services   115

CHAPTER

5

Marketing Strategies 141

CHAPTER

6

People   **193**

CHAPTER

7

Time and Personal Management Ideas 227

CHAPTER

8

Customer Service 243

Introduction

• •

In the absence of discontent, there is no creativity.

—*Deepak Chopra*

Why Is It a Good Time to Update *201*?

Eight years ago, when I last revised *201 Great Ideas,* many business owners were still bruised from the crazy "dot-com" era. Remember when billions of dollars were wasted on silly or copy-cat online business concepts? Luckily, we've figured out how to use the Internet to make connections and money.

I collected most of the new, great ideas for this third edition during a national speaking tour cosponsored by Bloomberg TV and local cable companies. The events, hosted by chambers of commerce, provided a wonderful opportunity for me to meet one-on-one with hundreds of business owners.

In 2008 and 2009, everyone I met was feeling pummeled by the Great Recession. Even if you had great credit, it was nearly impossible to borrow money. Millions of people were out of work and millions of homes were in foreclosure or "underwater." But, as the 2010 holiday season kicked off, the mood was definitely brighter in the small business community. We started spending money again and feeling more optimistic about the future.

Americans, especially small business owners, are extraordinarily resilient. We have the stamina, moxie, and plenty of great ideas to survive the worst of times. Despite massive national debt, two distant wars, and a trade deficit, America is still the best country to be a small business owner.

We have the biggest and strongest economy on the planet. Cash is flowing. Technology, equipment, and real estate are cheap. Amazing talent abounds. If you lost your business during the downturn, it's time to get back in the game.

This book is guaranteed to revive your entrepreneurial spirit. If this is your first venture, I promise *201 Great Ideas* will help you avoid the biggest potholes on the highway to success.

If you read an earlier edition of this book, you'll notice plenty of new ideas. Although my contract called for revising about 60 ideas, so much has changed in recent years, I updated every idea and included scores of new ones. This new edition of *201 Great Ideas* features great ideas from novice and veteran business owners. There are no theories. Every idea has been tested in a real business.

You'll meet the amazing business owners I met while traveling coast to coast, ranging from Skagway, Alaska, to Portland, Maine. In Victoria, British Columbia, I visited Smoking Lily, a boutique claiming to be the smallest small business in North America. It occupies 44 square feet of space in a cool, downtown shopping district. T-shirts and scarves hang on the wall. The young woman who rang up my purchases was perched on a platform about four feet off the ground in a corner of the closet-sized store. Crazy!

You'll meet Kesang Tashi, a wonderful Tibetan entrepreneur who has devoted his life to reviving the art and craft of rug making back in his homeland. He employs scores of craftspeople in Tibet, who now make a living by selling their handmade rugs, scarves, jewelry, and religious banners.

I met entrepreneurs who work part-time jobs to fund their dreams and people who share retail space to save money and serve similar customers.

Every year, no matter how rocky the economy is, about 500,000 Americans start a new business. We are fortunate to live in a country where you can wake up in the morning and be in business by the end of the day.

Sitting in a café with an Internet connection, you can buy a web site domain, order equipment, and open a bank account. Then, you can promote what you do or sell via LinkedIn, Facebook, and Twitter. Need help? Hire some virtual talent via Elance.com.

This book and new 201greatideas.com site is a distribution channel for great ideas. I try to practice what I preach. Unlike many financial journalists, I am a small business owner. I've founded three companies. I started The Applegate Group Inc. when I quit my job at the *Los Angeles Times* in 1991.

Three years later, I started a financial services consulting firm, eventually turning that venture over to my partner.

In 2000, with marketing support from CNN.com, we launched SBTV .com (Small Business TV), the first online video site devoted exclusively to small business news and features. We attracted blue chip sponsors including Merrill Lynch, IBM, and ING, and produced hundreds of broadcast-quality videos. After predictions of widespread broadband service failed to materialize, we sold the company trademark and assets—in 2003.

My company continues to evolve, reflecting my work as a writer, consultant, speaker, and producer. On the consulting side, I work with a handful of blue-chip corporations, helping them provide better products and services to small business owners. On the multimedia side, we produce original Web content for American Express's OPEN Forum.com, Cox Communications, and Montecito Bank. I also write and produce independent films, promotional videos, and videos for 201greatideas.com.

In addition to the scores of real business owners you'll meet in the following pages, you'll enjoy insights and advice provided by well-known entrepreneurs including Michael Bloomberg, New York City's mayor and founder of Bloomberg LP; USA Networks founder Kay Koplovitz; and management expert and author, Tom Peters.

You'll meet Lynn Tilton, a modern industrialist who is busy acquiring and reviving American manufacturing companies, and Nina McLemore, a dynamic fashion designer with a line of fabulous, classy clothes for professional women. If you attend any of my speaking events, you'll probably see me wearing her designs.

My search for great ideas doesn't stop here: if *you* have a great idea, please submit it via our web site: www.201greatideas.com. We'll be posting the best ideas and awarding prizes to the winners.

I look forward to hearing from you and wish you success on your journey.

Jane Applegate
Sharon, Vermont
March, 2011
jane@theapplegategroup.com

Management Strategies

Small business owners have to be like those plate spinners in the circus ring. You've probably seen those jugglers: they toss plates atop spindly poles. As soon as one plate starts spinning, the next plate wobbles, ready to crash. Plate spinners rush from pole to pole, trying to keep all the plates aloft.

Juggling skills are essential for running a small business.

Balancing life and work is nearly impossible, especially with all our electronic tethers. Smartphones are cool, but they make it easy to work nonstop.

This chapter on management strategies features great ideas about how to manage through chaos. I'll explain why creating an informal advisory board is a great idea and how a company retreat can boost morale and productivity.

You'll learn how to hire great advisers, including attorneys, accountants, and consultants. We'll explore how to keep employees healthy and happy by creating a safer, "greener" workplace. You may be inspired to move your business into a business incubator and cross-train your employees.

All these great ideas were suggested by business owners, so read on.

Always Deal with Decision Makers

An entrepreneur's goal is to operate at the highest level possible. You'll increase the odds of making a deal if you pitch the decision maker, whether that person is another business owner or a corporate executive. Your mission is to get to the person who writes the checks and move on to the next opportunity if the answer is "no."

Even when The Applegate Group Inc., my multimedia communications and consulting company, was based in the dining room of our suburban Los Angeles home, I resolved to always deal directly with the top person. My strategy raised eyebrows, but as a financial writer, I was interviewing and profiling decision makers every day. Companies claim to empower employees and work collaboratively, but the truth is, someone has to say "yes" or "no."

It took courage to quit my prestigious job at the *Los Angeles Times* to write a weekly small business column, write books, and consult with big companies selling products and services to small business owners.

I was very lucky. My first client was American Express. The corporate card group wanted to sponsor a weekly small business report on National Public Radio. I was upset when NPR turned us down, because they already had a corporate sponsor for small business coverage, but we took the idea to CBS Radio. My syndicated *Succeeding in Small Business* report aired for about four years and launched my speaking and consulting career.

We've flourished through the years by pitching marketing concepts, television programs, business events, and independent films to the people who can "green light" a project. You might be thinking, "Well, it's easy because you are Jane Applegate and people know who you are." Not so. No matter who you are, it's worth aiming high. You have nothing to lose by sending a short and focused handwritten note (not e-mail) to the founder, president, or chairman of a company you want to do business with. Worst case, your note will be read by an assistant and may forward it to the appropriate person down the chain of command.

I know everything is moving online, but letters cut through the clutter. I once sent a story pitch via Priority Mail to the executive producer at *60 Minutes*. Two days later, his assistant called me. She said my letter was the only piece of mail on his desk. He read it and asked a producer to call me right away. (They passed on the story, but I know it was considered, which impressed my client.)

And don't be shy about using all your contacts—even personal ones. For example, I was chatting with a neighbor who is executive vice president of a big bank. I mentioned that I was looking for companies to give this book away to small business customers. He passed along my pitch to his business banking team. No matter what happens, I know my proposal got to the right person, with a note from a top executive.

Remember, you have only a few seconds to make your pitch to a busy person. Focus on how your service, idea, or product can help their company beat the competition. If you don't get a response to your letter, call the company's main number early in the morning or after 5 PM. Ask the receptionist to connect you to the person's direct line. Powerful executives usually work longer hours than their subordinates and assistants. I've reached many top executives working at their desks during the lunch hour, too.

I should warn you that this "easier at the top" strategy has pitfalls. Even if the top person signs off on your project, middle managers may feel threatened. They will most likely sabotage your project. I've encountered this resistance to my projects many times, but most of the time, things work out if you keep the lines of communication open.

The "not invented here" issue can kill a good idea. I share this not to discourage you, but to emphasize how critical it is to have open and constant support from the decision maker who hired you. Keep in touch with that person and make sure they know how things are going.

Be creative and persistent. Find someone who knows your prospect and ask them to introduce you. Remember, people do business with people they know and like.

GREAT

2

Never Work with Anyone Who Gives You a Headache or a Stomachache

IDEA

This is my motto. Life is too short to work with people who make you miserable. You can't possibly do your best work when the people you have to deal with make you sick.

I know. I've tried. As a freelance writer and producer, I have worked on amazing projects for terrible people, including a greedy, obnoxious celebrity and the campus loony at an elite graduate school. The production company story involved a really famous person who misappropriated production funds raised by a nonprofit organization and is too upsetting to share. (I'll include it in my memoir.)

But lessons can be learned from my most traumatic work experience. In 2008, the Great Recession prompted me to accept what seemed like a dream job at a prestigious business school. I was hired to write white papers and articles, produce audio and video clips for a web site, and coproduce a lecture series on the future of television. Best of all, I was asked to write, produce, and direct a documentary based on interviews with top industry executives visiting the school.

My four-day schedule allowed me to still speak at Bloomberg TV–sponsored small business events a few times each month.

Unfortunately, six months into the job, I was suffering from blinding tension headaches and my stomach was in a twist. Every morning, as I walked past the security bars on the windows in the stairwell, I felt like I was heading to my prison cell. The chemistry between my boss and me was terrible. I knew I was toast when he called me into his office for a performance review.

He shut the door, sat down, and began listing my infractions: I walked too quickly down the hall, creating a "wake" that disturbed his secretary; at a staff meeting, my jacket accidentally brushed against her and I did not apologize. Worst of all—the day before our biggest public lecture (which drew a standing-room-only crowd of 250)—I left campus during my lunch hour to get my hair cut instead of helping her prepare the name tags.

I remember watching his mouth move but not hearing any sound. It was surreal. Not a word about my writing, public relations, or production skills. No mention of the interviews being conducted in the new studio funded by the dean's office. No mention of teaching students production techniques or producing a broadcast-quality film on a cable-access budget.

Of course, things went downhill after that. He desperately wanted me to quit, but I was not willing to give up this job without a fight. Naïve about academic politics, I met with the human resources director, the assistant dean, and an employee assistance counselor. The counselor told me my boss was well known for being "difficult and quirky," and my days were numbered. He also told me I was toast because my boss was a "rainmaker," who brought big money into the school. I begged the dean for a transfer to another department—any department where I was not being tortured and disrespected every day. I was desperate to keep the job, having given up all my freelance work.

Magical thinking took hold. Maybe if I worked harder things would improve? Every morning, I was the first one in the office. I risked my life driving to campus in a blizzard. A few weeks later, he called me into his office, reluctantly turning down the volume on the yodeling music he loved. (Yes, yodels streaming live via the Internet from Switzerland.)

This time I was reprimanded for asking a colleague whether she was going to meet an agreed-upon deadline for completing a brochure that had been languishing in the art department for *two* years.

"Jane, here's the problem," he said quietly. "You focus too much on performance and production. But my priorities are process and protocol."

Huh?

Slowly, he took away all my projects. I sat in an empty office for a few weeks waiting for the head of the department to return from a trip. It took sending a detailed letter to the dean detailing my former boss's unprofessional conduct and violations of the academic code of ethics to finally qualify for unemployment benefits.

After that demoralizing experience, I swore I would *never* work with anyone who made me sick. No amount of money is worth the pain. Success will evade you if you work in a toxic atmosphere. If you have made bad hires and you dread going to work, you need to take action *now*.

Work with people who admire you, work hard, and make you laugh when times are tough.

GREAT

3

IDEA

Don't Be Afraid to Reinvent Your Business

In the late 1990s, anyone wanting Sandra Nunnerley's elegant, custom-designed furniture had to have deep pockets as well as good taste. Long accustomed to serving the upscale market, with a single chair tagged at $10,000, Nunnerley said she was pushed into the retail market by copycats. "I started to notice that copies of my custom designs were appearing in retail outlets," said Nunnerley.

Fueled by the middle-class housing boom, Nunnerley teamed up with furniture giant Lane Upholstery to design a line of elegant sofas, beds, chairs, and tables.

Her furniture and interior designs, the subject of an upcoming book and featured in *Architectural Digest*, appealed to Lane Upholstery president Arthur Thompson.

"Sandra is a designer of remarkable talents, one who has consistently responded to a discerning international clientele," Thompson remarked when the line was launched. "Her simple, sophisticated designs fill a void in the marketplace for furniture that meets the demands of modern living without sacrificing elegance, style, and tradition."

Although her line for Lane was lucrative, Nunnerley said in 2005, her research showed that the U.S. housing boom was about to become a housing bust. "I did very well with Lane, but I could see the market changing, and by the end of 2005, I said this cannot last . . . this thing is a bubble."

"I saw the train coming and knew we had to rethink the company," said Nunnerley. "We were really making a profit on our high-end residential work, so I decided not to continue with designing products."

Colleagues who kept serving the mass market furniture, including Michael Smith, the Obama's interior designer, "got into a lot of trouble."

Since moving back to serve the highest end of the market, Nunnerley said the company has "never been so busy." The Manhattan-based firm has grown from 6 to 10 employees.

"At the level I work now, it's only for the very rich," she said. "That's the reality of it. We've become a boutique high-end residential firm, doing everything from interior architecture to design."

Her clients own multiple homes, boats, and airplanes. To keep them happy, she often commissions other designers to create one-of-a-kind pieces.

"We survived and have never been busier," she said. "Unfortunately, the architects are walking the streets. We advertised for an architect and received 700 resumes."

Nunnerley urges other business owners to "move with the times." She said, "You have to constantly rebrand, especially in this global market. It's a whole new world."

Looking back, she knows she did the right thing by moving away from manufacturing. "If I continued, I would have been out of business."

While Nunnerley saved her business by returning to the highest end of the market, long-time restaurant owners, the Ghios, continue to update the menu and operations at Anthony's Seafood Grotto in San Diego. The restaurant won the local best seafood restaurant award 14 years in a row.

Years ago, when they dropped the zabaglione cake from the menu, Rick Ghio told me he feared his dear, departed grandmother, Catherine, would send a lightning bolt down from heaven in protest. "We did it because we were throwing away more cake than we were selling," recalled Ghio, referring to the traditional sponge cake served with a rum custard sauce.

Dessert sales perked up when Anthony's started serving tiramisu and fresh fruit tarts. After 50 years in business, Anthony's dropped rosé from the wine list, switching to white Zinfandel. The Ghios continue to make changes every year. But why would a business founded in 1946 make changes?

"We were losing our market share," he said. "Our reputation was still strong, but people were not dining at Anthony's as frequently as they did in the past."

Families still booked tables for major celebrations and holidays, but the younger families and couples did not consider Anthony's a hip place to eat.

"Competition is fierce, relentless, and unforgiving," said Rick's brother, Craig, now responsible for business development. "Diners have more choices than ever, and tradition is no longer enough to keep them coming back."

The Ghios admit that making changes to an iconic eatery is a "scary process," especially since "there's a huge risk in saying goodbye to some of the things we had been doing, but we have been truly blessed by the response."

GREAT
4
IDEA
Add Spirituality to Your Business Life

Peter Oppermann studied mechanical engineering in Germany, but was always drawn to the arts, design, and Eastern philosophy. He moved to New York to marry a yoga teacher and started teaching yoga, but when the marriage ended, he followed his passion to create simple, elegant designs.

Today, he owns Shoji Living, a company that designs and manufactures Japanese-style sliding doors out of sustainable materials.

Oppermann said he's been inspired by *The Diamond Cutter*, a book written by Michael Roach, a Buddhist monk turned millionaire businessman. In fact, Oppermann teaches classes in "Karmic management," based on the book's principles, to ex-convicts learning new skills at the Osborne Association's Green Career Center in the South Bronx. (For more on hiring ex-cons, see Great Idea #145.)

Integrating his spiritual and work life is a top priority for Oppermann. In 2010, he took it a step further by joining a group of spiritually minded entrepreneurs who meet monthly. Together, they explore ways to integrate spiritual practice into their business and personal lives. The group calls itself Spirit Bus and is comprised of a former hedge fund manager, a former advertising executive, and two marketing consultants.

"Being an entrepreneur can be a little lonely," said Oppermann. "So, we get together once a month to exchange ideas, inspire, and support each other."

Taking a more spiritual approach to business is appealing to many business owners. Rabbi David Baron, founder of Temple Shalom for the Arts in West Los Angeles, said he started writing sermons about how the Bible relates to business issues as a way to connect with more members of his congregation. He said most business owners want their companies to reflect values they cherish.

But it's tough for busy business owners to incorporate key values into their day-to-day management decisions. Yet a truly successful business relies on the behavior and ethics of its owner and employees.

For instance, if you cheat your customers, you shouldn't be surprised if your employees do, too. If you tell white lies about why you were late or missed an appointment, your employees will think it is okay if they do the same. "The more I got into [these topics], the more it resonated with businesspeople," Baron told me. In one of his books, he asks readers to consider why God chose Moses for such an important leadership role when he was hardly management material.

"Imagine hiring a manager whose profile reads: reluctant to lead, stutters, distant, prone to long mountain-top vigils, temperamental to the point of smashing corporate mission statements, strikes out instead of speaking, settles disputes through swift violent means, and never reaches his ultimate objective."

Pretty funny.

If you are interested in exploring how business and spirituality align, check out Michael Roach's book, *The Diamond Cutter*, published by Doubleday Religion. Roach recently sold his diamond business to Warren Buffett for $200 million. A book about religion and business may inspire you to reconnect with your spiritual side, even if you haven't been to a church or synagogue in years.

GREAT
5
IDEA

Ask for a Quick "Yes" or "No"

Through the years, I've learned that a quick "no" is as important as a "yes" when it comes to dealing with clients and customers. While we all love to bring in new business, too much time is wasted in discussion and fruitless negotiation when people are reluctant to just say "no."

If someone isn't interested in buying what you have to offer, it's painful but better to know the truth and move on. The challenge is this: Most people don't like to say no, so they waffle, stall, and mumble. They don't return your phone calls, texts, or e-mails. This creates stress and frustration and wastes your time.

One strategy I've found to be extremely effective for getting a timely answer is to set a deadline for response. You may think this takes a lot of nerve, but it works in most situations. We set response deadlines on proposals submitted to the biggest Fortune 500 companies.

Setting a deadline is a grown-up way to do business. We ask our corporate clients, who usually need a lot of time to make a decision, to just tell us where they are in the process. Keeping us in the decision loop creates a respectful and honest relationship.

Of course, if someone asks for more time because they can't schedule a meeting or have to complete a new project, we wait for an answer. The goal is to manage the decision-making process in a professional, nonconfrontational manner.

Be polite and clear. Tell them you truly want to work with them or close the sale, but you believe a "no" is as important as a "yes." Try it.

Say Goodbye to Corporate Life

People leave their corporate jobs to start small businesses for all sorts of reasons, financial and emotional.

Liz Clarke was working for IBM as an organizational consultant when her son, Dana, died in 1994. To rebuild her life after his traumatic death, she moved to South Strafford Village, a tiny town in south central Vermont. Clarke purchased a couple of extra acres adjacent to her home, cleared the brush, and planted raspberries, blueberries, and currants.

Then, with scientific precision, she taught herself how to make jam, jellies, and *coulis* (a super-refined jelly). In the fall of 2010, she began selling U.S. Department of Agriculture (USDA) fancy-grade products under the Morrill Mountain Fruit Farm brand.

Clarke told me that digging in the dirt, driving a tractor, and picking berries cleared her mind. Slowly, she felt happier and brighter.

Across the country, Adam Dawson leveraged his experience as an investigative reporter into a successful small business. Dawson spent 12 years as an aggressive investigative reporter for the *Daily News* and the *Orange County Register*. His beat was white-collar crime, and he was relentlessly competitive. (I know because we battled it out covering federal court stories every day when I was a reporter for the *Los Angeles Times*.)

By the time Dawson was in his 40s, the newspaper industry was faltering and he was ready for a change.

"I could buy a toy like a sports car, have an affair, or reinvent my job," said Dawson. "I couldn't afford to buy a toy and my wife wouldn't let me have an affair, so I thought about what else I could do with the skills I had."

The attorneys and cops he worked with every day encouraged him to become a private investigator. Intrigued, Dawson looked into what it would take to obtain a license. He learned he needed 6,000 hours of investigative experience to qualify. Luckily, the director of the state licensing agency granted him credit for his many years of investigative reporting.

In 1989, Dawson passed a state exam and has since parlayed his reporting skills into a lucrative PI business based out of his Santa Monica, California, home.

He avoids marital cases ("too emotional") and hires other investigators to handle surveillance. Mostly, he focuses on what he did as a reporter: unraveling complex frauds and following the money trail. Still passionate about helping to put the bad guys in jail, he's making six figures a year and having fun.

Dairl Johnson was at the peak of his career and managing a product line with $1.5 billion in sales at IBM, when he "suddenly realized I was taking just as big a risk staying in my corporate job as I would if I left."

In the early 1990s, IBM was cutting staff. "The whole idea of the company being there forever was no longer true," said Johnson. "It rocks your whole perspective, and you suddenly say, 'there's no such thing as job security. I would rather trust my own skills and abilities.'"

He wasn't sure what his next step would be, but first he had to deal with a serious problem. Stressed out from too many hours at the computer, Johnson had developed a painful "executive slouch." Years before, he had injured his back when he bailed out of a Navy fighter jet and was hit by the ejection seat.

One day, his doctor suggested he visit a Relax the Back store in Austin. Johnson forked out $5,000 for a recliner chair, lumbar supports, and other back savers. Amazingly, his back pain eased.

Sensing a business opportunity, he checked out the franchise, cashed in his pension fund (see Great Idea #40), and maxed out his credit cards to purchase a Relax the Back franchise in Santa Monica for $184,000. "That business did $1 million in revenue in its first 10 months," recalls Johnson. "I knew there was really something going on here."

With southern California sales soaring, he started thinking bigger. "I said to myself, 'you know, I want to take this nationwide, and the only way I can do this is to purchase the entire company.'"

Turning to institutional investors, he raised $6 million to buy the operating company. The company now owns about 100 stores across the United States.

Back care is a growing field, since most sufferers are 60-year-old Baby Boomers with high-stress jobs and money to spend on relief. Relax the Back stores sell scores of products ranging from inexpensive massage oils to high-end mattresses and reclining chairs.

Looking back at his life as an executive, Johnson said he has no regrets about leaving the corporate life. "The most important thing is to be prepared for the risk," he advises. "It's a real free-fall, and sometimes you can't find the rip cord."

He said that once you make a decision to go into business, "you can't put one foot on the boat and keep the other one on land. Failure is not an acceptable alternative. Doubt and fear are okay but not failure."

Before you take your job and shove it:

- Do extensive research on businesses and industries that appeal to you.
- Speak to as many entrepreneurs as possible to get a sense of what it's really like.
- Work part-time for a similar business or be the world's oldest unpaid intern.
- Make sure you have enough money saved to live on for at least a year.
- Be sure you have the support of your spouse or significant other.
- Be aware that starting or buying a business is extremely stressful.
- Accept that things usually take three times as long and will cost you at least twice as much as you expected.

GREAT

7

IDEA

Create an Informal Advisory Board

The largest companies in the world have all sorts of advisory boards, but entrepreneurs are often reluctant to ask outsiders for help. An advisory board made up of industry leaders, deep thinkers, and trusted colleagues can steer you and your company through the choppiest waters—at very little cost.

Unlike a board of directors, which has legal and fiduciary responsibilities, advisory boards can be set up as formally or as informally as you like. You should offer to pay people a modest sum, perhaps $1,500, to attend one meeting every quarter or twice a year.

Years ago, I served on a small business advisory board created by the American Express Corporate Card group. About a dozen movers and shakers in the small business world met once or twice a year to brainstorm about new Amex financial products and services, review existing products, and share our insights with company executives.

When times were good, we met in five-star hotels. Warm cookies, cold milk, and monogrammed robes welcomed us when we checked into our rooms. During lean years, we met at a hotel across from the office and ate sandwiches. No matter where we met, we enjoyed the experience while providing valuable services and making our own business connections.

So how can an advisory board help your business? If you run a manufacturing company, for instance, invite representatives from your major suppliers, a marketing expert in your field, a retired executive with experience in your industry, and perhaps your accountant or attorney. (Be prepared to pay your advisers their regular fees to attend meetings.)

Meeting at least once a year in person is ideal. But if you have to meet via conference call or online, set a detailed agenda. Start by providing a brief overview of what's happening at the company. Before the meeting, send out a package or links to financial information, including a current balance sheet, marketing materials, and anything else to bring your advisers up to date.

After you've presented a brief overview, listen to their comments and suggestions. Don't get defensive. You want your "kitchen cabinet" to keep you on track and hold you accountable.

Seek out advisers who will help you take the pulse of your industry and monitor your competition. There's nothing better than feeling supported by a group of people who believe in what you're doing.

We rely on a core group of advisers to keep The Applegate Group Inc. on track. My dearest uncle, Steve Coan, a retired partner in a major Wall Street brokerage, is one of the smartest and most intuitive people I know. He's a whiz with numbers and terrific when it comes to solving sticky personnel problems.

One of my best friends, Kathy Taggares, is a successful entrepreneur and skilled strategist. She always has a fresh perspective to share. Although she's in the food processing business, she's media savvy, plugged into popular culture, and makes me laugh no matter how bad things are.

My husband, Joe, is my most trusted adviser. He's my ethical adviser, responsible for weighing the ramifications of every project I accept. He also calms me down when I start choking on what he calls "emotional hairballs." He reminds me not to take professional setbacks personally.

Whereas this kind of informal kitchen cabinet is essential for helping you make better decisions, consider establishing a more formal customer advisory board. A survey by Dr. Tony Carter, a professor of sales and marketing at Columbia University's Graduate School of Business, found that 21 of the 70 Fortune 500 companies surveyed had customer advisory boards. Nineteen of 21 said the boards were extremely useful.

In the 1990s, Swissôtel and Avis (now AvisBudget) both formed women's advisory boards to tap into the growing women's travel market. Based on recommendations from its board, Swissôtel began offering special services to women business travelers, including prime seats in hotel restaurants serving lighter, healthier spa-style cuisine. They extended health club hours to fit the women's busy schedules.

Susan Stautberg, a New York City consultant who helps companies create advisory boards, said Avis tried to make women feel more welcome by lowering sections of the check-out counters. In 2010, based on customer feedback, AvisBudget started offering the services of local drivers for an extra fee when you rent a car in certain cities. What a great idea that is, especially for people like me who hate to drive, especially in big cities where I don't know my way around.

So think about inviting some savvy experts and customers to provide invaluable advice to you and your staff.

GREAT IDEA 8 — Move Your Business into an Incubator

If you think incubators are just for babies and chicks, think again. Incubators offer entrepreneurs financing, real estate, mentoring, inspiration, encouragement, and a mix of compatible neighbors.

There are about 1,500 business incubators in the United States and thousands more abroad, according to the National Business Incubation Association, in Athens, Ohio.

Shapeways, an innovative company that provides rapid manufacturing or 3-D printing solutions to build low-cost product prototypes, began its life in an incubator in Eindhoven, Netherlands. The company, founded in 2007, was invited to participate in a "lifestyle incubator" operated by Royal Philips Electronics.

Life in the incubator meant low-cost office space and free, weekly counseling sessions with one of the incubator's managers, according to CEO Peter Weijmarshausen. The companies were all start-ups working on high-tech concepts. One company was developing a system to help patients manage their hospital stays. Another was perfecting an electronic gadget that tracked a person's movement throughout the day.

In September 2010, Shapeways announced it was ready to fly the coop. The company raised $5 million in Series A funding backed by Union Square Ventures in New York, which invested in Foursquare and Twitter, and London-based Index Ventures, which successfully backed Skype and Last.fm.

"Now, with the help of investors, Shapeways will be able to take the democratization of production to the next level," said Weijmarshausen. He said Philips plans to retain its investment in the company, but he would not disclose the amount.

Shapeways moved its headquarters to New York because most customers live in the United States. He said the company will spend the money raised to upgrade and improve the web site and hire more staffers to ramp up the marketing efforts.

Is Life in an Incubator Right for Your Company?

If you are thinking of moving into an incubator, take a tour and meet with other tenants. Then, get answers to the following questions:

- How long has the incubator been in operation?
- What kinds of businesses have occupied space in the incubator? How long do most businesses stay?
- What are some of the incubator's success stories?
- What specific services and support does the incubator offer tenants?
- Does the incubator intend to take equity in the businesses it houses? For how long?
- What financial resources are available to tenants? Access to loans? Introductions to private investors?
- Are there any hidden fees or charges?
- Do you require a contract? Can you move out sooner if your business grows too fast or fails to grow?

For more information, visit the National Business Incubation Association's web site at www.NBIA.org.

"We are revolutionizing personal production," he said in an exclusive interview. "If you think of a new product, you can put it on the market within a day."

The company 3-D prints more than 10,000 unique products every month, up from 600 a month in January 2009. (See more about how to design prototypes with affordable software in Great Idea #87.)

GREAT

9

IDEA

Organize a Company Retreat

An annual or semiannual retreat is an excellent way to measure the pulse of your business and tackle small problems before they turn into big ones. You don't have to book a Caribbean cruise, rent a fancy hotel suite, or even get on a plane. Instead, reserve a private room at a local restaurant, gather around a picnic table in the park, or go to someone's home. Hire a temp to answer your phones for the day. Tell customers and clients about the retreat. Believe me, they'll be impressed.

We planned our first retreat after signing a contract to produce a syndicated small business radio report for CBS stations. I knew the report, sponsored by American Express, would raise our profile and attract new business, so we needed to do some big thinking. I flew the key members of my team—all three of us—to Tucson for the weekend. We checked into a modest but comfortable motel, brainstormed at the pool, ate great Mexican food, and had some fun along the way.

If possible, hire an outside facilitator so you can participate. If you can't afford it and have to lead the discussion, that's okay.

Be sure to prepare for the retreat in advance. Decide exactly what you want to accomplish. Overall, you will want to review all customer accounts and current policies, and set specific goals. Create an agenda with space for notes.

Use flip charts or a white board to summarize the information and key points. Then open the meeting up to discussion. Go around the circle to encourage everyone's participation.

After you discuss what's happened in the past year, review what's working and what's not. For example, my colleagues told me that my tendency to micromanage projects was making them crazy. They couldn't do their work because I was constantly inquiring about their progress. This was painful but important criticism. I owned up to the problem, forced myself to stop hovering, and became a better manager.

Take time to discuss all those annoying behaviors, quirks, and patterns that interfere with productivity. Divide goals into short-term and long-term categories. Some tasks, like sending collection letters to clients, can be accomplished in a week; other jobs may take a month or a year. The most important thing is to make sure everyone agrees on what needs to be done, then set priorities and reasonable deadlines. At the end of the day, brainstorm about some pie-in-the-sky goals.

Try to inject humor into the discussion, especially if you are dealing with serious issues. Remember, listen more than talk.

GREAT **10** IDEA Create a Greener and Safer Workplace

Creating a greener, safer workplace can improve health and morale while boosting your bottom line. It makes sense because the Environmental Protection Agency estimates that every year indoor air pollution costs U.S. businesses more than $1 billion in medical bills and $60 billion in lost productivity.

Here are some great ideas to implement without spending a lot of time or money:

- *Design/landscaping:*
  - If you are building a new office, make sure your architect orients the building to take advantage of natural light to reduce lighting bills. Design a building that cuts down on unnecessary heating or cooling expenditures.
  - Landscape with native plants that require less water and suit your climate. Try to avoid the use of chemical pesticides and fertilizers to protect the local water supply.
- *Building materials.* Use materials that reduce indoor pollution. Avoid pressed wood products that are glued together or treated with form- aldehyde or other toxins. Be sure your building is well insulated with

recycled, nontoxic materials. Look for materials with a high R-value; the higher the number, the better the insulating properties. Reduce drafts with double- or triple-pane windows.

- *Lighting:*
  - Take advantage of sunlight whenever possible. Buy motion sensors that turn on when you enter a room. Replace incandescent and fluorescent bulbs with LEDs. One LED can last up to 60,000 hours. Use local, "task" lights rather than general overhead lighting. Install dimmers to reduce energy use.
  - Work with your local utility company or an independent energy auditor. Ask about rebates and other government-funded financial incentives available to business owners.
  - Keep computers out of direct sunlight to avoid glare and tilt monitors away from the window. Buy blinds with a silver coating on one side to reflect sunlight. Whenever possible, install glass above partitions to allow light to filter through the office.
- *Equipment:*
  - Look for "Energy Star–rated" copiers, computers, and other equipment that power down when you aren't using them.
  - When possible, print on both sides of the paper. Avoid printing out e-mail messages or documents whenever possible.
  - Check out the Energy Efficiency Rating (EER) and operating costs of appliances. Purchase a model that doesn't rely on chlorofluorocarbons (CFCs) to operate. These chemicals deplete the ozone layer.
- *Office supplies.* Whenever possible, buy nontoxic highlighters and dry-wipe markers. Buy recycled paper folders, notebooks, pencils, and pens.
- *Recycled products:*
  - Try using 50 percent recycled paper for everything from your printing to restroom needs. Reuse office paper for scratch paper.
  - Recycle all the paper you can: white paper, newsprint, and cardboard. Experts say it takes one-third less gross energy to make one sheet of recycled paper compared to "virgin" paper.
- *Recycling programs.* Paper is not the only office supply to recycle. You can recycle carpets, computer batteries, computers, printer cartridges, construction-site waste, floppy disks, glass, lightbulbs, holiday cards, light ballasts, and packing materials.

- *Telecommuting/transportation.* Encourage your workers to carpool, bike, or use public transportation. Try telecommuting at least one day a week to save time and fuel. Offer transit vouchers or other incentives to offset the cost of commuting.

GREAT
11
IDEA

Think Ergonomically

I'm usually the last one to urge any entrepreneur to spend money on fancy office furniture. In my previous life as a white-collar crime reporter, I quickly learned the glitzier the office, the worse the criminal who owned the company.

But with repetitive-motion injuries costing U.S. business owners hundreds of millions of dollars in lost productivity and millions more in workers' comp claims each year, it's important to make sure you and your employees are sitting on good chairs behind the right kind of desk. (Every year, there are more than 500,000 cases of repeated trauma disorders, such as carpal tunnel syndrome, affecting workers from white-collar executives to meatpackers.)

Providing a safe and comfortable workplace will boost morale as well as help you avoid lawsuits and complaints filed with state labor officials. So don't be cheap when it comes to outfitting your office.

"The most important investment you can make is in a chair with adjustable lumbar support and height features," said Mark Dutka, founder of a San Francisco design firm specializing in office furniture.

Rebecca Boenigk, chief executive officer and chairman of Neutral Posture Inc. in Bryan, Texas, is very familiar with comfortable, adjustable office chairs. Her father, Dr. Jerome Congleton, is a professor, national expert on ergonomics, and the person who designs most of the company's popular chairs.

"If you don't have proper support, you'll go home hurting every day," said Boenigk. "We want you to change the position of your chair all day long and make it easy to do so."

Recognizing that too many expensive chairs are not properly used, her company produces online videos and includes instruction booklets with every chair. "Some people think a $200 chair is expensive," she said. "But the chair is the most important part of the workstation."

Boenigk said treating a minor carpal tunnel injury, caused by too much typing or repetitive wrist movement can cost a company thousands of dollars in medical treatment and physical therapy. A serious injury can run into hundreds of thousands of dollars and may result in a lawsuit.

The market for comfortable office chairs is fueling the industry. There are about 100 ergonomic chair makers, with big companies like Steelcase selling more than $500 million worth of furniture and equipment a year.

"We are never going to be as cheap as chairs from China," said Boenigk. "If you go to a big box store and buy a $99 chair, six months later you are going to be throwing it in the trash can. We have 7,000 chairs that have been at UPS for 16 years. We wish they would replace them."

Being small and nimble helped Neutral Posture weather a 50 percent drop in industry sales during the 2008 recession. They cut costs and worked smarter but, rather than hunker down, hired a consultant to craft a three-year marketing and growth plan. "We rebranded the company with a new logo, new web site and new products," said Boenigk.

It worked. At a major industry trade show, the company's booth was mobbed with customers. Neutral Posture, with offices in Bryan, Texas, and Ontario, Canada, is a small player, but is considered a leader in its field.

How to Be More Ergonomic

- Hire an ergonomics consultant to visit and inspect your office.
- Determine what equipment you need to reduce back and wrist problems.
- Start by buying the low-budget items: back support pillows, wrist rests for keyboards, footstools, copyholders, and good lighting.
- Work your way up to buying new workstations and high-quality chairs.

GREAT IDEA 12 — Make Meetings More Productive

In this high-tech era, it's a bit surprising to learn that face-to-face meetings are still the most popular form of business communication. In fact, 44 percent of executives surveyed by Office Team, an office staffing service, said they preferred to communicate with people in person. E-mail ranked second, with 34 percent; paper memos, 12 percent; and voice mail, 7 percent.

Still, too many meetings drag on and accomplish very little.

"In these days of rapid change, time is precious, and you can't afford to waste it in meetings," said Dr. Mark Goulston, a Santa Monica psychiatrist, author, and business coach who works with both big and small companies.

One of Goulston's great ideas is to give a quiz at the end of a meeting. "We ask whether everyone really understands what was discussed," said Goulston. He also suggests asking, "What are you going to do differently and why?"

This strategy avoids "collusion" between meeting leaders and participants who sometimes just pretend to be listening or interested—or, worse yet, agree with their bosses to gain favored-employee status.

Here are some other tips to make your meetings more productive:

- Schedule meetings just before lunch so people will act quickly.
- Send out an agenda before the meeting.
- Invite the fewest number of people possible. Only meet when absolutely necessary.

GREAT IDEA 13 — Meet Clients in Elegant Public Places

The greatest thing about working at home is being able to spend more on high-tech, high-productivity office equipment, travel, marketing, and entertainment. But the challenge is where to meet with a client or customer?

If kids, dogs, or family members preclude you from inviting people to your home office, make reservations.

No matter where you live, you can meet in an elegant restaurant or hotel lobby. Be sure to scout out the location before you schedule the appointment. Check out the parking situation. Better yet, look for a place with valet parking.

Reserve a quiet table far from the kitchen. Make it very clear to the maître d' that your meeting is very important to your professional success. When you arrive and are shown to your table, be sure to give the maître d' a generous tip ($10 to $20).

Another classy idea: If sharing a meal isn't an option, invite your client to join you for tea or cocktails at a luxury hotel. Late afternoon is an excellent time for a leisurely business meeting because it doesn't interfere with lunch or dinner plans.

If your client prefers to skip the food and drinks, just meet in a secluded section of a fine hotel lobby. If you are well dressed and quiet, no one will ask you to leave. My favorite hotels for meetings are the St. Regis and the Regency in New York City. Poolside at the affordable and funky Sportsmen's Lodge in Studio City, California, is the perfect meeting spot for my film projects or auditions.

GREAT IDEA 14 Work the Phones or Walk the Floor

Publishers Weekly named Elaine Petrocelli, co-owner of Book Passage in Corte Madera, California, bookseller of the year a few years ago. She's earned a national reputation by battling nearby chain stores and online book sales. Book Passage, with stores in Marin County and San Francisco, is known for its stellar customer service and educational outreach programs and events.

Every year, Book Passage hosts about 700 author events, seminars, and workshops. They keep in close touch with 40,000 customers via newsletters and via their web site: www.bookpassage.com. (I will be signing books at Book Passage's San Francisco Ferry Building location in April.)

The original store, which opened in Larkspur, California, in 1976, now fills 12,500 square feet in Corte Madera, California. Petrocelli shared a great idea that anyone who owns a retail store or small business needs to do: get out of your office and work on the floor. In fact, she had just been working the floor when we spoke.

"The company execs here are scheduled like everyone else to get out and sell books," said Petrocelli. "Everyone here has worked on the floor as a bookseller."

Dealing with customers while your employees take a break is a great way to stay in touch with the front line of your business. Sit in for the receptionist and answer the phone.

"We had a marketing meeting, and so much of the information came from people saying, 'When I was on the floor yesterday . . .'" Petrocelli told me.

You'll be surprised how much valuable insight can be gained by working directly with your customers. Being on the front lines can generate the ideas and ammunition you've been searching for to beat your competition.

GREAT

15

IDEA

Join or Create a Peer Support Group

Tight budgets and soft sales during the recession pushed savvy business owners to turn to each other for free advice rather than hiring consultants. What began as a cost-cutting measure is still yielding invaluable benefits as business picks up, according to members of three informal, peer-to-peer business support groups.

Members say they look forward to their monthly gatherings to share contacts, tackle tough problems, and brainstorm together to dream up marketing strategies. They also rely on each other for motivation and inspiration.

"We always ask, 'How can we help each other and what information can we share?'" said Alison Raffaele, a makeup artist, beauty products entrepreneur and member of Beautiful New York. (Alison did my makeup for the photo on the back of this book.) "One member shared a contact that helped me get a $20,000 loan guaranteed by the Small Business Administration."

The members of Beautiful New York all make beauty or personal care products. Peace-Keepers Cause-metics sells natural lipstick and nail polish and donates its profits to organizations helping women. Juara Skincare makes and sells Indonesian-inspired complexion products. Raffaele is a makeup artist who sells a line of concealer and foundation. The only rule is that members can't compete directly with each other. In fact, they look for ways to promote each other's products as well as share distribution channels and sales reps.

Raffaele said sometimes members benefit by asking if a vendor is reliable or whether a boutique pays its bills on time. "We are all looking to increase our distribution channels at a time when the channels have changed."

Metta Murdaya, cofounder and owner of Juara Skincare, which sells skin and body care products containing ingredients found in Indonesia and elsewhere, said she looks forward to the monthly gatherings because they "keep everyone energized."

"The one thing we have in common is that we are female entrepreneurs in the New York beauty space," said Murdaya. "We meet to share resources, sales reps, distributors, and press contacts." She said they've also held successful joint marketing events such as opening temporary "popup" stores. (Juara provided the first prize for our "Great Ideas" contest.)

Two Minnesota-based entrepreneurs have taken the peer-to-peer counseling model a step further by serving as vice presidents of each other's companies.

Michelle Massman owns a marketing and event management firm in Minnesota. Every year, she produces a popular women's trade show. She also worked with me to round up sponsors for my book promotion tour and crafted our social media strategy. One of her other clients is Shaun Johnson.

Johnson is the founder and co-owner of Tonic Sol-fa, LLC, an entertainment company that owns and manages Tonic Sol-fa, a super successful all-male *a cappella* group. Tonic Sol-fa performs at sold-out concerts, sells thousands of CDs and song downloads, and produces popular holiday specials for PBS. I attended their holiday concert in Minneapolis and it was fantastic. A blizzard the day before did not stop fans from attending the concert.

"When Shaun and I first met, we were inches away from being totally burnt out," Massman told me. "The first conversation we had lasted three and a half hours. After that, we started looking at each other's companies in a different light. It is great to have someone to help you dig in and work on new strategies."

Although Massman and Johnson initially worked together informally to solve business challenges, they now serve as vice presidents of each other's companies and pay each other for services rendered. It's worked out well for both companies, which managed to keep busy during the Great Recession.

If you prefer to join an existing organization, check out The Alternative Board (www.thealternativeboard.com). TAB is an international franchise organization with more than 3,000 members in the United States, Canada, the United Kingdom, and Venezuela.

Founded in 1990 by business author Allen Fishman, TAB hosts monthly meetings as well as providing consulting services. Fees vary depending on the location, so contact TAB for details.

Ladies Who Launch has more than 100,000 members across the United States. This active group has a dynamic web site and newsletters designed to encourage networking and bootstrapping among members. Chapters across the country host monthly luncheons, seminars, and workshops. LWL is a national sponsor of my *201 Great Ideas* book tour. For more information, visit www.ladieswholaunch.com.

The Women Presidents' Organization (www.womenpresidentsorg.com) has 82 chapters and about 1,500 members in the United States, Canada, and the United Kingdom. Members are required to have $2 million in annual revenues ($1 million if it is a service business). WPO members meet monthly with a trained facilitator. The basic annual membership fee is about $1,650. Contact WPO for more information.

There are many other groups providing peer support and motivation for busy entrepreneurs. Joining your local chamber of commerce is a good place to start. Be sure to attend the monthly mixers and get to know as many members as possible. For more information visit the Chamber of Commerce of the United States web site (www.uschamber.org).

If you are interested in how politics affects business, join Women Impacting Public Policy (WIPP). The group tracks legislation and keeps tabs on elected officials (www.wipp.org).

Minority business owners can also contact the National Association of Minority Contractors (www.namcnational.org) and the U.S. Hispanic Chamber of Commerce (www.ushcc.com).

Franchise owners should consider joining the International Franchise Association. For more information, visit www.franchise.org.

GREAT

16

IDEA

Know When to Reach Out for Help

Every business hits a rocky patch once in a while; it's nothing to be ashamed of. But if you are worried about your business, please don't be afraid to reach out for help. If you don't set your ego aside, you could jeopardize everything—your business, your family, and your reputation.

This checklist will help you take the pulse of your business:

1. Are vendors or suppliers calling you and demanding to be paid immediately?   YES   NO
2. Has your banker reduced your credit line or demanded full payment of a loan?   YES   NO
3. Are you having trouble meeting your payroll?   YES   NO
4. Are you dipping into personal savings to pay your bills?   YES   NO
5. Are customer complaints increasing?   YES   NO
6. Do you have trouble sleeping and feel out of control?   YES   NO

If you checked more than one "yes," you need help ASAP. Ask whether your current advisers can help you sort things out. Your accountant may be able to suggest ways to boost your cash flow. Your attorney can send collection letters, which might help you get paid faster. You need to eliminate nonessential expenses, but consider hiring a freelance marketing consultant to create a low-cost, short-term promotion aimed at bringing in new sales.

If you feel your business is in serious jeopardy, consider hiring a professional turnaround consultant. These highly skilled and experienced experts step into your shoes and take charge. They work quickly to negotiate deals with creditors and vendors to keep them at bay. They deal with your banker, your suppliers, and your landlord, convincing them to give you more time to sort things out.

Bringing in an outsider to rescue your company is a dramatic measure, but it tells the world that you care enough about your business to step aside—at least temporarily. Turnaround consultants are not cheap. A good one may cost thousands of dollars that you probably don't have. Often, your bank will force you to bring in professional help.

One turnaround consultant I know told me he found $60,000 worth of checks tucked inside the desk drawer of a panicked controller. The moral of that story is: when your business is spinning out of control, it's tough to think clearly.

One caution: If you hire a turnaround consultant, you will have to relinquish day-to-day control. You can't disappear, though. You have to be available to answer questions and provide information.

For less severe problems, schedule some free or low-cost counseling at a Small Business Development Center (SBDC). There are about 1,000 centers around the country, jointly funded by the U.S. Small Business Administration and private organizations, usually colleges or universities. You can find the closest SBDC by visiting www.sba.gov.

And don't forget the free help offered by the Service Corps of Retired Executives (SCORE). SCORE has thousands of experienced businesspeople available to help you sort out any problems in person or online. Their services are free and their workshops affordable. Find a counselor who knows your industry at www.score.org.

Ignoring your problems is a sure way to kill your business. Send up a flare and save your company before it's too late. (Check the resource section at the end of the book for more ways to get help.)

GREAT

17   Hire a Great Lawyer

IDEA   One person who can help you in good and bad times is an experienced attorney. Save money when you can, but don't scrimp when it comes to getting solid legal advice.

Once you set up your business structure, you'll need a savvy lawyer to buy or sell real estate, form a partnership, create job applications, and write employee handbooks. (See the tip box on pages 28–29 for diversity tips.)

Working with a good small business attorney will help you avoid legal troubles involving staff, vendors, and customers. He or she can also prepare books and records when you are seeking outside investors or applying for a bank loan.

Finding a good attorney is not as challenging as you may think. There are about a million of them in the United States. The best way to find a good lawyer is to ask other small business owners, your banker, and your accountant for recommendations.

You can also find a lawyer through a legal directory or at various web sites. Most large libraries have a copy of the *Martindale-Hubbell Law Directory*, which provides brief biographical information about lawyers in your area. State bar associations offer free referral services. Be prepared to pay a fee for an initial consultation, although some lawyers won't charge you.

Remember, you have to feel comfortable telling your attorney everything, so choose someone you can confide in. Very important: work with someone who knows your industry.

My wonderful attorney, Cliff Ennico, is a small business expert, speaker, and author. He's kept me out of hot water for years. He not only drafts our contracts but provides excellent insights and legal advice. He's also one of the sweetest and funniest people I know.

Some attorneys who work with entrepreneurs may offer to provide legal services in exchange for stock in your company. That may be worth considering. The hourly fees you'll pay depend on where you live. Business owners based in New York City and Los Angeles generally pay higher legal fees than those living in Omaha, Nebraska.

Some questions to ask prospective attorneys:

- Are you a member of the state bar and licensed to practice law in this state? (If your company does a lot of interstate commerce, consider hiring an attorney who can practice in the federal courts as well.)
- What types of small businesses do you represent?
- How long have you been practicing law?
- Please provide three references for me to call. (If the person balks at this request, move on.)

How to Stay Out of Legal Trouble

Many business owners don't realize that federal rules and regulations affect them as soon as they have 15 or 20 employees. Julie Hickman, founder and CEO of Diversity Compliance & Testing Group in Shawnee, Kansas (www.diversitycompliancegroup.com), has created several online training and compliance programs for business owners and employees.

Not knowing the law is no excuse for not complying with the Americans with Disabilities Act, Title 7 of the Civil Rights Act, the Lily Ledbetter Fair Pay Act, and a laundry list of state and federal statutes.

"Unhappy employees can go right to the Equal Employment Opportunity Commission and file complaints," said Hickman. "Then, it can get ugly."

She said part-time and full-time employees have rights that can't be ignored. Her two-hour online training program for managers costs $29.95. Regular employees pay $19.95 and need to understand the material and pass a 25-question test.

GREAT 18 IDEA

Seek Help from a Restaurant Consultant

Isidore "Izzy" Kharasch is a skilled chef, but most of his clients don't even know he can cook. "I'm more comfortable managing the business end of a restaurant," said Kharasch, president of Hospitality Works, a Chicago restaurant consulting and turn-around company. Kharasch also teaches at Kendall College and has an MBA in hospitality management.

When I caught up with him, he was working with a tribal-owned casino in California. The Great Recession hit the restaurant industry hard, so he's been very busy.

No matter what the economy is doing, about 27 percent of all restaurants fail after the first year, and 60 percent close down after five years, according to researchers at Cornell and Michigan State University. It was worse between 2008 and 2009, according to Kharasch.

"I have clients who have lost between 5 and 50 percent of their sales," he said. "They only survived because they owned their property."

Although people still went out to eat, most trimmed their spending by not ordering appetizers and dessert. "Even if they order less, you still need 100 percent of your staff to serve them."

About half of his clients own struggling restaurants. The other half hire him because they want to open a restaurant. "Now, more clients are hiring me up front, before they start building," said Kharasch, who charges about $15,000 to review the demographics of the area and craft a realistic business plan. (Knowing how many prospective diners live near your restaurant is important.)

If you want him to manage your project from concept to opening, it will cost about $100,000.

"Our goal is to either have you committed to doing it or abandoning the idea," said Kharasch. "I teach people how to take general costs, like rent, and then figure out gross sales."

A few years ago he was hired by a couple who wanted to invest $1 million in a pastry shop in downtown Chicago. "By the end of the evening, I showed them that for them to make any money, they would need to have 600 people spending $7 per person, seven days a week," said Kharasch. "They were ready to sign a lease, but they spent $800 for one night with me and walked away with their $1 million."

He said dining habits have changed dramatically in the past 10 years. In the past, he would figure out who was living within a few miles of the restaurant. Now, he looks at who would be willing to drive to the restaurant in 15-minute increments.

There are many reasons a restaurant fails. Leading the list are poor design, poor location, overstaffing, and lax cost controls.

As soon as he's hired, he spends about three days "secret shopping," visiting the restaurant to observe operations. He recalled one night when the host seated him, but he was completely ignored by the wait staff for 30 minutes. Turns out the manager didn't believe in making table assignments for the waiters, so no one knew who should serve him.

"When I left, the host asked how I enjoyed my dinner," Kharasch said. "What dinner? I had never been offered a menu or a drink."

During these stealth visits he also reviews the quality of the food, portion sizes, and overall ambience. One of his recent success stories involved the remodeling and rebranding of Philander's, a 30-year-old, "white tablecloth" restaurant in Oak Park, Illinois. Mike Fox, the owner, hired Kharasch when he decided the eatery needed a major facelift. Together, they transformed it into Barclay's American Grille.

"We wanted to completely change the menu because people were not going out for $35 steaks," said Fox. "In 2009, we invested about $600,000 in the space and closed down for 90 days."

They updated the menu to include more casual, bistro food with an average tab of $25 including food and a drink. "The chef came up with a new menu with 30 new items," said Fox. His company, Fox Partners, is the landlord to 10 other restaurants, and he owns the Carleton Hotel where Barclay's is located.

Fox made another change: he stopped booking nightly live entertainment when the restaurant reopened. Although long-time patrons loved the music, Fox said "they would come in and buy one $5 drink" instead of ordering a meal. "The response has been very positive, although some diehards don't like it," said Fox.

Kharasch's Tips for Restaurant Owners

- Reduce the number of managers you hire by reorganizing the staffing schedule.
- Make sure the kitchen is designed to let the chef easily supervise cooking and to get the food out to customers fast.
- Make sure your menu is easy to understand, and promote high-margin items like appetizers and desserts.
- Insist that bartenders measure the alcohol they pour. Bartenders who don't measure "drain a restaurant of profit."
- Be sure your staff is well trained and motivated to provide great, friendly service.

One more tip: The owners of the Lyndonville Freight House in Lyndonville, Vermont, collect menus from other popular restaurants to get ideas for their menu. "We printed out 60 to 80 menus and compiled a list of 40 dishes we wanted to try," said Bonnie Paris, who runs the restaurant and a nearby farm with her parents and fiancé. "We try to use seasonal ingredients—heartier meals in the winter and lighter things in the summer."

GREAT IDEA 19 — Thank Everyone You Work With

Here's a great idea that doesn't cost a cent. Thank everyone you work with, whether they are an employee, supplier, vendor, or customer. It sounds absurdly simple, but a simple, heartfelt "thank you" goes a long way. Just saying it boosts your feelings of gratitude.

You can't be successful on your own. You need all those people you deal with all day to make your personal dreams come true. Another low-cost management tip: people love to hear the sound of their own name. So call a person by their name whenever possible. I make a mental note every time I'm on the phone with a customer service representative, whether it is someone at my bank or someone I'm placing an order with. You can hear them smile through the phone when I say, "Thanks so much for your help, Mary."

GREAT IDEA 20 — Move Your Business into a Main Street Revitalization Zone

Paul Curtain, owner of Raymond's Jewellers in downtown Sioux Falls, South Dakota, needed a loan to remodel his store a few years ago. So he borrowed money, below prime rate, from a revolving fund set up especially for downtown merchants. "As a small retailer, I couldn't have afforded to do what I've done in a mall location," said Curtain.

Merchants are moving from malls to Main Street across the country. Small business owners are taking advantage of a variety of state, local, and federal Main Street revitalization programs. For example, the merchants of Skagway, Alaska, with a year-round population of 300, applied for state and federal help to build new sidewalks that mimic the original wooden ones.

"There is a new breed of merchants, and they live in Downtown, USA," said Kennedy Smith, former director of the National Historic Trust's Main Street Center program.

Thousands of deteriorating and abandoned communities have been revitalized by funds and technical assistance provided by the program. Since it began in 1976, more than 2,000 communities in the United States and Puerto Rico have received help.

Cumulatively, the commercial districts taking part in the Main Street program have generated more than $48.8 billion in new investment, with 206,600 in building rehabilitations and a net gain of more than 391,050 new jobs and 87,850 new businesses.

Every dollar a community uses to support its local Main Street program leverages an average of $25 in new investment, making the Main Street program one of the most successful economic development strategies in America.

Main Street offers a four-point revitalization framework appropriate for communities of all types.

Communities across the country are revitalizing their downtown areas in a variety of ways. Peekskill, New York, for example, has created a downtown area filled with art galleries and art schools. Affordable rent and remodeled lofts are luring many artists from Manhattan and other areas, city officials said. Venice Beach, California, revitalized an ailing business district by encouraging galleries to move in, creating a mecca for art lovers along Abbott Kinney Boulevard.

White River Junction, Vermont, once a shabby railroad town, now boasts one of the coolest boutiques in New England. Revolution sells amazing vintage and designer clothing, as well as hosting wild fashion shows with customers modeling the clothes. Co-owner and self-proclaimed "revolutionary," Kim Souza hosts standing room only Oscar®-watching parties and lots of community events.

Down the street from Revolution, artists, printmakers, body workers, and health care practitioners coexist in the Tip Top Building, a former bakery, completely renovated by architect, actor, and filmmaker, Matt Bucy. The Tip Top Café, located in the lobby, offers delicious bistro cuisine and a cozy ambience that rivals the trendiest Manhattan restaurants.

For small retailers, moving downtown has many advantages. You can set your own hours and operate your store without being restricted by mall regulations. Rents are usually cheaper in downtown business districts.

If you are interested in improving your downtown area, here are some tips from the National Trust:

- Schedule a meeting with merchants, civic leaders, lenders, and restoration-minded citizens to start the conversation.
- Meet with public officials and city planners to gauge their interest in redevelopment efforts.
- Meet with a cross-section of community groups to enlist their support.
- Organize a downtown festival to focus attention on your downtown area. (We draw more than 1,000 people to downtown White River for one weekend in June for the White River Indie Film Festival.) David Fairbanks Ford, owner of the quirky and eclectic Main Street Museum, hosts parties and events year round. Tip Top Building owner Matt Bucy and Kim Souza of Revolution produce a fantastic Halloween street party and parade through the Junction. In 2010, the Tupelo Music Hall opened, bringing world-class artists to town. (Imagine Dave Mason and Judy Collins performing in a small town in Vermont.)
- Visit other Main Street areas to see what they are doing to liven things up.
- Create a task force of business owners, property owners, and government officials to set priorities and make plans.

For more information and technical assistance, contact www.preservationnation.org.

GREAT IDEA 21

Ask Your Staff to Evaluate You

Good managers are expected to evaluate their employees carefully at least once a year. These formal performance evaluations are used for awarding salary increases and promotions or for documenting problems prior to termination.

Great managers should be confident and open enough to reverse roles and let their employees evaluate them once a year. Asking your employees to rate your performance is not as scary as you'd think, and you will gain valuable insight.

In addition, human resources experts say that most unhappy employees quit rather than complain about their manager to their manager, so soliciting honest input from your staff may prevent a valuable employee from leaving.

The simplest way to collect honest feedback is to create a short evaluation form and ask employees to submit it anonymously.

Possible questions for your evaluation:

1. How would you describe my management style:
   - Tyrannical
   - Open to new ideas, inclusive
   - Rigid and uncompromising
2. Do I bring out the best in my employees?
   - Yes
   - No
   - Sometimes
   - Please elaborate:
3. What can I do to improve the way I manage the company? Please provide specific suggestions.
4. Would you recommend that friends apply for jobs here if their skills fit our needs?
   - If yes, why?
   - If no, why not?
5. Do I praise people publicly for their good work?
6. Do I often criticize people for poor performance in front of colleagues?
7. What is the best decision I've made this year?
8. What is the worst decision I've made this year?
9. How would you have handled the problem with _____ differently than the way I did?

Set a deadline for response, and remind employees that there is no need to sign their names. After you review the comments, schedule a staff meeting to discuss their suggestions for improvement and how you plan to respond.

GREAT 22 IDEA Cross-Train Your Employees

With so many online options for buying office supplies, why would anyone pick up the phone, place an order, and wait for a Magee's truck to deliver?

"We have 25 trucks on the road every day," said Peter Winslow, who bought the Randolph, Vermont–based company in 1963. Customers from 70 miles away rely on Magee's to keep their shelves stocked. One way they compete with office superstores is by belonging to a purchasing cooperative that serves 250 small office supply dealers.

Another secret of their long-term success is cross-training all employees to do multiple jobs. That way, people can fill in for each other as well as understand what it takes to get every job done. "The more and different jobs you can do, the more valuable you are," said Todd Winslow, Peter's son, who runs the company with his father's counsel but does not have a title.

"We don't have job titles," said Todd Winslow. "Everybody has a job to do, but they can all do more than one job. That's how we survive during recessions." (Bloomberg LP is another company that frowns on job titles.)

The Winslows also believe in rigorously testing people, from the time someone applies for a job to the day they leave the company. They rely on a variety of personality and aptitude tests, including Meyers-Briggs. "You never know what people are good at until you test them," he said. "We tested a guy for a sales job but he ended up being great at collecting (money)."

GREAT IDEA 23 — Create a Disaster Recovery Plan

Nobody likes to think about the possibility of disaster, but that doesn't mean you shouldn't have a comprehensive disaster recovery plan for your business. You may not be hit with a hurricane, tornado, or earthquake, but even a broken pipe or minor fire can temporarily wipe out your business.

Big companies have committees and consultants to deal with recovery planning. Smaller businesses are finally recognizing the need for similar plans, according to Judy Bell, founder of Disaster Survival Planning Network in Southern California. She's written several books, including *Disaster Survival Planning: A Practical Guide for Business*, available on her web site for $19.95 plus tax and shipping. Her company offers a seminar to help small business owners prepare for disaster at a cost of $6,000. The fee includes a software template to create your own plan.

"We see chief financial officers and company auditors wanting to do disaster plans," said Bell. "People who lease space are also asking their building managers how they can prepare." Bell, who has worked with hundreds of companies, said insurance companies encourage clients to plan for disaster recovery.

Check out a variety of do-it-yourself products offered on her site: www .disaster-survival.com.

Meanwhile, here's a list of questions to ask before developing a disaster recovery plan:

- Where would you work if you couldn't work in the office?
- Can you arrange to share office space with another business?
- How would you contact clients and customers?
- Do you have a list of every employee's name, address, and home phone number?
- Do you have copies of your client or customer database at someone's home?
- Do you have copies of your invoices and accounts receivable somewhere other than at the office?
- Are all your important business records, including corporate records, backed up and stored offsite?

As part of your plan, you should keep important records at your home or in another safe place. This includes tax records, returns, patents, training materials, policy manuals, personnel records, and payroll checks. Back up all data on thumb drives and give copies to one or two trusted employees. Be sure to include current phone numbers for your insurance agent, plus policy numbers and copies of your insurance policies.

Shoot digital photos of your computers and other equipment and create an inventory including serial numbers. This information will help your insurance company settle your claims quickly.

Before a disaster strikes, develop a plan for exiting your building quickly and safely. Install fire extinguishers and schedule a fire drill. Assign people to act as safety monitors. Speak to your insurance agent about buying business interruption insurance to keep the doors open after a crisis.

Money Matters

2

Entrepreneurs are obsessed with money. We fret about raising it, saving it, borrowing it, and spending it.

This chapter has all sorts of great ideas related to cutting costs and financing your business. One thing I've learned about money: many projects cost three times as much as you budgeted and usually take twice as long to complete—especially in the media and entertainment world.

Optimistic entrepreneurs often fail to consider how they can support their families while waiting to draw a salary. New business owners are notorious for overestimating revenues and underestimating expenses.

It's a blessing if you have someone else pay your living expenses—at least during the first year or two. My husband, Joe, has always had a "real" job, with good health insurance benefits. Through the years, he's provided a stable financial foundation and health insurance for our family while I've maxed out our credit cards and gambled everything we had on several ventures, including SBTV.com (Small Business TV), the first online television network exclusively covering small business news and Back on Track America, a cross-country speaking tour cosponsored by Amtrak in 2001 after the terrorist attacks on 9/11.

SBTV.com, launched in 2000 with marketing support from CNN.com, was way ahead of its time. We produced hundreds of high-quality video clips, but unfortunately, they were unwatchable on a dial-up connection. We sold that company in 2003 and now you can watch broadcast quality clips on 201greatideas.com.

Although I had a syndicated column, a book contract, and a syndicated radio report, my first years in business were challenging. I was lucky, though. Sales of my first book, *Succeeding in Small Business: The 101 Toughest Problems and How to Solve Them* took off after *USA Today* published an excerpt and an extensive profile, including a picture of me working in my new home office.

That story prompted American Express to sponsor my syndicated small business radio report. The radio report, which aired on CBS stations across the country, combined with my weekly column, served as a magnet for speaking engagements and consulting projects.

It's been an adventure. I don't regret quitting my job. But riding the entrepreneurial roller coaster is why both our kids work full-time for major media companies. Evan is a graphic designer for *Bloomberg Businessweek*. Jeanne is an assistant editor at Pixar Animation Studios. When she's not working hard on the next big animated hit, she creates animated and experimental videos for artists and musicians.

They vowed never to be entrepreneurs after an especially traumatic family vacation in Las Vegas. The phone rang while we were watching TV, and the kids (then 12 and 6 years old) were splashing in the groovy, in-room hot tub. The call was from our bookkeeper, and she was crying so hard I couldn't understand what she was saying. She finally calmed down enough to tell me we owned $91,000 in federal taxes—and it had to be paid within 24 hours. I almost fell off the bed. We packed up and checked out. Goodbye hot tub and mirrored ceiling. Goodbye Vegas. We stopped at Denny's for breakfast. I was crying so hard I couldn't eat, but Joe said the pancakes tasted soapy.

Thank goodness, I had the money in the bank. It turned out our flaky former CPA had forgotten to prepare the vouchers to make the required estimated tax payments! I was too busy running the business to keep track of when to pay the taxes. That's why *you*, the business owner, have to stay on top of everything, especially financial matters.

Most everyone reading this book has faced similar money challenges. So read on to learn the best way to court angel investors, how to collect debts, and how to reduce your tax burden without raising an eyebrow from Uncle Sam. Speaking of Uncle Sam, the U.S. government purchased $350 billion worth of goods and services in 2009, so think about whether you can become a government vendor or supplier.

The chapter begins with one of my favorite ideas: becoming a "profit enhancement officer," or PEO, for your business. If you've had it with your current business and are ready to move on, I share some good ideas about how to buff up your balance sheet before selling your business.

Meanwhile, here's a great money-saving tip from the American Institute of Certified Public Accountants: If you pack a lunch instead of spending $6 a day, five days a week, and put that money in the bank for 10 years, you would end up with $19,592, based on a 6 percent interest rate. That rate is not realistic, but the point is, every dollar saved really counts. Find more money-saving tips at www.feedthepig.org.

GREAT
24
IDEA

Become a Profit Enhancement Officer

We're all familiar with CEOs, but how about a PEO? A PEO is a profit enhancement officer, and that's what every business owner should be, according to Barry Schimel, a Maryland certified public accountant (CPA) who quit preparing tax returns to devote his life to boosting business owners' profits.

"If you ask employees what their responsibilities are, the word *profit* rarely comes out of their mouths," said Schimel. "People do their work, but there's often no relationship between what they do and how it affects the bottom line."

Beefing up the bottom line is the goal of Schimel's rigorous analysis and intense brainstorming sessions. Schimel says he's helped his clients reap more than $200 million in additional profits over the years.

The owner of an upstate New York moving company said "he gave us new ways of looking at things." For example, he encouraged the office staff to quickly complete all the move-related paperwork. Why? The faster they billed clients, the faster they were paid. This tactic added about $1,000 a week to the company's bottom line.

Next, Schimel recorded calls to the sales department. "That was a real eye-opener," said the moving company executive. "One salesperson was essentially giving away out-of-state business by referring customers to other movers."

Schimel's other clients reaped a windfall just by reviewing customer accounts. "We found a lot of customers with special discounts that no one had reviewed for years," said Gil Carpel, CEO of a DC-area delivery company. Schimel urged him to increase rates and charge clients more for mileage, round trips, and waiting time. Few customers complained about these minor adjustments, which brought in an extra $100,000 a year.

"It was really manna from heaven," said Carpel, who also "fired" some customers who rarely used his services. Based on Schimel's brainstorming sessions, they also installed a toll-free 800 number for drivers who had been calling dispatchers collect.

So look around your office today and find ways to cut expenses and boost profits.

G R E A T

25

I D E A

Write a Killer Business Plan

If two down-on-their-luck beggars approach you on the street asking for money, are you more likely to give money to the dirty, scruffy guy or the sincere, clean guy who asks politely for spare change?

Too many entrepreneurs circulate scruffy business plans and wonder why they never get funding. Remember this: your business plan has less than a minute to catch the eye of a serious investor. Messy, typo-filled, poorly written plans end up in the trash, according to the private, so-called angel investors and busy venture capitalists I've interviewed. Thousands of business plans hit their desk or inbox every year. They don't waste time reviewing second-rate pitches.

A veteran venture capitalist (VC) agreed to share some insights, but asked not to be identified. She said, first of all, she looks for succinctly written plans printed in an easy-to-read font. "The less the plan weighs, the better," she said. "I always read the two-pound business plans last."

She and other professional investors interviewed said the most important element is the executive summary. If it's not concise, yet comprehensive, the potential investor will go no further. If you aren't a great writer, hire one to help.

"The content is critical, especially in a technical area like biotechnology," she said. "Always include the most compelling research results and data. Your plan must explain why someone should invest in *your* firm and not the competition."

Remember to write your plan with the investor's perspective in mind, not yours. Be sure to include all the perks beyond making money. For instance, some investors like to be invited to glitzy parties and industry trade shows when they have money in a high-profile deal. Others want to be quoted in the press when the deal closes.

Good products and great writing aside, luck and personal contacts play a significant role in raising capital. Despite the soft economy, U.S.VCs invested $18.2 billion in 2,469 companies in 2009, and $16.9 billion through the third quarter of 2010, according to the National Venture Capital Association.

Like anything else in life, timing is essential. Your company has to have a great scalable product or service and the right team in order to appeal to venture capitalists (also known as *vulture capitalists*).

But, because people lend money to people, not companies, savvy investors always consider where the deal came from. "The source of the deal is very important to a venture capitalist," said the VC. "If we like the source, we'll definitely pay attention to the deal."

So, if you want your business plan to land on the right desk, take advantage of every possible contact you have. Attorneys, accountants, and successful businesspeople can often help you get your business plan to the appropriate investor. Then it's up to your plan to be a magnet for money.

GREAT
26
IDEA

More Insider Tips to Woo Investors

Carol Nichols invests in fast companies and fast horses. As managing director of Circle C Ventures LLC, Dallas, she is always looking for attractive investment opportunities. But before she invests, she needs to hear "the story."

"Often, a small business owner doesn't have the financial staff, a CFO, or controller to tell the company story in a way that is persuasive to a sophisticated lender or investor," said Nichols, who worked as a banker for 26 years prior to cofounding the Texas Women's Venture Fund.

Nichols said step one on the road to securing financing is to determine how much and what kind of capital you need to grow your business.

"If you don't have personal assets, then you need other people's money, or OPM," said Nichols. "That's when I ask company executives, 'Who is going to listen to your story?'"

So, ask yourself who knows you, who trusts you, and who has made money with you before?

Nichols said this question often stops business owners cold. "But if friends and family won't lend you money, why should a stranger?"

Raising money in the past two years has been extremely tough. The Great Recession created by the mortgage and Wall Street meltdown severely impacted the venture capital market. And, finding a bank to finance a small deal is even tougher, Nichols said.

Another barrier to financing: if you are lucky enough to find investors, be prepared to step aside. "Often, the person who has invented the product or the company's current CEO is not the one who can take the company to the next level," Nichols cautioned.

When it comes to her own investments, Nichols said she looks for well-managed, fast-growth businesses, including "leading edge biotech."

"Companies needing $5 to $10 million are my sweet spot," she said, noting that as soon as the money is in the door, the management team needs to be able to discuss who will buy the company down the road.

"Private investors are all about the exit," said Nichols. "They want to know 'when am I going to get my money back and how much?'"

Despite the recession and limited number of venture-backed deals, VCs still want to earn 10 times their initial investment.

When she's not working on her own deals, Nichols does business development for vCFO.com and works with Golden Seeds, an angel investment fund. (See Great Idea #28 for more about vCFO.com.)

GREAT IDEA 27 — Find Yourself an Angel

Bettina Hein is the perfect person to ask about raising angel capital. She's raised $9 million to start two small, high-tech companies—with about $6 million coming from angel or private investors. After founding a speech technology software company in her native Switzerland, she moved to Boston to start another venture,

Pixability Inc. (www.pixability.com). Pixability helps customers quickly and affordably edit and post high-quality video clips to the Web.

"I do not come from a rich family or have any special connections," Hein told me. "In fact, I was a young female with no previous business experience. If I can do it, you can do it."

If your company is too young, too risky, or too offbeat to qualify for traditional bank financing or won't grow fast enough to intrigue a VC, you probably need angels. Angels are private investors, usually successful entrepreneurs, who prefer to invest in small businesses in their industry and close to home.

Hein said the first step toward raising money from angels is to have a well-written business plan (see Great Idea #25), a compelling executive summary, up-to-date financials, and at least one real customer. Dress well, get a good night's sleep, and rehearse your presentation. Plan to prepare a slide deck with about 15 slides. Make hard copies of the deck to leave behind, or give everyone the presentation on a USB drive.

"Remember, you are a salesperson, and you have to have your act together," she said. "Finding angels is all about relation-based selling."

Since you are dealing with private individuals, it is important to be introduced by personal contacts. This is why building up your professional network is essential. Be a detective. Find out who the potential angel knows, what schools they attended, groups they belong to, and so on.

Hein said angels are usually very social people and respected industry leaders. It is crucial to find a "lead angel" who will vouch for you and make introductions to other angels. Once you have an angel investor, invite them to accompany you to meet with other potential investors. Their presence adds credibility to your pitch.

"Angels serve as their own investment committee, so it's important that they like you and feel an affinity for you," said Hein. Since she operates in a high-tech world, most of her angels are retired telecommunications executives who need to "feel like they are still in the game."

"First, I ask them for advice—not for money," said Hein. "I truly listen to what they have to say, acknowledge their tips and advice, and give them progress reports."

Remember, the average angel invests about $25,000, so you don't need to pitch only the super-rich. Finally, Hein reminds us not to take rejection personally, but be persistent. "You are never going to get the check on the first date."

If possible, invite your angel to become a member of your formal board of directors or an advisory board. Many angels like to keep a close eye on their money; plus, they can offer you invaluable advice.

Tips for attracting angel investors:

1. Prepare a well-researched, detailed business plan that explains what you plan to do with the money.
2. Your executive summary needs one page explaining *why* someone should invest in your business. Explain, too, how you plan to repay the money and when.
3. Join a professional association or trade group for your industry to start meeting the movers and shakers. Be an active and high-profile member.
4. Discreetly inquire about which members have invested in small businesses.
5. Once you meet a prospect, request a short meeting to discuss your proposal.
6. Be prepared to answer all questions and bring along extra copies of your business plan and executive summary.
7. Rehearse your presentation before the meeting. You want to be as confident and relaxed as possible.
8. If the investor is interested, move to the next step. Bring in your accountant and attorney to close the deal and draft the agreements.

Note: Some angels prefer to make loans at rates comparable to banks or at a slightly higher rate. Others may want to be repaid in stock if your company eventually goes public. Be sure to tailor the financial arrangements to fit your angel's needs.

Howard Sherman, CEO of Inventure Holdings LLC, a Los Angeles–based investment company, has invested in nearly a dozen small companies. He said he is personally attracted to companies that offer solutions to problems. For instance, he's invested in two medical device companies; one involves a new technology to cool down overheated bodies, and the other company makes a new surgical scalpel that reduces scarring and virtually eliminates bleeding. The cooling device has many applications, including cooling soldiers in the battlefield and for people suffering from multiple sclerosis. People with MS often find their symptoms worsen in hot weather.

How to Raise Money from Your Family or Friends

While it's usually better to raise money from professionals, most business owners start with money invested by friends and relatives. But taking money from people you know can be sticky. So here are some tips:

1. Make sure the person understands your business concept and all the risks involved in investing—put it all in writing.
2. Treat a family member or friend like all the other investors.
3. Provide frequent updates explaining what's going on with the business. Be honest.
4. Don't discuss business matters at family gatherings or social events.
5. Never offer an investment opportunity to anyone who can't afford to lose it all.

Sherman, who prefers to sit on the board of the companies he invests in, said angel money is usually based on a personal relationship. The investor also has to feel some affinity for the product or service. "Sometimes you can position a product as something that will change lives, and then investors view it as almost donating to a charity."

GREAT

28

IDEA

Hire a Virtual Chief Financial Officer

Fourteen years ago, while working as a chief financial officer, a friend introduced Ellen Woods to Tommy Davenport, who was also working as a CFO. Frustrated by only being able to work with one or two companies at a time, they started discussing how they might leverage their skills to help more companies. That's how Virtual CFO was born. The company now has about 100 employees, 1,500 clients, and offices in Dallas, Austin, Houston, Seattle, and Denver. In addition to providing bookkeepers, controllers, and CFOs, the company has a division to help companies recruit permanent financial employees and executives.

The company has flourished by offering a variety of professionals who can determine what kind of help the company needs and provide "a slice of the right level of (financial) expertise," said Wood.

So when should you consider hiring a virtual CFO?

"If you don't have a CFO on your team, you need someone to do pro forma projections and be able to tell your financial story to make it believable," said Carol Nichols, a veteran VC who does business development for Virtual CFO.

"Fractional CFOs," earn between $55 and $250 an hour, depending on their level of expertise. Small companies may just need a controller two days a week. They may later hire a temporary CFO to help with strategic transactions.

"Our concept allows the company to get the right person at the right time," Nichols said.

GREAT IDEA 29 — Choose the Right Bank

The myth is that bankers don't like entrepreneurs. The reality is that bankers have nothing against entrepreneurs, but bankers tend to be conservative and risk-averse. As we know, entrepreneurs tend to be risk takers and able to deal with uncertainty. If you view this situation as a communication gap, not a personality clash, you'll be on your way to building a strong relationship with a banker.

But how do you find the right bank for your company? The first step is to determine exactly what services you need from your bank. I like the idea of starting with a community bank, where you can get to know your banker and they can get to know you and your business.

That personal relationship is critical. I was once hired by Wells Fargo Bank to research what was most important to small business owners about their banking relationship. We were surprised to learn that most business owners want a bank with a personal banker dedicated to their specific needs.

Unfortunately, given the massive consolidation among banks and the push to doing most transactions online, it's tough to find a real person.

Despite these drawbacks, it's still possible to find a good business banker, especially at a community bank like Montecito Bank & Trust in Santa Barbara. I've been working with the team there on a variety of marketing projects and they really do care about their customers. Choosing a banker is like choosing a good doctor. You want someone who is competent, personable, and a good listener. Your banker should be a member of your management team.

What you need from a bank changes depending on where you are in the business life cycle. In the first year or two, you'll probably need a business checking account, a savings account, and, if you process credit card orders, merchant card services (see Great Idea #50).

Other services to consider:

- Letters of credit (domestic and international)
- Notary public service
- Traveler's checks
- Commercial line of credit
- Small Business Administration–guaranteed loans
- Wire transfers
- Direct deposit of payroll checks for employees
- Payroll tax deposits

Some tips on finding the right banker:

1. Ask friends and colleagues to recommend their favorite bankers. Many bankers move around, so if you find someone you like, you may be forced to follow that person from one financial institution to another.
2. Set up interviews with a few potential bankers. Meeting face to face is critical to making an informed decision. Ask for references, and call other clients.
3. Open your accounts and, if possible, link your checking and savings accounts together.
4. Ask for perks. If your deposit is large enough, you'll probably qualify for a free safe-deposit box, free bank checks, and so on.
5. Once your money is safely tucked away, invite your banker to visit your office and meet your team.
6. If you can't find a reputable local bank, consider a "nonbank" alternative, like a brokerage house.

GREAT IDEA 30

Create a Sensitivity Analysis

Want to impress a banker when you apply for a credit line or loan? Walk into the meeting with a sensitivity analysis. It sounds hard to do, but it's not especially complicated, according to Denise Howard, a former banker who now works as a financial planner for many business owners.

"You basically need to look at what will be your break-even point," said Howard. "Figure out the minimum dollar amount you will need to break even. Then, look at the worst- and best-case scenarios."

Howard said if you are prepared to discuss the impact of these various scenarios, "you will blow the banker away."

Before you meet, bring along or submit in advance a pro forma balance sheet and a profit-and-loss statement. These are *not* the same thing.

"Many small business owners don't understand the difference between an income statement and a cash flow projection," said Howard.

The bottom line is this: You have to show a potential lender where, when, and how their loan will be repaid in a timely manner.

Howard has another tip: "Bankers don't like surprises. We'd much rather have you call and tell us what's going on—even if it's bad news."

She has this cautionary tale: one of her former clients was making so much money, he started buying two or three new gas stations and convenience stores a year. He used cash from his existing stores to open the new ones. "Unfortunately, he wasn't monitoring expenses, including the rising price of gasoline."

Everything began to fall apart. He was about to file for bankruptcy protection when Howard helped him find someone willing to invest in the crumbling gas station empire in exchange for equity.

"Just because you have money in the bank doesn't mean you are making money," she warns.

GREAT IDEA 31

Find a Good Accountant

Now that you have customers, clients, and money to grow your business, it's time to hire an experienced accountant or tax professional. A good accountant does much more than help you file your taxes. They should lead your financial advisory team.

A good small business accountant keeps up to date on all state and federal tax laws. He or she should understand your business and serve as your confidant. You should consult them before you buy any equipment, sign a major deal, or sell or relocate your business.

John D'Aquila, founder of D'Aquila & Co. LLP, with offices in Jacksonville, Florida, provides a range of services to his entrepreneurial clients. He not only prepares our tax returns, but helps me manage all my finances. Best of all, he steers me away from making financial mistakes. I appreciate his expertise, candor, and integrity. He brilliantly orchestrated the sale of SBTV.com by setting it up as an installment sale that benefited both us and the buyer. He also helps many of his clients attract outside investors to fuel growth.

So how do you find the right accountant for your particular business? If possible, hire someone with experience in your specific industry. So, if you are in the apparel business, you want someone who knows fashion. If you are in the construction industry, you want someone who knows the ins and outs of leasing heavy equipment and dealing with subcontractors.

Word of mouth is the best way to find a good accountant; so start by asking your friends, neighbors, and business associates for recommendations.

Remember, in order to do a good job, your accountant has to know nearly everything about you, your family, and your business. You need to work with someone you feel comfortable confiding in.

Once you assemble a list of potential candidates, check out their web sites and profiles on LinkedIn.

If you like what you see, schedule a meeting. Many entrepreneurs prefer to work with small accounting firms because they are more apt to work directly with a partner. But if your business requires a big company with international offices, don't rule out a big firm. A reputable accountant should not charge you for the initial meeting.

Make a list of questions you want to ask during your interview. Do you feel comfortable with the person? You'll be sharing very personal and financial information.

If you like what you see, ask for a short list of other clients to call for references. If the accountant is reluctant to give references, move on. Ask if they are up to date on the professional courses they are required to take by their accrediting organizations. If you like the person and their references check out, discuss these specific issues:

1. What are the fees for various projects and services?
2. Who, specifically, at the firm will do the hands-on accounting and tax preparation? Can an introduction to that person be arranged?
3. How does the firm expect information to be provided to them? Via e-mail? Paper copies?
4. Is the firm experienced in handling disputes with the IRS?
5. How does the firm expect to be paid? Net 30?

Remember, if things don't work out, don't be afraid to change accountants. There are thousands out there who would be happy to have your business.

GREAT
32
IDEA

Work with an Enrolled Agent to Do Your Taxes

I want all the CPAs to skip this section. I'm about to suggest an alternative tax preparer: an enrolled agent (EA). Although they've been around since 1884 and prepare millions of tax returns a year, enrolled agents are a well-kept secret. While certified public accountants (CPAs) and public accountants (PAs) are licensed by the state, enrolled agents are licensed by the federal government. EAs specialize in preparing tax returns and can represent taxpayers before the Internal Revenue Service, just like CPAs and tax attorneys.

They have to renew their license every three years after completing 72 hours of education in taxation. Despite their background and education, EAs tend to charge lower fees than CPAs or PAs.

EAs are definitely outnumbered: there are only about 35,000 in the United States, compared with 500,000 CPAs and PAs.

There are probably so few because it's tough to become one. There are only two ways: pass a tough, two-day exam given once a year by the IRS (only about 30 percent of those who take it pass it) or work for the IRS for five years. Through the years, EAs have had to battle CPAs who have pushed legislation aimed at limiting an EA's ability to prepare balance sheets and financial statements for business clients.

CPAs contend that EAs should do only tax returns. EAs insist they can't do a good tax return without an accurate financial statement.

"CPAs treat us as a subspecies," said Sid Norton, former president of the California Society of Enrolled Agents. In 1986, Norton said California CPAs launched a major political battle to keep EAs from preparing financial reports for business owners. The EAs fought back and prevailed, but similar battles have been waged in other states.

"CPAs are very upset when we use the word *accounting*," said Sharon Flynn, who has been an EA since 1969.

If you are curious about working with an EA, check it out. Just don't call any tax professional in March or April, when they're working 24/7 on tax returns. "Trying to interview a tax pro during the peak of tax preparation season can be like chatting with a doctor during brain surgery," joked Sid Norton.

GREAT 33 IDEA

Find a Strategic Partner to Invest in Your Company

Jay Whelan's "lightbulb" moment hit while he was undergoing physical therapy for a shoulder injury. He was bored and staring out the clinic window as he spun a wheel with a hand pedal attached. The device was designed to strengthen his shoulder muscles.

"I thought, 'What if I could capture the energy I'm expending on this exercise and put it into the (electric) power grid?'" recalled Whelan, who has an industrial engineering background and an MBA from Boston College.

Whelan knew electricity could be generated from fitness equipment, including spinning bikes, but he wasn't sure how long it would take to develop the right equipment and technology.

"It was a matter of hiring engineers to take my vision and make something workable," said Whelan, founder and CEO of eGreen Revolution (www.egreenrevolution.com).

Once they had a prototype, they tested it with positive results at a local sports club. Then, he approached the New York Sports Club.

"People in spin rooms are a passionate group who show up consistently and train hard," said Ed Trainor, vice president of business and product development for Town Sports International (TSI), which owns the New York Sports Club and other clubs around the country.

TSI installed the first eGreen Revolution equipment on spin bikes in New York City and Washington, DC, in 2010. So far, response has been positive.

"The spin classes were the perfect place to start using the technology," said Trainor. "It gives people a way to measure their effort and performance. It's a hard workout but great to know at the end of the class that they've generated power." So far, it's just enough power to run the video screens attached to the cardio equipment.

Trainor declined to say how much money the company has invested in the eGreen Revolution technology, but said it was thousands of dollars. "Our company has a strong green initiative and this fit right in. It is an investment, and it will take a while to recover that investment, but it's definitely worth it. . . . It has added real value and people like it."

According to eGreenRevolution.com, 20 people participating in a spinning class could collectively generate about 3 kilowatts of electricity. A spinning room, with four classes of 20 people a day could generate 300 kilowatts a month—enough power to serve a typical home for six months.

Prior to starting his own business, Whelan spent 18 years as a consultant for Accenture.

"After 18 years on the road, living in hotels and airports, my two kids didn't really know who their dad was," said Whelan. At 46, he cashed out, planning to retire and putter around. But six months later, he was bored. He looked into buying a franchise, but decided he'd rather start something on his own.

So far, he's invested close to $1 million in cash and time. He has also been reluctant to collect a salary.

Testing the concept on spinning bikes at clubs has been invaluable. "It's one thing to develop a product that works in the lab, but another to make it commercially viable," explained Whelan, who was lucky to connect with the big fitness company.

Finding the right strategic partner is a critical key to success for many small companies. Teaming up with a bigger, financially strong partner can provide a source of cash for growth, marketing, and expansion.

So, consider joining forces with a bigger, well-financed partner to bring your product to market.

Here are some things to consider before you craft a strategic alliance:

- Set clear goals for what each partner hopes to accomplish.
- Clarify exactly what each party has committed to do to move the project forward.
- Specify who will be the key players and how they intend to communicate with everyone involved.
- Try working on a small project together before launching a major initiative.
- Regularly review the success of the project and make changes to improve it.

GREAT IDEA 34
Even Out Your Cash Flow

Running a seasonal business is challenging, but there are strategies to manage cash flow in order to make it through the slow times of the year.

Paula Wolff, a former certified public accountant (CPA) with a major firm who also served as an interim chief financial officer (CFO) with a biotech company, agreed to help her son, Barry, expand Seasonal Solutions, his Overland Park, Kansas–based landscaping business. After he lost his job when Lehmann Brothers collapsed, he went into the commercial real estate and property management business.

Landscaping companies in the Midwest are busier in the summer than the winter, so the mother-and-son team needed to figure out more ways to keep their six full-time employees busy all year round. (They hire more help during the summer.)

"We expanded our services to think out of the box," said Wolff. "We are also good about asking for business."

For example, in addition to doing lawn care and maintenance, Seasonal Solutions can install a sprinkler system or build an outdoor kitchen.

"We try to package our services into a menu, so we are not just knocking on doors doing a onesie or twosie service."

They take credit cards and thank American Express for helping them manage cash flow with small business–oriented financial products. Wolff said their Business Platinum card offers cash rebates that are credited against the monthly bill. The card also permits them to make monthly payments versus paying off the balance every month.

"We are using the American Express Business Platinum card with a $20,000 limit as our line of credit," said Wolff, adding that she also bills clients twice a month and encourages clients to sign up for automatic bill payments.

In the winter months, the company provides snow and ice removal. "We sign a contract and ask for level payments over time, which helps us stretch our cash flow over a 10-month period, rather than six months."

In addition to requiring payment the day a project is completed, "we offer a bundle of services versus a discount," she said. "For instance, we'll say, we'll do this job and provide the first chemical treatment for fertilization and weed control at no charge. That guarantees us more work because you can't just do one chemical treatment—you need to do five."

For more info, visit www.seaonsalsolutionskc.com.

GREAT IDEA 35 — Consider Buying a Franchise

Franchising in the United States is a $2.3 trillion-a-year industry employing about 21 million Americans. Franchise companies offer thousands of different businesses, from janitorial services to beauty salons to business coaching.

Between 2001 and 2005, the franchising sector expanded at a faster pace than many other sectors of the U.S. economy. Direct economic output of franchised businesses grew by over 41 percent, while economic output of all businesses grew by 26 percent, according to the International Franchise Association (IFA).

The number of franchised establishments grew by 18.5 percent compared to 15.9 percent for establishments created by all businesses.

But operating a franchise is not for everyone. A franchise provides people training and a firm structure for running a business. It's not recommend for people who prefer to do their own thing.

Here are some tips from the IFA to help you do your homework:

- Meet with the franchiser; get to know key players.
- Consult any and all advisers who can help you make a decision.
- Ask questions. No question is too trivial.
- Compare other franchise systems in the same field.
- Make sure you'll be comfortable doing what the business model requires.
- Read and understand the Uniform Franchise Offering Circular, and know all the details and terms of your contract.
- Check the references of the franchise's officers and managers.
- Research, research, research. The more you know, the better your decision is likely to be.

Contact the International Franchise Association at (202) 628-8000 or visit www.franchise.org.

GREAT IDEA 36

Franchise Your Business Concept

Maybe you've thought about franchising your business? Even if your business is wildly successful, it may not work well as a franchise. For the inside scoop, I turned to Rammy Harwood, a successful entrepreneur who took his first venture, Cosi, a chain of 80 popular sandwich and coffee bars, public in 2000. He went back to business school for an MBA and, after graduating, launched Kidville, a franchise with about 35 outlets in the United States and abroad.

Harwood said everything changed when his partner, Andy Stenzler, and his wife, Shari, had a baby. When Kylie was six months old, Shari took her to a music class for babies. The class met in the dirty basement of a Fred Astaire dance studio. She was so upset over the grungy location, she told Andy, 'You have no idea what I just went through.'"

That was the lightbulb moment for Andy and Rammy. "We thought, there's got to be a better way to offer enrichment programs for kids zero to five," recalled Harwood.

A believer in extensive market research, Harwood visited most of the 60 places on the Upper East Side of New York City that offered early childhood activities. The partners quickly recognized a need to create something wonderful for parents and kids up to five years old. Their business plan called for bright, well-designed centers with classrooms, perhaps a café, and a retail store. Some locations would also feature indoor playgrounds, a space for birthday parties, and a kids' hair salon with plasma screen TVs.

"We wanted to create a place that people would feel comfortable visiting with their kids," said Harwood. "The Upper East Side is unique, and those families deserve the best quality and cleanliness."

To launch Kidville, they tapped their own funds and attracted some very high-profile investors, including the Tisch family and tennis star Andre Agassi, who was a new father at the time.

"It is a privilege to be in this business," said Harwood. The company owns five locations in New York City. There are Kidville locations opening up around the world, including in Cairo; and Dubai. (A former customer bought the right to open several in Dubai and nearby countries.) It costs about $50,000 to buy the franchise and several hundred thousand dollars to build the facility, depending on the size and location. Franchisees also pay a percentage of sales to the parent company.

To make sure they did everything right, they hired renowned franchise consultant Michael Seid, who also sits on the company's board.

Harwood, who earned his MBA at the Stern Business School, said he loves his job because he gets to see his preschool age kids, Cameron and Xander, almost every day.

If you think you have a successful and easy-to-teach business concept, here are some questions to ask yourself:

1. Does my concept work well?
2. Can I create a network of owners versus hiring general managers? "If you don't have the right partners, it can make or break your concept," said Harwood.
3. Do you love what you do?

"I had 3,000 employees in the restaurant business, but no one working for us wanted to be doing what they were doing," said Harwood. "Now, I'm surrounded by people who love what they do and really want to work with kids."

Opening new locations has not been without challenges, including a revolution in Egypt and where to park the fleet of strollers at every Kidville location. "We had to use part of the café to park strollers, which makes it by far the most expensive parking area per square foot in New York City."

Harwood said his favorite thing is teaching new franchisees how to run the business. He is totally hands-on, helping create 19 training manuals, all available online. He said a secret of running a franchise is to make everything "idiot-proof." That's why Kidville spends millions of dollars on its information systems.

Instead of struggling with complicated forms and software, Harwood said, "I want them (the owner) to focus on knowing little Johnny's name and giving him a high five when he comes through the door."

So why should you buy a franchise rather than start a business from scratch?

"It works if you want to be an entrepreneur but you don't have the guts to do it on your own," said Harwood.

GREAT
37
IDEA

Barter for Goods and Services

Jason Greis, co-owner of Greis Jewelry in Farmington Hills, Michigan, admits he was reluctant to accept "trade dollars" for his high-end merchandise when a new customer asked him about it. "He wanted to make a purchase using trade dollars, but I was a little bit worried," said Greis. "If I took $10,000 in trade dollars, what would I do with them?"

Well, Greis has used those trade dollars and more for advertising, printing, and painting. And, best of all, everyone who has used trade dollars to buy jewelry has been a new customer at the store he opened in 1974.

"My fear was that current customers would switch from cash to trade dollars, but that has not happened," said Greis.

Barter is a popular and safe way for business owners to move excess inventory and swap their services for products and services they need.

There are hundreds of barter exchanges around the country. TradeFirst .com, which operates in Michigan, Ohio, and Florida, has been around since 1978. Members pay a $475 annual membership fee and a 10 percent commission on all transactions. Transactions are handled via a card that looks like a credit card with a magnetic strip.

The company has a big warehouse in Michigan with about $4 million worth of office supplies, building materials, tools, and just about everything else a business owner needs or wants.

"It's like a mini club store," said Gail Bernhardt, a senior account executive based in Oak Park, Michigan.

TradeFirst.com's president, Fred Detweiler, said the company's 5,000-plus members are using barter to exchange excess inventory for services they need, including print and cable television advertising. "When the economy slows down, advertising goes out the window," said Detweiler. But, with trade dollars, members can barter for ads to keep the flag flying.

Members also use barter dollars for travel and hotel expenses. Barter seems to be a win-win proposition for its fans. The IRS considers barter dollars the same as real dollars, so all transactions are treated the same tax-wise.

GREAT

38

IDEA

Seek Vendor Financing

Ivan, a white Samoyed with really, really bad breath, was the inspiration behind Greenies®, a dog chew that refreshes even the worst doggie breath.

It's a great story. Ivan's owner, Joe Roetheli, was working as a research manager for the U.S. Department of Agriculture when his wife, Judy, asked him to please do something to cure Ivan's stinky breath. Joe contacted researchers at the University of Missouri dental school, who were using dogs to test a variety of new dental products for humans. One researcher suggested Roetheli try a substance that he declined to identify. Amazingly, it worked.

The couple obtained the formula and started making Greenies. Judy would keep the dog treats in her pockets and give them away. They rented a booth at a local home show and left samples at pet stores. Believing they had a hit, they hired a salesperson, who brought in 150,000 orders in three days. That should have been good news, but the problem was, they had no equipment to fill the orders.

Roetheli frantically started calling injection mold manufacturing companies, desperately trying to buy a machine and a custom mold that would allow them to mass produce his invention. "The mold was going to cost $35,000," he recalled. "I finally talked one guy into saying yes, he would make the mold for us. Then, I did it with 17 different companies."

Roetheli promised to pay them for the machine when the checks cleared. "Most said yes just to get rid of me."

At the beginning, the family would package the dog treats while watching television. "We paid our sons, Steffan and Michael, a few cents for each one they packaged," said Roetheli.

By relying on a network of mold makers willing to make the molds and be paid after sales picked up, Roetheli was able to mass produce Greenies. It was such huge hit with dog owners, sales reached about $1 million a month. At that point, the company was finally able to obtain bank financing.

"It would have been so easy to give up, but persistence paid off," said Roetheli.

By 2005, Greenies was ranked the eighth-largest pet treat company in the United States. In 2006, Roetheli sold Greenies to Mars for an undisclosed sum. He would only say it was "millions of dollars"—enough to open a variety of new businesses, including a day spa and resort, a printing company, and a café. He also supports a foundation that builds villages in South America.

His advice to anyone trying to manufacture a product with limited capital: "If you are passionate about it, keep going. Somebody will do it for you."

GREAT
39
IDEA

EB-5 Visas for Foreign Investors

Did you know that foreign investors with at least $500,000 cash can "buy" themselves a green card? It's true. Under the EB-5 visa program, foreign investors with a minimum of

$500,000 to invest in an area experiencing high unemployment can invest in an American business as long as they create at least 10 full-time jobs.

"These (foreign) investments are creating jobs for qualified U.S. workers," said Lara Baharlo, an associate at the Global Law Group in Los Angeles, which handles dozens of these visa applications a year.

The investment visa program is not without controversy. In fact, several consultants who make these lucrative matches declined to be interviewed. One West Coast business owner, who explained in detail how he attracted $1 million from a Chinese investor and then sold his company two years later to a big German firm, called me back in a panic and begged me not to use his quotes in this book. I agreed, but I still wonder why people are so reluctant to discuss this novel way to attract foreign investment.

On the positive side, the immigration visa process is highly regulated and managed by the federal government, through the U.S. Immigration and Customs Enforcement agency (ICE). U.S. business owners must submit their proposals for federal approval before they can seek investors.

"There are 114 regional centers, which can be found on the immigration service web site," said Baharlo.

At the other end of the deal, wealthy foreign investors must apply for a green card, which initially grants them residency for two and a half years. If all goes well and the jobs they create are real, they can apply for a 10-year permanent residency card.

Foreign investors, mostly from China, are taking full advantage of these investment visas, according to Baharlo.

It's no surprise that China is the number one source of investors. "Investors and business owners work with a network of immigration visa brokers in China," explained Baharlo. "The investors go to a 'dog and pony' show to find U.S. companies to invest in."

Most of the companies seeking foreign investment are privately held, mostly involved in retail, manufacturing, hotels, and light industrial.

Not all companies receiving foreign funds are so profitable. Most have profit margins around 2 percent. Still, hundreds of foreign investors are still motivated to fast-track their way to the American dream.

"It's a win-win situation because the investors are creating jobs in America," said Baharlo.

Invest in Yourself by Tapping Your 401(k)

After losing his engineering job at Whirlpool in 2009, Mike Tilley decided it was time to work for himself. He researched a variety of franchises before he and his wife, Cathy, bought an existing Mr. Handyman franchise in Kalamazoo, Michigan, by cashing in his 401(k) retirement fund.

Tilley used the money to pay the $60,000 franchise fee and invested another $158,000 to buy equipment and to cover other business expenses.

"You really need to believe in yourself to do this," said Tilley. He was lucky. His franchise was breaking even by the third month and was on the road to profitability by the end of the first year.

Tilley is one of thousands of former corporate executives taking advantage of a little-known transaction called a "rollover as business start-up" by the IRS. It is also informally known as the "entrepreneur rollover stock ownership plan" or ERSOP. Although pension experts say the IRS might scrutinize taxpayers who tap into their retirement accounts to fund businesses, it is still an attractive option to consider, if done right.

"The penalties for not complying with the rules are staggering," said Cliff Ennico, an attorney based in Fairfield, Connecticut, who counsels clients cashing in their retirement funds to purchase businesses. "If the IRS determines that a 401(k) rollover is a prohibited transaction, it can trigger excise taxes on top of taxes, interest, and penalties for premature distribution of 401(k) funds."

It's a good idea to work with a company that specializes in these transactions. BeneTrends Inc., founded by Leonard Fischer, is based in North Wales, Pennsylvania. Every year, the company helps thousands of new entrepreneurs execute these rollover transactions.

"At the end of the day, all we are doing is helping clients invest in themselves," said Fischer, who has been dealing with pension and profit-sharing issues for 50 years.

Fischer said it works like this: clients set up a new corporation with a defined contribution plan and roll over the money from their 401(k) into the "qualifying employer securities" or stock in the new company. "It's their job to make the money," said Fischer. "It's our job to make sure they are in compliance with all tax laws."

BeneTrends charges a flat fee of $4,995 to handle the paperwork. Then, they charge a monthly fee of about $100 to make sure the company remains in compliance. "Maintaining these plans seems deceivingly simple, but it is incredibly complicated."

Fischer cautions that not everyone should risk investing their nest egg on a business.

"It's not like gambling in Las Vegas, but there is an investment risk," he said. "The person has to feel comfortable investing in himself."

He also points out that the average 50-year-old has about $175,000 in a company-sponsored retirement account, which is not really enough to live on after retirement. "It makes sense to build a business that will outperform the stock market," said Fischer.

He also said that if you start withdrawing retirement funds to live on, most people will pay 30 to 40 percent in income taxes.

Ennico, a small business attorney and author of several books on small business, said it is critical to proceed with caution. "If your franchised business ultimately fails, the profit-sharing plan will be left holding worthless stock, which may have a catastrophic impact on your financial future."

It is important to understand all the risks of "betting the ranch" on a franchise, because "that's exactly what you are doing."

Meanwhile, Tilley admits he's working harder than he ever did before, especially since he has no retirement fund to fall back on. "I've got to give it a shot and do everything in my power to make this successful."

GREAT 41 IDEA Apply for a Government-Backed Bank Loan

In the fall of 2010, right before the midterm elections when Republicans regained control of Congress, President Obama shamed legislators into freeing up a package of $30 billion in tax credits and loans and other programs aimed to help small business owners dig out. Main Street finally got what Wall Street had received years before.

It took a lot of wrangling, but the measure is aimed at encouraging community banks to lend money to qualified business owners. The U.S.

Small Business Administration (SBA) also raised the maximum limit on several loan programs.

The changes are permanent for general small business loans under SBA's 7(a) guaranteed loan program, fixed asset loans through the 504 Certified Development Company program, Microloans, and International Trade, Export Working Capital, and Export Express loans. The SBA permanently increased 7(a) and 504 limits from $2 million to $5 million, and for manufacturers and certain energy-related projects seeking 504 loans, to $5.5 million.

The maximum for International Trade and Export Working Capital loans was increased from $2 million to $5 million. SBA also permanently increased microloan limits from $35,000 to $50,000, helping larger entrepreneurs with start-up costs and small business owners in underserved communities.

The SBA boosted the limit on Export Express loans, from $250,000 to $500,000, and made the program permanent. Check www.sba.gov for updates and loan details.

GREAT
42
IDEA

Invoice Bimonthly and Add an Overhead Charge

Susan Pepperdine, a veteran public relations consultant, has two great ideas for boosting cash flow. She bills clients twice a month and adds a 2 percent overhead charge to cover postage, shipping, and printing, so you don't have to keep track of all that small stuff.

"If you bill more frequently, you don't have to wait until the end of the month to be paid," she said. "The longer you stretch it out, the less likely you are to get paid. Plus, consultants are not like the phone or electric company; we can't cut the service off, so you have to do something."

Pepperdine's clients range from a well-drilling and mineral exploration company in Kansas to a church and an investment company. She also writes newsletters and annual reports.

The bimonthly billing strategy has other advantages. "If you wait until the end of the month to send a bill, clients will forget what you've done for them lately," she said. "Bimonthly bills are also in smaller chunks, which is easier to get through the accounting department. There's not as much sticker shock."

43 Ask for a Deposit

If you want Diane Dunn to play angelic harp music at a wedding, funeral, or party, you have to pay a 50 percent deposit when you book the date.

"If clients balk, I tell them that once I book a date, I turn away other opportunities to play," said Dunn, who lives in Walled Lake, Michigan. She charges $300 for the first hour and $75 an hour after that.

I love deposits. If you want to book me to speak at an event, I require a 50 percent deposit to hold the date. No matter what you do, requiring a deposit is a great way to boost your cash flow. If handled fairly and properly, it shouldn't alienate good customers.

Professional consultants often require 50 percent of the first month's fee when they are retained. Progress payments are made along the way, and the balance is due when the project is completed.

If you haven't required deposits before, here's what to do. Send a letter (not e-mail) to all your customers or clients. Be clear about your new deposit policy, and don't play favorites. Make sure every customer or client complies with the policy. Your customers shouldn't object to paying 20, 30, or even 50 percent down when they place an order or sign a contract. They know you are running a business, not a charity.

44 Lock Your Supply Cabinet

Profit-meister Barry Schimel shared this idea. If your office supply bill is skyrocketing, and the supply closet shelves are always empty, try locking the closet. Give the key to one responsible person, the office manager, or if that's not feasible, to a couple of managers or supervisors on different shifts. This way, no one can just root around for an armload of supplies. Add a sign-out sheet, too, to monitor who is taking what and when.

If employees balk at this, here's what to do: at the end of your next staff meeting send everyone back to their desks to collect all the pencils, pens, and markers under piles of paper or tucked into the backs of drawers. Have a group "show and tell." Look in your backpack, briefcase, or purse. I guarantee you'll find a stash of writing implements.

GREAT

45

IDEA

Set Up a Retirement Plan

Paperwork and complex tax filings discourage many smaller companies from offering even minimal retirement benefits for workers. But no matter how small your company is, you and your employees should be saving for the future.

Many small companies set up simple 401(k) plans and match employee contributions. Because so many people change jobs (the average worker may have 12 jobs in a lifetime), 401(k) plans make sense.

The plans, named after the tax code provision, are easy to set up. Most companies try to provide some sort of matching contribution. It varies from 1 or 2 percent to much higher. Financial planners encourage clients to set aside and invest the maximum amount possible every year to create a robust retirement account.

In 2010, you could deposit up to $16,500 in a 401(k). People over 50 could contribute up to $22,000.

If you are self-employed, look into setting up a simplified employee pension plan–individual retirement account (SEP-IRA). Be sure to work with an experienced financial adviser, no matter what kind of retirement plan you choose.

Saving a few thousand dollars a year may not sound too impressive, but consider this scenario offered by one financial adviser: if your employee earns a salary of $50,000 a year and contributes $6,000 a year to his or her own retirement account, if you contribute just $1,500 a year, after 20 years, the employee would have about $400,000 if the investments selected generated a 9 percent rate of return.

Establish an Employee Stock Ownership Plan (ESOP)

When a small business owner wants to cash out or pull some equity out of his or her business for retirement, one of the best options for employers and employees is to set up an employee stock ownership plan, or ESOP.

ESOPs allow business owners to sell company shares to employees at a fair price. ESOPs also provide significant tax benefits for owners while providing retirement benefits for workers. Workers who own shares usually feel more loyal and driven to perform, so productivity increases and, as a result, their stock increases in value.

"Ninety-one percent of ESOP companies declared that creating employee ownership through an ESOP was a good decision that has helped the company," said J. Michael Keeling, president of the ESOP Association. "That's saying a great deal in these challenging times."

An ESOP can also help finance the expansion of the business, so everyone benefits. ESOPs work especially well for small, stable companies with fewer than 100 loyal, long-time employees. The employees get all the economic benefits of being a shareholder without the liabilities.

America has about 11,500 ESOPs, covering 10 million employees, according to the ESOP Association, based in Washington, DC (www .esopassociation.org). Total assets of U.S. ESOPs at the end of 2007 was estimated to be $901 billion. About 20 percent of ESOP companies are in the manufacturing sector. Most ESOP companies also have retirement and savings plans in addition to employee stock ownership.

One huge perk for business owners is the ability to deduct both the principal and interest on any loan used to finance an ESOP. If you borrow money to create the ESOP, you can use the entire distribution tax free.

If you are thinking of creating an ESOP, you'll need an experienced team comprised of an attorney, an accountant, and a bank or brokerage house to provide the cash to buy the shares.

You'll also need a skilled administrator to keep track of the paperwork and distribute shares when employees quit or retire. Most employees are vested in the plan after five to seven years.

Contact the ESOP Association at 1726 M St., NW, Washington, DC 20036; (202) 293-2971; via e-mail: esop@esopassociation.org; or at their web site: www.esopassociation.org.

Find a Good Independent Insurance Broker

Your insurance broker should be "part of your financial inner circle," according to Richard Butwin, copresident and CEO of the Butwin Insurance Group in Great Neck, New York.

Meeting with a savvy insurance broker at least once a year can protect you and your business from disaster. Business-related insurance is not a luxury—it is a necessity, especially if you interact with the public, which most businesses do, either online or in person.

"During the meeting, you should describe your business, ask questions, and then let the broker design an insurance program," said Butwin.

Most small companies are underinsured, which can be a big mistake. Have you heard of employment practices liability insurance? I hadn't. It protects your company if you are sued for firing, not hiring an applicant, or violating an employee's legal rights. (The policy covers legal costs, but does not cover fines levied by state or federal agencies).

What about business income or business interruption insurance? A comprehensive policy can provide money to keep the lights on and the payroll covered if your business is hit by disaster. (See Great Idea #23 on disaster recovery planning.)

Butwin said a small business owner who sells filters for camera lenses, was extremely grateful he listened to Butwin and bought this coverage. A few years ago, a worker in the office below left a hot plate burning—and nearly burned down the entire building. Firefighters saved the building, but everything was soaking wet and covered with a thick layer of inky soot.

Luckily, the business income policy covered the cost of cleaning up the office. They missed a few days of work but few customers even knew what happened.

"Brokers are supposed to diagnose a loss before it happens," said Butwin, who also takes credit for encouraging a major travel agency client to keep paying for coverage related to telephone and Internet service outages.

A few months later, the hard drive controlling the agency's phone system crashed. Based on past bookings and telephone records, Butwin could prove how much money was lost and filed a successful claim.

His biggest claim involved a defunct car dealership. "A city water main broke and the entire building began to sink into the ground," he recalled. Although the policy excluded claims related to underground water, he was able to prove that the water came from a broken pipe, not a natural spring.

Although it sold cars, most of the dealership revenue was generated from service and repairs. So, Butwin said, it was imperative that the service department reopen as soon as possible. It cost about $1 million for the dealership to move its service department across the street into a vacant building. They had to build a ramp up to the second floor, but the insurance company paid for everything.

"They were back in business within a matter of weeks," said Butwin.

So, no matter what you do for a living, find yourself an experienced independent insurance broker and sleep better at night.

Buy Disability Insurance

Once you find a reputable independent insurance broker, ask them about a very important kind of insurance for yourself: disability insurance.

Insurance industry experts estimate that only 30 to 40 percent of the nation's small business owners have disability insurance. This is a chilling statistic, especially when you consider that at age 37—the prime age for an entrepreneur—the probability of becoming disabled is three and a half times higher than the probability of death.

Virtually all personal disability policies offer the same kinds of benefits. They generally pay a monthly benefit that is slightly less than what you would earn if you were healthy and working. This gap is intentional: insurers want you to have an incentive to get well and return to work. The kind of policy you qualify for depends on what you do for a living.

Professionals, such as attorneys and architects, usually have the easiest time buying disability insurance. Automobile and real estate salespeople, subject to the ups and downs of the economy, have a tougher time. People in risky professions—such as private detectives, construction workers, and actors—may have to look a long time for a policy.

Insurance companies tend to distrust home-based entrepreneurs, thinking they are less stable and more likely to fake accidents. When my firm was home based, I managed to buy disability insurance only because my insurance agent visited my office several times and convinced his bosses that I was running a legitimate consulting business.

Insurance underwriters look at the probability and length of possible disabilities when determining the type of policy you might require. They also consider the number of employees, the length of time you have been in business, and your industry's disability claim history.

One way to save money on insurance premiums is by choosing a 60- to 90-day elimination period. This means you will have to wait a while before your payments begin. Insurance companies think if you are willing to wait for benefits to kick in, you might be less likely to claim a disability. Normally, disability benefits are tax free. Always pay with a personal check. If your company pays for the premium and takes a tax deduction, your benefits will be taxed.

Make sure your policy covers your specific occupation, not just any occupation. If you have a stroke and can't do your old job, you can collect your benefits even if you take up a less demanding, lower-paying occupation. Although it's cheaper to buy a policy that provides benefits to age 65, many agents recommend paying a bit extra for a policy with lifetime benefits.

Finding the Right
Disability Insurance

* Figure out how much you need to cover all your personal monthly expenses.
* Obtain estimates from several insurance carriers.
* Check the financial stability of the company.
* Although it costs more, try to buy a policy with lifetime benefits.

GREAT

IDEA

Hire a Debt Arbitrator

At 10 years old, Robert "Bobby" Blumenfeld was already working the sales floor of his parents' retail store in the Catskill Mountains. At 12, he was selling men's suits. So Blumenfeld isn't bragging when he says he knows every aspect of the retail business. He's worked both inside and outside of companies as an investor, owner, and consultant. And, through the years, he's watched too many companies drown in debt when they could have been saved.

He said many creditors misinterpret a company's failure to pay as a lack of desire to pay. These misunderstandings lead to costly litigation and aggravation. That's when he steps in to help.

"I always enjoy trying to save a business, versus shutting the door on them," said Blumenfeld, a veteran debt arbitrator, who now works as a consultant. His mission is to negotiate a settlement to help both sides resolve their financial distress. Most debt arbitrators work on a contingency basis for the debtor, earning a percentage of the money he saves them.

For example, if you owed a creditor $100,000 and Blumenfeld settled the debt for $30,000, you would pay him about 35 percent of the $70,000 you saved. "A settlement provides creditors with immediate cash and avoids the enormous financial and human costs of litigation," said Blumenfeld. "Debtors have the opportunity to reduce their debt burden, improve their balance sheet, and increase cash flow."

Arbitration can often save a small, struggling business from disaster. "Large companies can turn to an army of internal specialists who can often negotiate highly favorable terms with creditors," he said. "That leaves small-to medium-sized businesses without the resources to assist them in debt negotiation."

Blumenfeld said American business owners are often in a cash crunch because they aren't paid for 30 to 60—or even 90—days after they deliver the goods. In contrast, many European companies require payment in 15 days, which really keeps the cash flowing.

Collect the Money People Owe You

If you can't find or afford a debt arbitrator, you'll just have to do it yourself. When I ask the people at my events if anyone owes them money, way too many hands go up. Unless you are a bank, you should not be financing your customers.

The key to collecting money from customers is to handle it diplomatically and not jeopardize a good business relationship. So, here are some tips:

First, determine exactly how much each customer owes you by reviewing every account. Next, contact the responsible person in writing—not via e-mail. You need to determine whether the client or company has temporarily fallen on hard times, or if they are in serious trouble and have no ability to pay up.

If a good customer is experiencing a short-term cash-flow crunch, you might want to be patient. But speak directly with the business owner and tell him or her that while you are prepared to wait a few weeks longer for payment, you expect to be paid in full. Ask for a partial payment as a sign of good faith.

If you hear that a customer is struggling, move quickly to collect something before all the assets vanish. Doing nothing is not an option. If there is no immediate response to your demand for payment, look into filing what is called a "writ of attachment" in court.

This step puts the matter before a judge, who can call a hearing to determine whether there are any assets to attach. You may not end up being paid in cash, but if the business is liquidated, you could end up with office furniture, a truck, or some equipment.

A good collections letter:

- Clearly states how much is owed your company.
- Spells out exactly what action you want them to take.
- Outlines your course of action if they don't pay right away.

Discount Accounts Receivable

If people owe you money, try offering to discount the amount owed—if they make a payment immediately. This incentive works well if the client or company has cash but is holding back.

This works best if you propose a significant discount—at least 10 percent. Put your offer in writing and set a deadline for response. Include a self-addressed, stamped envelope or overnight mailing slip. Even if just a handful of customers respond, it may bring in some cash.

To avoid deadbeat customers, don't extend credit. Accept credit cards instead (see Great Idea #51). If you really need to extend credit, pay for a credit check and call their bank. Require a deposit up front so you can sleep at night.

Most collection agencies work on a contingency basis, usually keeping about 35 percent of what they collect as payment for their services. Ask for a client list; call other clients for references. Visit the company offices to meet with the owner or manager. Don't base your decision solely on price. Paying a higher fee to work harder on your behalf may actually bring in more cash.

GREAT

51 IDEA

Accept Credit Cards

One excellent way to boost cash flow is to accept credit cards. Many customers prefer to pay their bills with credit cards. That's good for everyone. You get paid quickly while your customers can pay off the bill over time, as well as take advantage of rewards and points for airline tickets, hotels, and other perks.

If you run a retail business or restaurant or offer professional services, such as consulting, production, or design, I suggest setting up a merchant account to accept credit cards. The biggest benefit for you is this:

Credit card payments speed up cash flow because the money will hit your account within a day or so. Although you will pay processing fees ranging up to 3 percent, you won't have to wait 30 or 60 days to be paid. Most commercial banks can set up a third-party merchant account within a few days. There may be minor set-up fees and you will have to pay for the terminal and portable "swiper."

If you want to accept American Express cards, you may have to set up an account directly with Amex. Remember, the best thing about accepting credit cards is that the payments are automatically deposited into your business bank account.

If you are home based, you may have a tougher time being approved for a merchant account, but if you provide financial statements and tax returns showing you are a solid business, you will most likely find some bank willing to help you set up a merchant credit card account.

In most cases, the more charge volume you have, the less you will pay the credit card company in processing fees.

Before selecting a merchant account provider, ask these questions:

- With so much credit card fraud, what kind of security do you offer customers? Are transactions encrypted? Your customers want to feel secure when sending their personal credit card information.
- What kind of fraud protection do you offer? Will you reject a card that is stolen or expired?
- What other services do you provide?
- Will I be able to reach customer service 24/7?
- Are processing fees refundable on returns? What is your policy if a transaction dispute arises?
- What's the average wait time for money to reach my account? Can I monitor my account online?

GREAT

52

IDEA

Work Part Time to Support Your Business

Cori Giacomazzi works in a brothel to support her vintage clothing shop in Skagway, Alaska. Well, actually, she's a part-time curator at the brothel museum inside the Red

Onion Saloon. The Saloon is a major tourist attraction in this funky, isolated Gold Rush–era mining town. (We visited Skagway during a fantastic Alaskan cruise my family embarked on to celebrate my father, Marty's 80th birthday.)

I was wandering around town, when I stopped in to check out Wandering Wardrobe, a tiny shop on a side street. There, I met Giacomazzi, a skilled seamstress and fashion designer. To supplement her income, she restores and repairs the antique corsets and gaudy dresses worn by prostitutes who worked at the saloon in the 1800s. The original dresses are on display, but she creates replicas of the colorful "saloon girl" dresses for the women who give tours of the museum. She also makes costumes for the funny live show depicting the colorful history of Skagway.

"I love what I do at the museum, but here in my shop I can create what I want," said Giacomazzi, who has a degree in textile design from the University of Alberta. She opened the vintage and designer clothing shop about five years ago, squeezing racks of clothing and mannequins into the 180-square-foot space. (It's so small it doesn't have a bathroom, so she uses a neighbor's.)

Giacomazzi is one of many small business owners who work another job to keep the lights on.

Across the country in Enfield, New Hampshire, Steve Fulton works as a freelance mechanical engineer to supplement income from his Blue Ox organic farm. "I'm still doing engineering projects and enjoying it, but I prefer being outside," said Fulton, who holds six patents on a variety of machines. "There is a lot more immediate gratification and feedback from farming compared with engineering projects."

He grows about 30 different vegetables on 10 acres, including lettuce, squash, tomatoes, and eggplant. Fulton sells everything he grows to local grocery stores. In 2002, he started cultivating soybeans, which became his first cash crop.

Although he is a successful farmer, he still can't support himself by farming alone.

"Last year, I made some money farming, but it's definitely not paying all the bills," said Fulton. "I wish I had known how slim the (profit) margins would be. Still, selling vegetables does cover the farm expenses."

Unlike engineering, which is detailed and precise, farming is totally unpredictable. "The weather is a huge factor," said Fulton. "Most of my land is pretty wet, so rain is a bad thing."

Working hard outdoors isn't a problem. He has a few part-time helpers during the busy summer season. However, his biggest challenge is keeping up with all the paperwork associated with running a small business. "You get into farming because you want to be outside growing things—not filling out paperwork."

Hollywood actor Mark Cross teaches cardiopulmonary resuscitation (CPR) between acting jobs and voice-over gigs.

"It works because I'm an actor who wants to inspire and educate people," said Cross, who teaches classes at many small businesses. "Most business owners don't know that if you have 10 or more employees, OSHA (the federal occupational health and safety agency) requires at least 10 percent of your staff to be trained in CPR."

Cross, who has taught CPR to about 2,000 people, charges $525 for up to a dozen employees to attend a four-and-a-half-hour class. He said his biggest challenge is to overcome students' fears about getting sick if they help someone who is unconscious.

"I talk about the Good Samaritan law, which protects people trying to save a life from being sued," said Cross. "I also tell them to wear gloves and safety glasses to avoid blood spurting into their eyes."

Teaching CPR all around southern California provides Cross with the flexible schedule he needs to attend auditions and rehearsals and perform in the evenings at the Sierra Madre Playhouse, among other venues. "There's a little bit of juggling back and forth between my teaching and my acting, but it works."

GREAT

53

IDEA

Expand Your Vendor Network

Is your business overly dependent on one or two suppliers for the things you need on a regular basis? What would happen if your primary supplier called today and said he or she unexpectedly ran out of the materials you need? What would your employees do if the delivery truck broke down in Ohio, and your raw materials were sitting on the side of the highway for three days?

Although most small business owners prefer to establish stable, long-term relationships with vendors and suppliers, savvy entrepreneurs always find alternative sources for key products. Being loyal to vendors is important, especially if what you need is in short supply. But things change. You have to protect yourself and your workers by having alternative sources on tap.

Seek new sources of supplies and raw materials:

- Google companies selling what you need. Download catalogs and price lists from competing companies.
- Keep track of all the information even if you don't think you'll need it.

When you start comparing prices from suppliers, you might find you are paying too much. If you do find a better deal, there's nothing wrong with going back to your primary suppliers and asking them to meet or beat the prices you found. Of course, your current suppliers don't want to lose your business, so, they may propose a discount or extended payment terms to maintain the relationship.

Remember, the quickest way to expand your business horizons is to attend an industry trade show or professional meeting. You'll get up to speed on all the new products, suppliers, and gossip—all in one place.

GREAT

54

IDEA

Check Out Economic Development Incentives

If you are thinking of relocating or expanding your business, it's time to investigate a variety of economic incentives and tax breaks. Hundreds of local, state, federal, and private agencies offer scores of programs designed to entice business owners to move into economically disadvantaged areas.

Former President Bill Clinton supported a high-profile initiative that designated distressed communities across the country as Empowerment Zones and Enterprise Communities (EZs and ECs).

In 2001, he moved his office into one of the first EZs in Harlem, which had been selected for $1.2 million to stimulate tourism by developing a tour package and gift shop for the Apollo Theater.

Similar initiatives rely on public and private partnerships to attract the investment necessary for economic and community development. Billions of dollars have been poured into communities in the past 10 years.

New or expanding companies can qualify for programs where the state helps pay part of the cost of training workers. There are thousands of state, local, and federal tax credits and incentives available for employers. For more information about initiatives in your area, contact the Department of Housing and Urban Development web site at www.hud.gov, or contact your local SBA office.

GREAT
55
IDEA

Produce an Independent Film

It's time to share a secret. During most summers, I take a break from the real world to work on an independent film. I love being part of a creative team, especially because writing books and columns can be lonely.

Although producing an independent film can be stressful and exhausting, there's something magical about transforming a script into something tangible with the hope that the film will be seen by at least a few people who think it's fabulous. (By the time you are reading this, *Brief Reunion*, the John Daschbach feature film I worked on in the blistering summer of 2010, may be in theaters or at least available online and on DVD.)

First, let me explain what the various producers do. Executive producers are usually major investors or entertainment attorneys. They raise the production money, visit the set to schmooze with the cast and fret about finishing and distributing the "picture." (Films are called "pictures" by people in the industry.) Other producers help raise money or provide connections and favors, such as a securing a great location. There are also associate producers who are real worker bees, helping out on all aspects of production.

I have been both an executive and supervising producer on television programs and a money-raising producer. On *Brief Reunion*, written, directed, and edited by Daschbach, I was the line producer. The line producer has the most exhausting and thankless job on the set. After serving as location manager because we didn't have one, my primary job was feeding and watering about 40 cast and crew for 19 days during a blazing heat wave in New Hampshire. It's no wonder the crew was crabby. Our shooting schedule was aggressive to say the least. The crew lived in rustic cabins without air conditioning or Internet service. Although we warned the urban dwellers that it would be like summer camp, no one paid attention. Most of them were from New York City and were seduced by the thought of shooting a film in rural New Hampshire.

In addition to handling all food and logistics, me and a couple of terrific production assistants (Olivia and Chuck) were responsible for driving cargo vans around to the various locations. We collected and hauled enormous amounts of trash to various dumpsters, taped protective paper to the floors of the house where we shot the film, cleaned the house, and rented portable toilets and tents. (I insisted on renting a big tent to serve as shelter during rainstorms and a comfortable place to serve our meals.)

Amy and Seamus Good were the mother and son team who ran our "craft services" department. Craft services is the crossroads and central meeting place on a film set. The Goods provided nonstop refreshments, first aid, and counseling. Our biggest challenge and eventual triumph was finding local restaurants willing to deliver a hot and hearty dinner at midnight to the rural farmhouse where we were shooting overnight. Turns out money talks, and the hot, delicious meals kept coming. (Special thanks to the Orient and Gusanoz in Hanover, N.H.)

Ben Silberfarb, a very talented Norwich, Vermont–based director and filmmaker, was the money-raising guy. He was amazing. During a recession he managed to raise more than $150,000 from friends, family, and film lovers who believed in the project. It was impressive that we could make such a high-quality film on such a small budget. Having a great director of photography, Joe Foley, and a talented cast helped. The cast included Scott Shepherd, Alexie Gilmore, and Joel del la Fuente.

Everyone pitched in to make this happen. Daschbach's parents moved out of their charming farmhouse for a month so we could paint the kitchen and use their property as our set. Ben's parents, Ann and Peter Silberfarb, were my official shoppers, making endless trips to the big box stores for food and supplies. Ben's vivacious mother-in-law, Isabel, was a driver and runner of numerous errands.

Between doing hand surgeries, Ben's wife, Diane, drove cast members all over as well as serving as the set doctor and unofficial psychologist. (We had a few health problems, including asthma attacks on set.)

Making an independent film requires asking favors of everyone we knew, from the manager of the Hanover Co-op market who let us shoot a scene after hours, to Ledyard Bank and King Arthur Flour. King Arthur deserves a trophy for donating the most delicious salmon and pasta dinner on July 3 after we shot an amazing fireworks scene on the beach at Post Pond. Jay and Amy Kelly, managers of Loch Lyme Lodge, where we housed the crew, were also heroes. More than 100 people contributed something to make the film. That's why the credits are so long.

The question remains: Why do people invest in independent films when so few make any money?

I call it the "stardust" factor. People like to feel they are part of a creative effort. There are also tax incentives for film lovers. Thanks to a quirky provision in the federal tax code, investors can write off their investment during the year they write the check to help finance a film.

In many cases, as hard as you try, it takes years to make a film. My dear friend, Nora Jacobson, is a talented screenwriter and director. We worked for a couple of years trying to make a film about adoption that would be shot in Vermont and Korea. It's a family drama based on the life of a friend of Nora's who adopted a Korean girl.

We invested our own money and then raised about $60,000 in development funds from friends and fans of her work. We visited Korea twice to do research, scout locations, and raise more money. Some of our travel expenses were covered by the Seoul Film Commission, which still supports the project. Although Nora's film, *The Hanji Box,* has yet to be made, I learned so much about film production from working on Nora's project. We retained Steven Beer, a respected New York-based entertainment attorney who also tried to bring in investors.

Unfortunately, our most promising investor worked for Bear Stearns, which blew up at the exact moment we needed a check. I have no regrets about devoting two years of my life to that project. We had wonderful experiences during two visits to South Korea. We attended the Sundance producer's program to learn how to produce an independent film. And best of all, we walked down the red carpet at the Pusan Film Festival, and our picture appeared above an article about the project published in the Asian edition of *Variety.*

Why do I make independent films? The "stardust" factor makes up for hauling all that trash.

GREAT

56

IDEA

Buy Prepaid Legal Insurance or Make a Deal with a Law Firm

Did you know that 52 percent of all Americans have some sort of legal problem and one of every three people will need legal advice in the next 12 months?

With attorneys charging an average of $175 per hour, legal bills can gobble up your profits. Even a small legal problem can drag down your morale and create a major distraction. That's why many small business owners are signing up for prepaid legal insurance. One of the oldest providers is Pre-Paid Legal Services® Inc., based in Ada, Oklahoma. The company sells coverage to both individuals and small businesses. For under $100 a month, businesses with fewer than 15 employees and $250,000 or less in net income can have access to experienced business attorneys.

Lawyers can draft and review contracts, write debt collection letters, and deal with leases, partnerships, creditor harassment, and bankruptcy, among other issues. Clients contact the company and within a day or so, get a call back.

Pre-Paid Legal Services, a publicly held company, was founded in 1972. It contracts with 2,700 law firms in 46 states.

You may also be able to cut a similar deal with a small, local law firm. The recession forced many firms to discount their fees, so don't be afraid to ask. You will probably be asked to pay a monthly retainer, but if you have legal issues, it may be worth it. Also check out RocketLawyer.com, an online legal services company.

GREAT

57

IDEA

Find the Right Office Space

Entrepreneurs often cringe at the thought of leasing office space. It's scary and expensive and takes time to find the right space. That's why so many of us work at home until we get thrown out by our loving spouses or families. The Applegate Group, founded in the den of our home in Sun Valley, California, outgrew that space within a year. Taking a big risk, we invested $10,000 to remodel the garage. It was a great commute—down the driveway.

We worked in the renovated garage until we moved to Pelham, New York. Our temporary world headquarters there were in a basement—it was either blasting hot or freezing cold. When my husband, Joe, and I bought a spacious, three-bedroom apartment in a stately stone building overlooking a country club, it was evident that the company was going to be evicted—the condo association prohibited operating a commercial enterprise in your apartment.

We were lucky to find a big, sunny corner office in the funky Pelham, New York, post office building. We moved in early 1997 and ended up renting three very cheap offices there (no hot water, ghosts, and a nonworking elevator kept the rent affordable).

So, if it's time to move out of your home, explore all the options. First, look for a business incubator in your area (see Great Idea #8). There are hundreds of private, university, and government-sponsored roosts for small companies. The rent is affordable, and there is great comfort to be found in the company of other crazy entrepreneurs.

Most cities have a glut of office space, so with some persistence, you can find affordable digs.

Here are some tips to help you find the right space:

- Drive around neighborhoods that appeal to you. Look for "For Rent" signs.
- Check the neighboring buildings to see if they are well maintained. Take notes on the parking situation, proximity to mass transit, and street lighting.
- Check out the lobby. Is it well lit and clean? Remember that deodorant commercial that warned, "You never get a second chance to make a first impression"? Well, you don't want a building with a dreary lobby.
- Visit the restrooms and check the fire exits and hallways for cleanliness and accessibility for disabled workers and customers.
- Speak to other tenants before you meet the building manager. They will usually give you the scoop on what it's like to work in the building.
- If you are renting retail space, find out whether the landlord expects a percentage of gross sales as well as rent.

- Find out exactly what the landlord pays for and what you are financially responsible for.
- It may make sense to work with a commercial real estate broker, especially if you are renting more than a small office.
- Ask a lawyer to review a lease before you sign it.

For more information on using a savvy real estate broker, see the next Great Idea, #58.

Hire a Savvy Real Estate Broker

Moving into commercial space is a serious financial commitment. In many cases, rent is the second-highest expense after payroll. If you're feeling cramped now, consider hiring a commercial real estate broker to help because it can take six months or more to relocate.

If you need only one office, you can probably find one on your own, but if you have a dozen employees and need more than 1,500 square feet, working with a broker makes sense. Plus, in most cases, landlords pay the broker's commission.

"Since small business owners are not in the real estate market day in and day out," said Steven Swerdlow, a real estate expert. "It's very important to work with a team that you can trust."

He recommends working with both a broker and a real estate attorney because very few business owners are familiar with real estate law or jargon. "People who work with leases every day know how the game is played."

Being able to sublet your space is very important, he said. "I can't tell you how many lease transactions we've been involved in where we did all kinds of planning for long-term leases and, invariably, the world changes, and your company is either too small or too big for the space."

Before you call a broker, sit down with your employees and decide exactly how much space you need. Brokers say figure on renting about 250 square feet of rentable space per employee as a rule of thumb. Write down what else you need in terms of private offices, conference rooms, a reception area, storage space, kitchen, parking, and security.

Be sure to factor in growth. The worst thing is to move in and realize you will soon outgrow your new digs. If you end up with an extra office or two, you might consider subleasing to another small business owner. But be sure your lease allows you to sublease.

Feeling good about where you work is essential. It's well worth your effort to find the right broker to help you locate space and sign a lease that suits your needs.

GREAT

59

IDEA

Share Space with a Compatible Business

Another great option is to share space with another small business. I once met two happy bakers who shared a commercial kitchen in Orange County, California. The gourmet brownie baker and his friend, a cheesecake baker, worked around the clock. The brownie guy baked during the day; the cheesecake guy worked nights. They split the expenses and kept the ovens hot around the clock.

In downtown Hanover, New Hampshire, Shackleton Thomas, an upscale furniture maker and a high-end pottery company, share space with Khawachen, a Tibetan rug and gift store. The three entrepreneurs began sharing space in an old mill building in Bridgewater, Vermont.

Charles Shackleton, the custom furniture maker and his wife, Miranda Thomas, a potter, decided to open a store on the main street of the college town. Selling compatible wares, they thought it was a good idea to extend the relationship with their friend, rug and decorative items importer, Kesang Tashi.

It makes sense that anyone who can afford a bedroom set for $30,000 would be open to buying a handmade $15,000 rug to go with it.

You don't have to sell high-end furniture and rugs to share space. Bankruptcy attorney Renee Sophia Coulter set up a small office in a copy center located in a strip mall in Livonia, Michigan. Although she also works at home, being in the copy center is perfect because bankruptcy clients need lots of copies of records for their court cases. The owner of the shop, Cathy Anderson, answers Coulter's phone and rents her a small office in the back of the shop for just $300 a month. It's truly a win-win situation for both women.

Buy Used Office Furnishings

When I was an investigative reporter at the *Los Angeles Times*, my beat was white-collar crime. I had the best job in the world. I was paid to track down the slickest, sleaziest business criminals in the country as they defrauded investors out of millions with precious metals scams, stock frauds, and real estate schemes.

They had two passions: stealing money and working in glitzy offices. To impress prospective victims of their schemes, they usually rented the top floor of a modern office building with a spectacular city or ocean view.

My favorite con man had a reception area the size of a small apartment, with plush gray carpeting and stained glass panels. His perfectly coiffed secretary sat behind a massive cherry wood desk. His private office was about 2,000 square feet and featured a panoramic view of the Pacific Ocean. Of course, visitors were convinced he was a legitimate commodities dealer—only a successful businessman would have such a fabulous office!

So he's the reason why I equate fancy offices with criminal behavior. There is no reason to buy new stuff with so many bargains out there. Unfortunately, you can take advantage of the furniture abandoned by hundreds of thousands of companies that closed during the Great Recession.

If you run an advertising or modeling agency, you might need to present a super groovy image, but in my opinion, the funkier the office, the smarter the business owner.

Think of all the money you'll save every year by renting office space in a building a bit off the beaten track or in a less-than-desirable area—as long as it's safe for you and your employees.

One last tip: Before you spend a dime on furniture, buy some graph paper and draw up a simple floor plan. Take inventory of everything you have and make a detailed list of what you borrow or buy.

When you know what you need, find the nearest used-office-furniture company or shop online. Be sure to look for bargains in the local classified ads.

Buying tips from Steelcase, a Grand Rapids, Michigan–based firm:

- Define your furniture requirements by what your employees need to work effectively rather than by the features of a particular furniture line.

- Ask these questions: What kind of furniture do we need? Tables for meetings? Acoustical panels for privacy?
- Inventory all the furniture you have to avoid buying things you don't need.
- Buy furniture for its functionality.
- Consider leasing or renting furniture. This will increase your flexibility as your company grows or shrinks.

GREAT 61 IDEA — Sell Your Business at the Right Time and Price

Business broker Colin Gabriel has this advice for entrepreneurs: hire someone to audit your financial statements and constantly update your business plan. Why? You never know when a buyer will show up.

"The best buyers are the ones who come knocking on your door because they have an interest in your company," said Gabriel, founder of Gwent Inc. in San Diego, California.

In today's global economy, there are no boundaries for buyers. (See Great Idea #39 about foreign investment visas.) For example, Gabriel said he once brokered the sale of a New Jersey firm to a company in France that he found on the Internet. It gets even better: it didn't matter to the French buyer that the New Jersey–based company was making all its electronic products in a Taiwanese-owned factory.

Savvy sellers know they will be put under a microscope during a transaction, but they turn the tables on the buyer by learning as much as they can about them. Doing your homework may reveal what Gabriel calls "nasty surprises." But it's better to know about any problems, so you can call off the deal.

Don't be afraid to ask the prospective buyer for a current balance sheet and details about the financing. Gabriel said many deals are highly leveraged, and the new owner may be planning to saddle your company with debt the minute the deal closes.

"With a leveraged buyout, someone will borrow 70 to 80 percent of the purchase price and load the company with debt. The astute seller has to decide in advance whether to engage in a deal like that," said Gabriel.

Tips for Sellers

- Place a realistic value on your business.
- Work with a business appraiser to determine the value.
- Be patient. Art is auctioned; houses are sold slowly. Most businesses are like houses.
- Estimate future profits and document these expectations.
- Invest in audited financial statements.
- Understand how the financing will work.
- Disclose everything; hiding problems can kill the deal.
- Be vigilant until the contract is signed.
- Listen to your advisers, but don't give up the helm.
- Sell the assets or sell the shares. It's usually better to sell shares rather than assets. If you sell the assets, you may face double taxation.

Your buyer may also ask you to provide some of the financing by taking back a promissory note. If you don't want to end up owning the company again, refuse to finance the deal. (However, we sold SBTV.com on an installment basis. The buyers paid us on time, every month for about two years and never missed a payment.)

GREAT

62

IDEA

Sell Your Company to an Industry Giant

Two seconds after 3M issued a news release confirming its acquisition of Lingualcare Inc. in 2007, Lea Nesbit e-mailed the release to everyone who had ever turned down her request for money.

The company, which developed a proprietary technology for the mass customization of invisible braces that attach to the back of the teeth, was founded in 2003 by Nesbit and Ruedger Rubbert, a German mechanical engineer. They worked with a doctor to develop the proprietary technology and intellectual property needed to launch the company.

From the beginning, Nesbit said she made sure all the major players in the industry knew who she was and what Lingualcare was all about. "I made a point of knowing all the big fish," she said. "I would introduce myself to people at trade shows. I had relationships with every major company in my industry."

With a great product but not a lot of cash to spare, Nesbit said Lingualcare had to be agile and creative to compete with bigger players. From the beginning, she and other company executives planned to eventually sell Lingualcare to a big public or private company. They relied on skilled financial advisers to make sure the books were in order. That data helped Nesbit's team come up with a realistic valuation for the firm.

In 2005, a few years prior to the sale, Nesbit moved the factory operations to Calexico, Mexico to cut costs. (See Great Idea #184.) In 2006, Lingualcare was gaining market share and growing. That year, a friend sent Nesbit a press release announcing the sale of a competitor to 3M for $97 million.

"I asked myself, 'How did a company that didn't have a nickel of revenue make that deal?'" Nesbit recalled. She quickly tracked down the investment banker who sold the other company and convinced him to meet with her.

They eventually presented the company to eight potential buyers. "We took bids for the first round and then let the top bidders into our electronic due diligence room," recalled Nesbit. She worked closely with the investment banker throughout the process. "His job was to bring people to the table. My job was to get them excited."

In the summer of 2007, four companies went through the due diligence process. "We took final bids at the end of August. I knew I wanted cash. 3M wasn't our highest bidder, but they were willing to pay cash."

Nesbit declined to disclose the terms of the sale, but said, "I was happy and everyone else was happy." The day the deal closed was bittersweet; it was the same day her divorce was finalized.

She agreed to work for the newly acquired company for about three years and left in 2010. "I reported to someone who was two levels down from the CEO," said Nesbit. "I learned a lot. It's been a good acquisition." (The company is now part of 3M's Unitek division.)

A serial entrepreneur, in 2009, Nesbit started raising money for a new dental company she founded, Celadon Dental. She closed a round of financing in 2011.

Nesbit offers this advice for anyone trying to sell a company they built: "Don't apologize for what you are asking for. And when people start picking your company apart, know they are just negotiating. There's a lot of emotional manipulation and gamesmanship. You can't take it personally. You have to be willing to walk away."

No matter what happens: "Believe in yourself, believe in your deal, and stand strong."

How to prepare your business for acquisition:

- *Explore ways to increase value.* Your business could be made more attractive to prospective buyers if changes are made in the organization, key personnel, or marketing strategies. Understand when the market is ready.
- *Be ready when buyers are active, money is plentiful, and interest rates are low.* Don't assume the best buyer is local. Document the growth potential of your business. Consider which perks you'll miss after selling your business.
- *Hire a reputable person to appraise your business.* Work with a competent attorney, investment banker, and accountant. This is not a time to scrimp on professional help.

Technology and Tele- communications

3

By cutting the cord to the office and home, we can work and play anywhere, completely changing the game for small business owners. Sitting on a balmy beach, we can visit about 200 million registered web sites or download more than 500,000 smartphone applications.

It's tough to keep up with all the new technology. It's hard to believe, but in 2007, only 11 percent of Americans used a smartphone to access the Internet. By 2009, it was up to 38 percent, according to a 2010 report by the Pew Research Center. In the next five years, industry analysts predict Apple alone will sell around 185 million phones, not counting all its aggressive competitors. In 2011, Verizon started offering iPhones to customers, challenging AT&T's monopoly.

Now, being online 24/7 is the norm, not the exception. American adults spend an average of 13 hours a week online versus 7 hours a week in 2002, and that doesn't include dealing with e-mail, according to a poll by Harris Interactive.

I keep in close touch with family and friends online, but here's a disturbing statistic from a recent poll: a third of women between the ages of 18 and 34 years old check their Facebook accounts in the morning *before* they visit the bathroom or brush their teeth. That's scary.

Facebook, which boasted 621 million users in 2010, can definitely raise the profile of your business, but its effectiveness depends on whether your customers and clients use Facebook to look for information. I have a regular Facebook account and a "fan" page to promote this book, share tips, and provide information about where I'm speaking. Debra Dakin, my makeup consultant, uses Facebook to promote her "In the Pink" salon and services by posting photos of herself and clients on her page.

Social media works only if your customers use social media sites. If they embrace social media, you need a dynamic, integrated online presence. If they don't, rethink your online marketing strategy.

Twitter is great if you have time-sensitive information to share, such as when fresh cornbread is ready to be sold at your bakery. Posting your professional credentials and company contact information on LinkedIn is a great idea. The human resources department at Bloomberg LP found my 23-year-old son, Evan, on LinkedIn. A self-described "visual journalist," he posted his portfolio online. They were impressed by his work, set up a round of interviews, and offered him a terrific job as a designer at *Bloomberg Businessweek.*

With all sorts of affordable tools and content platforms, there is no excuse for having a boring, static web site. In this chapter, you can learn how to take advantage of content management systems (CMSs). A CMS allows anyone who can read and write to upload and distribute content across multiple platforms in real time.

My new site, www.201GreatIdeas.com, is powered by HubSpot.com.

HubSpot provides inbound marketing applications designed to help prospects looking for a particular product or service find your company. Their technology generates leads and then converts those leads into qualified prospects.

Business owners are taking advantage of all the fast and affordable, super-lightweight, shiny, and brightly colored computers. You can manage your digital life on a tablet, including an iPad or Dell Streak. I wrote this book on a sturdy and reliable Asus brand "Eee PC." It has a full-size keyboard and a battery that lasts six hours. (At home, I hook it up to a Samsung 20-inch flat screen monitor.)

All these new tech toys and tools can be overwhelming, but on the plus side, affordable technology levels the playing field, opening doors for small companies to compete with much bigger firms.

But please don't let technology rule or ruin your life. Even Mari Smith, one of the top experts on how to use Facebook for business, admits to having to "log off" once in a while. "I take periodic fasts and don't touch technology for days," she told me. "I ban the iPhone from my bedroom and leave it in my office."

And Julie Lenzer Kirk, a self-described nerd says: "I admit to having a 'Crackberry' and a low-end netbook. But I'm not an early adopter, even though I have a degree in computer science and ran a software company for 10 years."

Kirk, CEO of the Fast Forward Center for Innovation and Entrepreneurship in Maryland, admits that keeping up with the daily deluge of e-mail is a constant challenge.

"E-mail is a vortex you can get sucked into," she said. "I try to manage it, but still spend three hours a day handling e-mail."

Super-stressed entrepreneurs always ask me what gadgets I think they should buy. The answer is this: it depends on what you need the technology to do. Unless you are in a high-tech business, I recommend hiring an expert to research all the options and help you make smart purchasing decisions.

While writing this revised edition, I asked everyone I spoke with to share their favorite web sites and software apps. My son, Evan, the graphic designer, recommends DropBox.com for storing big files "in the cloud." We use Doodle to plan meetings for the White River Indie Film Festival. I've used Google Docs to keep track of the Web content I commission and edit for a client. It's also great for things like keeping track of all the credits and thank you notes for *Brief Reunion*, the independent feature I helped produce last year.

Gist.com is a cool application that integrates all your social media interactions. FlipBoard is another great application, which aggregates articles in a magazine-like format.

Many small business owners rely on Constant Contact, Survey Monkey, and eVite.com. Traxco.com lets you organize all your travel information. You can buy and design stamps online at www.usps.gov.

Since being accessible is essential to business success, this chapter includes information about Ring Central, which provides affordable cloud-based phone services.

At this writing, Groupon, the mass discount shopping site, made headlines by rejecting a $6 billion offer from Google. Although thousands of small restaurants, salons, and retail businesses are signing up to offer discounts to groups of customers, it's very important to know what you are getting into. Two restaurant owners I met in Minneapolis told me they lost money on the deals they offered through Groupon and a competitor, Living

Social. Instead of boosting business, the promotions actually backfired—regular customers who weren't savvy enough to sign up for the group discounts were angry about paying full price. Many of the bargain hunters never came back.

So, turn off your smartphone and read on for some really great ideas from respected tech and social media gurus, including my friend, Guy Kawasaki, best-selling author, speaker, and founder of www.alltop.com.

GREAT IDEA 63

Twitter for Business: Tips from Guy Kawasaki

Guy Kawasaki told me he believes business owners don't need a web site anymore.

Really?

"Web sites are a total waste of time," declared Kawasaki, a best-selling author and keynote speaker. He was one of Apple Computer's first employees and later returned to the company to craft its innovative marketing strategy. "Twitter is fast, free, and ubiquitous. If a businessperson doesn't get it, that person is an idiot."

No one wants to be an idiot, so I asked him how exactly can Twitter help boost sales? Kawasaki says it's simple: only tweet when you have something interesting and important to share. "If all you do is promote yourself on Twitter, no one will care."

I asked Kawasaki to provide examples of how Twitter posts can translate into dollars. "Dell Outlets use Twitter to advertise discounts on computers," he explained. "Koji BBQ is a street food vendor in Los Angeles. They use Twitter to tell followers where to find their truck every day."

He contends that Twitter works so well for business because it's an opt-in platform. Clients and customers who sign up to follow you or your company are obviously interested in what you are doing or selling.

Kawasaki also pointed out that Twitter works really well for experts in a particular field. For example, if you are a human resource consultant, you can build a following by sending out practical personnel tips. Once you have a few hundred followers, use Twitter to promote a seminar or workshop. The session can be online or in person, depending on the response.

Always an innovator, Kawasaki founded alltop.com, a cool news aggregation site. He's a thought leader with more than 40,000 Facebook fans. His latest book, *Enchantment,* will be published by Portfolio in March, 2011. It provides a range of insights and strategies for attracting customers and generating goodwill.

GREAT

64

IDEA

Facebook Tips for Business Owners

Talk about a great idea. Mark Zuckerberg was a Harvard undergrad when he launched a web site as a way to rank the appearance of women on campus. Now, Facebook is the social media powerhouse of the universe. But how can you use Facebook to promote your business?

The secret is having a separate "fan" page for your business—in addition to your personal Facebook page.

"First, you have to understand how Facebook works," said Mari Smith, a social media expert and author. "You get started by building a fan page for your business." (Visit: www.facebook.com/pages.)

"Your fan page is really an extension of your brand," said Smith. Once you have built a cool-looking fan page, then, she said it's time to push compelling content out through all your social media networks, including Twitter and LinkedIn. Your fan page is the place to highlight what's new, different, or special about your company's services and products.

Remember, your fan page should *not* feature the same stuff as your personal page. (For example, post Aunt Tillie's 90th birthday party pictures only on your personal page.)

No matter how hard you work on promoting your business via Facebook, be patient. Smith cautions that it takes time to build an online presence, so don't expect to see results overnight.

"It takes three to six months to see some solid, measurable results," she said. The key is to constantly refresh the content. You have to post new material several times a week, if not every day. If you have nothing new to share, you'll quickly lose fans.

Smith shared another great idea: monitor what's being said about you and your business in cyberspace. Set up Google Alerts. The service is free and can help you avert a disaster. Or check out these sites—www .socialmention.com and www.scoutlabs.com—to see what is being said about your company.

"Many companies now have CLOs, chief listening officers, who trawl the Internet for information," said Smith. (Her web site is www.marismith.com.)

Use Skype for Business

After interviewing Kawasaki and Smith, I was ready to build customized social networking pages to promote this book. Since I am not a tech-head or a designer, I contacted Brian Hanson, an Indiana-based Web designer who has several companies, including www.customtwit.com.

Although I spoke with him once on the phone, he prefers to work with clients via Skype. I was a bit skeptical. I love Skype and use it to chat with my kids and friends, but I was puzzled about how we would use it to design my customized Facebook, Twitter, and YouTube.com pages.

"I find Skype much easier and personal than e-mail," said Hanson. "It lets me communicate directly with clients in real time."

Working with Hanson on Skype was a great experience. We set a time to "meet" on Skype. Before the session, he asked me to have all my photos, logos, and book images ready to upload. I also gave him the password to my accounts so he could access the pages.

Via the chat function, Hanson told me when to use the "share" function to upload the next image or photo. A total pro, he works very fast. Within a few minutes, he sent me a link to my new Facebook fan page.

Every time he added or changed something on the page, he instructed me to refresh my browser so I could see what he was doing. If I wanted something changed, I just sent him a note.

The pages came together quickly. It took about four hours over two sessions. I paid him $208, about $50 an hour, for three very cool pages. My only challenge was learning "Web-speak." Now I know *k* means *okay* and *LOL* means *laugh out loud.*

Hanson totally rocked the design process. He's been designing sites for his own business, including www.nationwideclassifieds.com, for about 17 years. In recent years, he's created custom social media pages and Word Press sites for about 50 clients, including Facebook expert Mari Smith.

Working with Hanson proved to me that Skype is a viable tool for collaborative work. I will definitely use it for other projects. Obviously, lots of people are using Skype 24/7. In fact, while we were working online, there were 23 million people using Skype.

Right after he finished my three customized pages and sent over the files, he shared this poem:

"Skype, Skype, the wonderful tool, the more you use it, the more you drool."

GREAT

66

IDEA

Set Up a Teleconference

Videoconferencing is another great option for collaborative work or a virtual meeting. Years ago, only big companies could afford the technology, but now you can, too.

FedEx/Kinkos offers videoconference services at many locations. You can also try Logitech's LifeSize Communications or Cisco's TelePresence, which is more expensive. If you have $300,000 you can install your own Cisco video conference suite. Many Fortune 500 companies have done so. Most major cities have a variety of more affordable videoconferencing services available.

If you need to use the technology frequently, IBM, Cisco, Avaya, and Microsoft all sell desktop-based video technologies. You can video chat on your iPhone or other smartphones, but the quality isn't spectacular.

For a group meeting, FedEx offers affordable videoconferencing services at more than 120 locations. If everyone on your call meets at a FedEx location, the cost is about $150 per hour per site, with a half-hour minimum. That's a lot cheaper than a plane ticket and a hotel room. (In 2010, Americans took 427 million business trips at a cost of $228 billion, according to travel industry reports.)

In addition to broadcasting images, you can transmit graphics, slides, video clips, and other data. "It's the second-best thing to being there," said a Kinko's spokeswoman. If using Skype isn't an option, here's more information about the various FedEx options. Prices may change:

- *Point-to-Point.* Two videoconference locations, either FedEx Office to FedEx Office or FedEx Office to an outside location. Cost is $225 per hour per FedEx Office location.
- *Point-to-Point with Conversion.* Two videoconference locations, FedEx Office to outside location with conversion required. A conversion is the method used to connect incompatible equipment or networks with a FedEx Office location. Cost is $295 per hour per FedEx Office location.
- *Multi-Point.* Three or more videoconference locations. $265 per hour per FedEx Office location.
- *Multi-Point with Conversion.* Three or more videoconference locations, with conversion to a non–FedEx Office site required. A conversion is the method used to connect incompatible equipment or networks with a FedEx Office location. Cost is $335 per hour per FedEx Office location.

There are other fees to consider, including adding an audio participant to a videoconference call for $55 per hour per audio port. A FedEx Office "conference producer" can also provide introductions for all parties and verify that video and audio are acceptable. The cost is $55 per conference. FedEx also offers DVD recordings of videoconferences at a cost of $35 per conference, plus shipping fees.

You can find a videoconferencing location by using the online store locator. Or, call (866) 828-4563 and request videoconferencing information.

Here are some tips from FedEx/Kinko's for making your videoconference a success:

- Schedule the conference in advance and make sure everyone knows what needs to be accomplished.
- Send out an agenda and other materials prior to the conference.
- Choose one person to act as moderator at each location.
- Avoid wearing bright red, white, plaids, stripes, or prints, because they are distracting and create visual problems on camera.

- Speak naturally and clearly. Pause briefly at the end of your remarks; there is a slight lag-time in transmission.
- Don't cough into the microphone or hold side conversations during the session.
- Let everyone know when you are about to share graphics.
- Identify yourself from time to time so everyone can keep track of the participants.

GREAT

67

IDEA

Make the Most of Voice Mail

I love voice mail. For a few pennies a day, you can change your outgoing message, receive multiple messages while you're on the phone, and call in for messages from anywhere on the planet.

It can be your best friend when you have to finish a project without interruptions.

Unfortunately, most people don't take the time to update their greeting daily or even weekly. (My friend Pam Engebretson, a land use planning consultant based in San Diego, updates her outgoing message daily, which I love.) Show you care by telling callers when they can expect a return call. Remember, not everyone tracks business associates on Facebook or Twitter.

Best of all, voice mail helps reduce or eliminate telephone tag. (See Great Idea #175 for tips from the "Telephone Doctor.")

I always leave detailed messages, including my phone number, even if I think you know it. I also mention the best time to reach me live. Voice mail is great if you don't want to engage in a long conversation. Just leave a message after hours on the person's office line—if they still have an office phone.

Voice mail is extremely effective when you are working on projects with people in multiple time zones. Through the years, I have relied on voice mail to execute six-figure projects without ever meeting certain members of my client's team.

A robust, professional voice mail system can forward a message to the right person so problems can be resolved quickly. Individual mailboxes make it easy for callers to leave messages. No matter how great your voice mail system may be, make sure callers can reach a live person by pressing 0.

Remember, businesses lose millions of dollars in sales because frustrated callers hang up when they can't speak to a company representative.

If your staff needs to put callers on hold, consider adding a "messages on hold" feature to your phone system. These systems allow you to fill the hold time with music, product information, or even trivia games (see Great Idea #98).

GREAT IDEA 68

Don't Let E-Mail Rule or Ruin Your Life

It's hard to imagine life without e-mail. It's a great tool, but when people have to work late into the night to make up for not getting anything done during the day, you know e-mail has gotten out of control.

One of my closest friends is president of a large business advocacy organization. She admitted that she often spent eight hours a day responding to e-mail! That means she has to work another six or seven hours every night to actually get any work done. That's crazy. She finally hired a full-time assistant, who spends most of her time responding to e-mail. Does it really make sense to pay someone $40,000 or $50,000 a year, plus benefits, to manage your e-mail?

I believe we make really poor decisions when we feel pressured to respond to e-mail within seconds. Unless you are a trauma surgeon or top military officer, you don't need to respond right away. Just take a breath and *think* before you hit reply. Here's another tip: never, ever write an e-mail if you are angry, high, or drunk. I've received some crazy messages from people who were obviously out of their minds.

You may be too young to remember that just a few years ago we conducted business via letters and faxes. If a matter was truly urgent or we needed a contract signed, we sent overnight letters. (When I was a reporter at the *Los Angeles Times,* receiving a FedEx package was a big deal and meant you were writing an important story.)

More strategies for taking control of e-mail:

- As hard as it may be at first, try checking e-mail every two hours instead of every two minutes. Try this on a day when you need to write a proposal or complete a project. You'll be amazed at how much you can accomplish when you take a break from your e-mail.
- Don't reply to every message, especially if you just need to say "thanks."
- The fewer messages you send or respond to, the fewer you will receive.
- Just write your message in the subject line, not the body.
- Ask an assistant to screen and prioritize your messages. Respond quickly to messages from clients or customers.
- Notice how your stress level will plummet once you stop checking e-mail every two minutes.

GREAT

69

IDEA

Take This Technology Checkup

Computers and telecommunications equipment has never been cheaper. So, there's no excuse not to buy the best hardware and software available. You can boost productivity and morale and improve customer service by having the right technology.

Use this quick checkup to determine what you should buy:

1. *What do you need to be more productive?* Do you prefer to work on a tablet, desktop, or laptop?
2. *What do your employees need to be more productive?* Don't buy anything without asking them what they need.
3. *Assign one staffer to research products and prices.* Ask other business owners for their recommendations. Read reviews and blogs.
4. *Ask your customers, clients, and suppliers how they prefer to communicate with you.* Try Survey Monkey or another free survey tool. Keep the questions short. Most customers will be happy to tell you how they prefer to communicate with your team. Just ask.

Smart Technology and Telecommunication Toys to Buy for Your Business

Based on your tech checkup, here are some products and online services to consider:

- *Online data storage and a physical backup system.* Why risk a complete meltdown if your computer crashes? Buy hard drives or USB drives to store data. Back it up by sending it to a server in the cloud (try DropBox .com). You can buy 8 GBs of storage for about $50.
- *Wireless router.* An affordable way to share an Internet connection.
- *Toll-free, 800 number.* I resent paying for a call when I'm ordering products from your company. A toll-free number is affordable and classy.
- *Smartphone.* Everyone needs a phone that can make calls, text, take photos, shoot video, and access the Internet. The key is matching your phone to your work style. I like texting, so I have an LG phone with a full QWERTY keyboard. I'll probably have a 4G smartphone by the time you read this, but I don't like typing on a glass screen.
- *A femtocell.* Sounds like a weird scientific term, but it's a mini cell tower than plugs into your router to boost cell phone reception. When you live in the middle of nowhere, Vermont like we do, you need one. Industry analysts say there are about a million femtocells in use in the United States. Verizon charges $249 for one, but when I threatened to switch providers, the salesperson knocked $100 off the price. The rectangular black box took five minutes to install. It's a miracle—I can now use my cell phone in my home office!
- *Wireless Internet card.* If you travel a lot, consider buying a card that gives you Internet access from just about anywhere. Some hotels still charge for Internet access, which is particularly irksome. All the major carriers offer cards at competitive rates. They average about $50 a month. You can also buy a mobile wi-fi system that lets about five people log on from just about anywhere.
- *A tablet computer.* There are all sorts of cool choices other than an iPad. Sony and Dell sell tablets that are great for viewing content. The Dell Streak costs about $1,400. It has a five-inch screen and includes a full-functional 3G phone with instant messaging and short message service (SMS)/text capabilities.

Post Videos and Photos on Your Web Site

With so many affordable digital cameras, there's no excuse not to have lots of photos and video clips on your web site and social media pages. I have a Flip HD camcorder, which cost about $200. It's very easy to use and comes with simple editing software.

Just shoot something and, within minutes, you can post clips to your YouTube.com page. If you prefer to pay someone to edit and post video clips, check out Pixability.com.

Ask your clients and customers if you can post their photos on your site. If you sell products online, it might be best to hire a professional photographer to shoot the pictures. Be sure shoppers can enlarge and rotate the images.

Stock photos or illustrations are a great way to jazz up your site. I use iStock.com. That site is terrific. It makes it easy to access hundreds of thousands of affordable, royalty-free photos and images. You use a credit card to buy credits for your account. Then, you review images and store the ones you like in a "light box." Once you find the perfect image, download and purchase the size you need.

Small jpeg files download within seconds. You can also purchase large, high-resolution files for print or animation projects. Check out the cool animation based on my book cover image on the 201GreatIdeas.com site. We bought the rights from Getty Images for under $100. Scrolling through stock photos can give your brain an inspirational jolt.

Consider a Cloud-Based Telephone Service

With so many options for telecommunications, it's tough to figure out what's best. Small business owners are canceling their land lines and relying solely on mobile phones. Others use services like Google Voice, which forwards calls to multiple phones until it catches up with you. Other businesses are looking to the "clouds" for telecommunications services.

One of the leaders in this space is Ring Central, which offers cloud-based business telephone systems at an affordable rate.

"We do a lot of call recording for training purposes, so that was a big feature for us," said Bobby Martyna, CEO of Travado.com, based in Lakewood, Colorado. His company, which sells snacks and amenities to small retailers, hotels, and campgrounds around the country, has about a dozen employees—many of whom are on the road making deliveries.

He said he switched because he was tired of the phones not working on top of poor call quality.

Ring Central shipped Travado preconfigured telephones and tech support to make the switch. Martyna said he spends about $400 a month on his phone service, which includes call forwarding and voice mail messages forwarded to e-mail. (Ring Central also offers 800 numbers and virtual PBX service.)

"The customer support is great," said Martyna. "You can go online and look for a solution, or someone calls you back within 24 hours," he said.

"Our sweet spot is businesses with fewer than 20 employees," said Praful Shah, vice president of strategy for Ring Central. He said that, unlike bigger phone companies, the company doesn't require customers to sign long-term contracts. "They only time a vendor ties you up is when they don't trust you to stay."

For more information, visit www.ringcentral.com.

GREAT

73

IDEA

Create a Dynamic Web Site

No matter how big or small your company is, your web site has to be functional as well as provide compelling content.

"You need to set up a content management system, customize your content by using landing pages, track all visitors, and write a blog to be distributed to all your social networking sites," advises Joe Zarrett, founding partner, president, and CEO of Verndale, a Boston-based consulting firm.

Zarrett has been building and optimizing web sites since 1998. In 2010, Verndale had about 300 big and small clients. Even during the recession, the company posted impressive growth of 30 to 40 percent a year.

The biggest challenge facing most small business owners is that their sites have been cobbled together over the years. "They end up painting themselves into a corner with islands of information that don't work well together," Zarrett said.

So what can you do? He recommends hiring an experienced Web developer who can reorganize your site and add a content management system. Some content management systems are free; others can cost up to $40,000 for a license. These new platforms organize information in a hub-and-spoke fashion. The cool thing is that you just upload the information once, and then it can be distributed to multiple places.

Leave the technology to the experts. Focus instead on tailoring content to fit your customers' needs. Do everything you can to position yourself as an expert in your field.

"One of the simplest things you can do is write a blog for your web site, then distribute the blog via Facebook and LinkedIn," said Zarrett. "Then, you can consolidate the blog posts into a monthly e-newsletter."

Content is king. You need to come up with interesting things to share with your clients and customers. No one wants to read useless blather. If you sell something, try highlighting new features or offer a discount.

Zarrett said too many business owners waste time and money trying to attract visitors to their sites. That's where search engine optimization (SEO) comes in. SEO sounds scary, but it is just a way to improve your rankings on various search engines.

Although many small businesses buy Google Ad Words, Zarrett questions whether it's worth it. "They are throwing good money out the window in almost every case," he said. "Instead of buying ad words, the trick is to define a set of keywords that are appropriately targeted, then set up a landing page specific to the user group you are targeting."

In other words, if you put a link on your Facebook fan page or send out a tweet via Twitter, be sure the link takes visitors to a specific page, not the home page.

To get started, here are some of Zarrett's recommendations for finding the right content management system:

Open Source (free):

Joomla: www.joomla.org
Drupal: www.drupal.org
DotNetNuke: www.dotnetnuke.com

Licensed:

Kentico: www.kentico.com
SiteFinity: www.sitefinity.com
Sitecore: www.sitecore.com

For more information, visit these CMS review sites: www.cmsreview .com and www.cmsmatrix.org.

For more information, visit Joe Zarrett's blog: www.verndale.com/Our -Thinking/How-to-Select-The-Best-Content-Management-System.aspx.

GREAT

74

IDEA

The Truth about Search Engine Optimization (SEO)

Sean Rusinko, director of search engine marketing for Verndale.com, told me something shocking: there are new ways to manipulate search engines and you better know what to do.

"In the past, we used information on Web pages, keywords, and words hidden in texts to gain visibility," said Rusinko. "These were called 'black hat tactics.' But, since the Google revolution, it's not the case anymore."

Before Google ruled the universe, Rusinko said "bots" would trawl web sites to gather information and rank sites based on keywords. Now, Google ranks sites based on the *links* people use to get there. "So now the quantity of links pointing to a web site is what determines its ranking."

You still need keywords, but it's more important to create a compelling and memorable experience for your users. You do that by figuring out what they need to know about your products or services.

The challenge is this: most small companies don't have the financial resources to devote to SEO. Big companies spend hundreds of thousands of dollars a year on SEO, but most small businesses don't have the budget. Still, since 95 percent of Internet users rely on search engines, you have to do something to boost traffic.

It surprised me to learn that SEO is actually related to your marketing strategy, not the back-end coding of your web site. "SEO has to be integrated into your overall marketing plan," said Rusinko.

Your challenge is to attract visitors to dedicated landing pages where they can find fresh content. "That's why social media is such an important part of a Web strategy," he explained. "When you publish timely content on the Web, it pushes up the ranking of your site. Remember, things get stale and old very quickly."

So how can you improve the search engine ranking of your site?

"First build the content, then focus on getting other people to link to you," Rusinko advises. Contact other web sites that serve the same customers and see if you can work together.

"The key is to understand what the audience is looking for in terms of an online experience," he said.

Things really shifted in 2010 when Google and Bing started to index and integrate social media content into search engines.

"Facebook pages (not profile pages) can be crawled and indexed," said Rusinko. "So that's why you have to use social media marketing to reach your audience."

Even if you just have a few thousand dollars, hire an independent contractor who is willing to work on a project basis. But make sure the person has legitimate SEO experience.

"It comes down to executing a strong strategy," said Rusinko. "People will go to your site because you are going to provide or add value."

GREAT 75 IDEA

Hire a Great Web Designer

If you are in the process of designing or redesigning your site, here are some things to consider:

- *Check out a variety of web sites to see what appeals to you.* Figure out what you like and don't like. Some sites take forever to load because they are laden with clunky graphics and animations. The best sites, in my opinion, are very simple and elegant. Make a list of your favorites to share with a designer.

- *Outline all the elements you want to feature on your site.* Do you need product photos, audio or video clips? Will your customers be able to place orders and track their shipments?
- List all the sections of your site and create an outline of each page. Most web site designers base their fees on the number of pages.
- *Once you've outlined what you want to feature on your site, meet with at least two or three designers.* Ask friends or colleagues to recommend designers. Contact companies whose sites you like and ask them who designed their sites. Ask for references before you set up any meetings.
- *Before the meeting, go online and review their work.* Then, get answers to these questions:
  - Will they actually do the work or farm it out to others?
  - How and when do they expect to be paid? Do they require a deposit?
  - How much do they charge to update and maintain a site? Can you maintain it yourself with a content management system?
  - Will they host your site or find a host for you?
- *Ask for a detailed estimate in writing*—including a "site map" that shows you how all the pages flow from the home page.
- *Design and development prices will vary considerably, depending on what you want your site to do.* Designing a new web site can cost as little as $600 or as much as $500,000 or more, depending on the complexity. Many Web registration companies, like GoDaddy.com and Network Solutions, offer free or low-cost, template-based sites. If you are interested in a Word Press site based on a template, Brian Hanson at Customtwit.com (www.customtwit.com) will build one for about $600. He did a fantastic job customizing my YouTube, Facebook, and Twitter pages.
- *Watch out for hidden costs.* Don't be afraid to ask questions to really understand everything you'll be paying for.
- *When your site is uploaded, ask the designer for a copy of all the files.* The designer doesn't own the site—you do. Having the files protects you from losing all the work if you need to hire someone to take over.

76

Run Your Business in the Cloud

Emily Borders, cofounder of Borders + Gratehouse, a San Francisco–based public relations (PR) firm, practices what she preaches. "We work with technology companies across a number of industries that are providing technology solutions for small businesses," said Borders, who left a big PR agency to start her own business in 2007.

Borders works with six people in San Francisco. Four other professionals in her firm work from their homes in Chicago. "When we started the company, we were faced with a lot of questions about how to set up the infrastructure of the business," she said.

To walk the talk, she relies on her clients' services to manage her business every day. For example, she's hired freelance talent through Elance.com. She uses Ring Central's "cloud-based" phone service and turns to RocketLawyer.com for legal services. They use Fresh Books for bookkeeping.

Since public relations relies on collaboration, they need to share files. Borders said they started using free platforms like Google Docs, but soon realized they needed something more professional. Now they use Egnyte, an online file server that works like a big company file server.

"We have people in Chicago and Atlanta who are all unified and able to share files with our clients, for a monthly fee of $10 to $60, based on the number of users."

She has other favorite cloud-based tools, including a program called Slide Rocket. "It allows you to create a Power Point® presentation online," she explained. "You can integrate a Twitter feed and then link it to YouTube."

The company also uses High Rise, a customer relationship management tool developed by 37signals.com. "We put all our contacts in there and we can easily see what anyone on the team is doing for clients and prospects. I really love it."

Borders said, "It can be daunting to put a new business together, but these cloud-based services have helped us establish our business."

GREAT
77
IDEA

Use Online Mailing Solutions

On March 31, 1999, the U.S. Postal Service outlawed the mechanical postage meters used by most small businesses. The Postal Service's decision to ban mechanical meters was aimed at eliminating about $100 million a year in postal meter fraud. I remember lugging that darn postage meter to the post office and waiting in line to load it up.

Now, you can manage mail from your desktop. You can download postage online in less than a minute for a small fee. You can buy and print stamps with customized images for holidays or special promotions.

Industry leader Pitney Bowes is working hard to create solutions for business owners.

"Our products are designed to help customers communicate with their customers, both physically and digitally," said Lisa Somer, senior director, small business marketing for Pitney Bowes.

She said if you are sending about 60 pieces of mail a month, it makes sense to use a postage meter. The smallest models cost about $20 a month.

A postage meter isn't just convenient, Somer said, but may qualify your business for discounts of up to 5 percent on certain packages.

In addition to being able to download postage, Pitney Bowes has a cool product called AddressRightNow™. It's an online list management service for smaller-volume or infrequent mailings.

The service lets you upload your mailing list to Pitney Bowes for updating based on the change of address information submitted to the U.S. Postal Service. It works like this: You upload your mailing lists to Pitney Bowes's secure web site. The address verification service scans the lists for changes, makes corrections and formats addresses to meet U.S. Postal Service standards.

This is important because more than 45 million Americans change their address every year, according to the Postal Service. This makes it tough to keep track of customers and clients. Being able to verify an address before a mailing not only saves you money, but helps you meet new Postal Service quality standards.

Starting in 2010, the Postal Service requires mailers to apply a USPS®-approved address correction method on First-Class Mail® and Standard Mail® submitted at discount postage rates.

If you don't update addresses 95 days prior to the mailing, you will be charged an additional seven cents per assessed piece.

"Mailing lists are the lifeblood of a customer's mail communications," said Mark Pollack, vice president, marketing, U.S. Mailing, at Pitney Bowes. "Our AddressRightNow online list management service can help mailers easily and quickly improve the quality of addresses in their mailing lists, which can lead to improved response rates and reduced mailing costs."

For information on Pitney Bowes products and services, check out their web site at www.pb.com.

GREAT
78
IDEA

Train Employees Online

In the rush to use new programs, many business owners forget that people need to be taught how to use the program before they can be more productive.

An employee can lose up to three weeks of work time trying to tackle a new program on their own, according to a survey of 400 PC users by SCO, a British software firm, and Harris Research. In fact, the first month after a new program is introduced, employees spend an average of 100 minutes a week trying to figure out how to use it.

If you are looking for an alternative to sending your employees to community college classes or hiring private instructors, try online training.

"I like to work on my own," said Barbara Epstein, who signed up for an online tutorial that taught her how to use Microsoft Office. "I really don't enjoy reading instruction books," said Epstein. "This has given me confidence with the computer."

Because everyone learns differently, many online tutorials include audio instruction as well as visual demonstrations. ElementK.com is one of the biggest online training companies.

Some Training Tips

- Ask your employees to research the programs they believe would boost productivity.
- Compare prices before you buy or sign up for anything.
- Schedule time during the workday for training.
- Share the expense of hiring a trainer with another small business owner in your area.

Online training is great: it's like having a virtual tutor who never sleeps and isn't on the payroll.

GREAT 79 IDEA

Sell Products Online

Consumers buy billions of dollars' worth of stuff online, so you should consider selling your products and services, too.

Your challenge is to make the online shopping experience both enjoyable and lucrative. One trend is to find out exactly what your customers want in advance, then push out the information.

One cool site, www.shopittome.com, asks new customers to complete a detailed questionnaire about their fashion preferences, including sizes, colors, and styles. Then, once a week, they send you a personalized e-mail with photographs of the clothes and special offers.

No matter what you sell, you need sharp, color photographs of your products, accompanied by well-written copy, detailed descriptions, prices, and shipping information. If you can, ask happy customers for permission to post testimonials. If you get reviewed in the press, post the positive reviews on your site.

Another tip: Be sure to include your phone number on every Web page so customers can call if they're having any issues. Offer a variety of payment options, including PayPal®, so you don't scare customers away.

Make sure all your back-end systems are functioning perfectly. In the early days of online shopping, nearly 80 percent of customers failed to complete transactions due to technical problems. Those high failure rates soured people who were trying to save time by shopping online. Test and retest your shopping cart program and check it every day.

Consider offering online-only specials and post coupons.

GREAT

80

IDEA

Visit My Favorite Web Sites

People often ask me what sites I visit frequently, so here's what's on my list:

- BizSugar.com aggregates small business content in an easily accessible manner. Readers rank the articles and provide feedback.
- OpenForum.com is the American Express small business site. I'm a contributor. You can find dozens of other experts, including author and marketing expert Guy Kawasaki, and John Jantsch, founder of Duct Tape Marketing. If you have an American Express card, you can create a business profile. It's easy to do and you may make a few connections.
- Check out SmallBizDaily.com for great tips and advice from Rieva Lesonsky and other experts.
- Bloomberg.com features quality content on all sorts of business topics and issues. There are video clips, audio downloads, and stories. *Bloomberg Businessweek* also has a great web site.
- I subscribe to the daily *New York Times* news feed. It's a great way to start your day, even if you just scan the headlines.

And, of course, I hope you'll visit my site and submit a great idea: www.201greatideas.com.

Develop and Launch New Products and Services

4

• •

Y ou might think that only big companies with deep pockets can launch products. Not so. More products are dreamed up and executed by small, innovative companies or individuals. In 2007, small companies invested about $50 billion on research and development (R&D), according to the National Science Foundation.

In 2010, as the economy improved, all U.S. firms were projected to spend $260 billion on R&D, down slightly from the $268 billion spent before the recession in 2008.

Often, just one or two people dream up a staggeringly great idea. Facebook was founded by Mark Zuckerberg, a Harvard undergrad, and some friends. A few years and several lawsuits later, he turned down a billion-dollar offer to sell Facebook, and by 2010, the privately held company was estimated to be worth about $33 billion.

Feisty entrepreneurs founded Napster, the company that pioneered digital music sharing. Napster's colorful history included high-profile lawsuits filed by musicians and music publishers, bankruptcy, and an ultimate revival and sale to Best Buy for about $130 million. (My friend Chris Gorog resurrected the bankrupt company when he served as CEO and turned it around before it was sold.)

Being a pioneer isn't easy. Jann Wenner dropped out of UC Berkeley to start a new music magazine called *Rolling Stone*. He borrowed $7,500 from family and friends to print 40,000 copies of the first issue. It was a flop. Magazine dealers sent 34,000 back. Undeterred, he worked on the second issue. The magazine is still around and kicking ass.

In this chapter, you'll meet the cab driver/composer who invented Magnetic Poetry as a way to overcome writer's block. You'll learn how Frieda Caplan, a mom who wanted to spend more time with her baby, pioneered the importation of exotic fruits and vegetables, bringing new tastes to the American table.

With tens of thousands of practical and zany ideas floating around out there, it's no wonder the U.S. Patent and Trademark Office is overburdened with applications. The backlog is estimated to be 700,000. It can take up to three years to obtain full patent protection, prompting David Kappos, the patent agency's director, to admit at a public hearing that "we are currently operating the most senseless system of delayed and delinquent examination imaginable."

Congress is supposedly trying to speed up the patent process, including a fee for "fast-tracking" an application. Although the fees for small companies are modest, it can cost about $10,000 or more to hire a patent attorney to navigate the complicated process.

Small business owners and inventors are launching and promoting new products every day. They push products on eBay and buy ads on Google. They line up to pitch their products to QVC and other popular shopping channels. It's tough to land a spot and even tougher to be invited back. If you are selling beauty products, you need to sell thousands of dollars' worth of products a minute, according to entrepreneurs who gave it a try. Direct selling is tricky and you have to be prepared to fill orders quickly.

Don't be discouraged. Bringing your vision to reality is easier than ever. If you've ever designed a piece of jewelry, picture frame, napkin ring, or flower vase, you can buy software for about $100 and design a 3-D model. That digital file can be e-mailed to a company like Shapeways (see Great Idea #87) for "rapid manufacturing," or 3-D printing, as it is known. Within a day or so, you can post the product for sale in the Shapeways' online store.

Read on to learn how to license your product to a bigger company or make a distribution deal with an industry leader. You'll meet two women from New Jersey who fell in love with handmade Italian pottery and ended up importing it for use in gardens and homes across the country.

This batch of great ideas will inspire you to go for it: develop a product, create a prototype, mass produce it, and sell it.

GREAT IDEA 81 — Create a Fad

Even when they weren't hungry, friends stood in front of Dave Kappel's refrigerator, mesmerized by his poetry created by a collection of words stuck on magnets. That simple, great idea spawned a wildly popular product that is still around.

Kappel's original Magnetic Poetry kit is the perfect example of how a brainstorm leads to a moneymaking venture. In the late 1990s, Kapell was a songwriter and cab driver. He told me he made the first poetry kit to combat a bad case of writer's block. Then, he started making kits for his friends.

"Instead of bringing wine to a party, I'd bring a magnetic poetry kit," said Kapell. Next, he started selling poetry kits at craft fairs, and then to local retailers.

Sales took off. Soon, he had 30 people making kits in their homes, while he worked 90 hours a week getting the company off the ground. Hard work paid off: the company has sold millions of kits and a variety of related products.

Kapell said one of his greatest moments was when a Magnetic Poetry set appeared on Jerry Seinfeld's apartment refrigerator on *Seinfeld*.

So what advice does he have for you?

"Little guys should get a product out there quick and sell the hell out of it," said Kapell. "Don't worry about legal protection—people are paralyzed by it. It costs a lot of bucks to patent something and it's not that important."

Although the kits are copyrighted, he says you shouldn't get bogged down with legalities. "The big boys aren't going to pay attention or try to compete with you until you sell millions of items."

Check out what's new at www.magneticpoetry.com.

Import Something New and Different

About 45 years ago, a homely, brown fuzzy fruit known as the Chinese gooseberry spawned a new industry. The egg-shaped fruit, now called "kiwi fruit," because it resembled the flightless, fuzzy bird that live in Australia, inspired Frieda Caplan to start a successful exotic produce business.

In the 1960s, apples, bananas, and oranges were pretty much the only fresh fruits Americans ate. Today, you can thank produce pioneer Caplan every time you munch on alfalfa sprouts, macadamia nuts, sugar snap peas, spaghetti squash, and dried blueberries. Frieda's Inc. also popularized the succulent, oversized Portobello mushrooms that sell for up to $12 a pound. And in 2009, Frieda's introduced American's to black garlic from Korea.

Frieda's Inc. brokers about 300 fruits and vegetables from growers around the world, according to Karen Caplan, president. During the recession in 2008, she said the company, which employs about 80, downsized and reduced the number of products they handled. But things started picking up again in 2010. The privately held company has an 81,000-square-foot warehouse in Orange County, California.

One secret of Frieda's success is asking grocery store clients to share sales data so they can quickly track what's selling and what's not.

"You really want to be focused on your best sellers," said Caplan. "There is a limited amount of space in supermarkets, so we are narrowing down the product list."

Adding new items to the produce department is much tougher than it was 10 years ago. For example, Caplan said it can take up to a month to get a new product approved by a buyer and logged into the distribution system. "Fast-tracking" a new fruit or vegetable into the produce section can take a week.

Fruits and vegetables are tracked by those little stickers with a numerical code.

In 2010, fingerling potatoes, hot chili peppers, and a variety of spices used in Latin and Asian recipes were strong sellers.

Karen's mother, Frieda, began introducing Americans to tastebud-tingling delicacies in 1962. Needing a job with flexible hours after Karen was born, Frieda started working nights in the Los Angeles produce market. She made contacts and enjoyed the work. She decided to go out on her own when a space became available, starting the company with about $10,000 in loans.

In 1986, daughter Karen Caplan joined the business. Importing produce doesn't seem like such a revolutionary concept, but in the 1990s, most grocery store produce departments featured fewer than 100 items. Today, the average market stocks about 350—thanks in part to Frieda Caplan's vision.

In addition to offering offbeat fruits and vegetables, Frieda's Inc. has set itself apart from the competition through its use of a distinctive signature purple color in packaging and advertising.

"When mom started, she needed a sign for the store," recalls Karen Caplan. "She had to have it up over the weekend. The guy who painted the sign only had one color in his truck—lavender. Now it's our trademarked purple. It is like subliminal advertising. When I show up places, people say things like, 'I really expected to see you in a purple suit.'"

The produce boxes are purple, too. "A unique design is okay," said Caplan. "But that purple color is especially effective."

Check out what's new at www.friedas.com. You can also read Caplan's blog on the site.

GREAT

83

IDEA

Turn Your Hobby into a Successful Business

Many hobbies evolve into successful small businesses. Even the most offbeat pastimes can prove profitable. For example, Roz Watnemo and Sue Meier turned their passion for an obscure form of Norwegian embroidery into a successful retail and mail-order business. Nordic Needle, based in Fargo, North Dakota, has grown from a 400-square-foot storefront to a 9,000-square-foot space with 24 employees.

The 35-year-old company has been honored by the U.S. Small Business Administration for boosting exports from North Dakota. Nordic Needle's

50,000 retail customers live in 600 countries. They can purchase about 19,000 items via mail order, in person, or online.

I met Roz and Sue a few years ago while visiting Fargo to speak at a conference. They told me they never thought that signing up for a class in Hardanger embroidery, a traditional form of white thread-on-white fabric stitchery used to decorate tablecloths and aprons, would change their lives.

Embroidery is very popular in the Plains states, where winters are long and cold and people seek out something fun and productive to pass the time. Tired of driving to Minnesota or sending away to Norway for supplies, the partners decided to buy and sell a few Hardanger necessities. Thinking they'd sell a few items to friends, they opened a tiny shop in downtown Fargo.

About 13 years later, when they were—bad pun—bursting at the seams, they moved into a suburban shopping plaza. The bright, cozy store is a stitcher's paradise. Every inch of space is filled with yards of fabric, rainbows of thread, patterns, samplers, and sewing kits.

"I know a lot of partnerships don't go well, but Roz and I are very different from each other, and we complement each other," said Meier, who is retired but still involved in the business.

Watnemo, the Hardanger expert, produces new pattern books each year. She designs by hand, but relies on a software program to create the actual pattern graphs. Most years, hardcore fans of Nordic Needle gather for a retreat in Fargo.

Across the country, former real estate broker Sally Wright Bacon turned her love of beads and thread into a lucrative one-of-a-kind jewelry business.

In 2010, she stopped renting space at craft fairs and opened Oodles, a boutique in the sleepy town of Orford, New Hampshire.

Bacon never intended to be a jewelry designer. A friend took her to a bead store as a way to help her overcome the paralyzing grief she felt after her 16-year-old son, Aaron, died of starvation in 1994 while participating in a wilderness boot camp for teens.

"I was on the verge of ending it all," said Bacon. "I had never been in a bead store. I wandered around and became fascinated by the beads." She took it as a good omen when "Wind Beneath My Wings," was playing in the store because she and Aaron loved that song. "My son had sung it to me many times, and it was the song we played at his funeral."

Bacon started beading that weekend and hasn't stopped.

She designs elaborate rosaries and dramatic necklaces made with African trade beads and chunky, rare semiprecious stones. One of her special rosaries was presented to Pope John Paul II. "When I'm in my studio, I'm just so centered," said Bacon. "It's all about the beads. They have traveled continents to get to me."

Check out her work on her web site, www.sallywrightbacon.com, and visit Oodles in Orford, New Hampshire.

Here are some tips for turning your hobby into a small business:

- Look for others who share your passion and connect with them to see what they are doing.
- Attend a hobby or craft trade show to check out the trends and competition.
- Subscribe to magazines and newsletters that cover your hobby.
- Find out if you can rent the publication's or web site's e-mail list. Do a test mailing to promote your best product.
- Start small. Don't quit your job.
- Check with your accountant about the IRS rules on tax deductions for hobbies versus businesses. If you don't make any money doing what you love, it's not a business.

GREAT

84

IDEA

Become an Exclusive Importer

Being first to introduce a unique product to the United States is one of the best ways to establish a successful small business. This was the strategy used by Mara Seibert and Lenore Rice, two former high-powered Wall Street players who traded in their briefcases for a New Jersey warehouse full of handmade Italian terra-cotta pottery.

Mara Seibert was on the fast track as a mergers and acquisitions specialist at Chase Manhattan Bank, structuring big leveraged buyouts and hostile corporate takeovers during the 1980s.

Tax attorney Lenore Rice was working as a Wall Street lawyer during the 1980s mergers and acquisitions boom. Tired of the rat race, Seibert and Rice opted to quit their jobs to stay home with their young children.

Seibert spent her free time collecting ceramic art, remodeling her home, and working in her garden. Rice studied Italian prior to booking a villa in Tuscany. She invited the Seiberts to join them on the vacation, beginning their long-standing friendship.

In Tuscany, the women wanted to go somewhere while their husbands played tennis. The women drove to Impruneta, a tiny village located about two hours outside of Florence. The town's signature craft, deep orangey-pink and white-tinged pottery, intrigued them. They selected pots to buy and dragged their husbands back to the village. Their husbands agreed that the pots were beautiful and durable. Thinking big, the women called customs brokers to figure out whether it was feasible to buy a pallet full of pots. If they couldn't sell them, they would just keep them. They spent $3,000 on pots and another $1,000 to ship them back to New Jersey by boat.

Tips for Becoming an Exclusive Importer

An exclusive importing relationship is based on trust. The people you buy from have to honor the relationship, and you have to make every effort to sell their products. Here are some tips on how to establish a trustworthy arrangement with an overseas company:

- First, confirm that they don't have any existing relationships with other U.S. companies.
- If necessary, hire an interpreter to help you negotiate the agreement. Work with a local attorney to draft an agreement in the local language. Make sure you understand all the terms and aren't breaking any local or national laws.
- Start with a short-term deal to test the market for the product. If things look promising, extend the contract.
- Find a reputable customs broker to handle the shipment of goods from the manufacturer to your warehouse.
- Set up a system to track sales and shipping information.
- Communicate frequently with your supplier. It's easy to keep in touch via e-mail, Skype, and telephone calls.

Back home, they showed the pots and planters to landscape designers and upscale nurseries. Everyone loved them, and the pottery, which averages $500 for a small pot and $1,500 or more for a big planter, spawned a successful business.

Knowing presentation was important, the partners spent $5,000 on a high-quality brochure. They sold $20,000 worth of pots in their first year in business. Sales reached several million dollars in 2008, despite the recession and business is picking up again.

Looking for a new angle, they launched a line of Italian pots designed by American designers. In a recent interview, Siebert said their biggest challenge is keeping their business going, since the potters who craft their exclusive line of pottery are getting old. Unfortunately, only two of the potters' children intend to stay in the pottery business.

Siebert and Rice are so concerned about other companies poaching their suppliers, they decline to reveal the surnames of their potters. The relationship is much more than commercial. The women consider the potters and their families close friends, not just vendors. And once or twice a year, they visit the village to place orders and visit with the potters they know and love.

Check out the company's beautiful pots at www.seibert-rice.com.

GREAT 85 IDEA Launch a Green Product

On a rainy morning in 2005, Reza Tourzia was jogging around his Los Angeles neighborhood when he noticed how many automatic sprinklers were watering lawns despite the downpour. He realized many homeowners relied on automatic timers, but timers couldn't tell whether it was sunny or sprinkling. That's when his great idea hit.

An experienced software developer, Tourzia decided to develop a smart device that could go online to check the local weather. Then, it would turn the sprinklers on and off depending on the need rather than the time or day of the week. Cyber-Rain hit the market in 2008.

"Launching a small business in 2008 was not the best time in the world, but we are alive," said Diana Schulz, chief executive officer of Cyber-Rain, which is based in Encino, California. "Our success is a testament to the technology and the fact that there is a growing awareness of the water crisis and increasing water rates."

Schulz said that 39 states will be facing drought by 2013, according to the U.S. Environmental Protection Agency. That's another reason she believes homeowners and landowners will be willing to pay $399 for a system that controls eight sprinklers.

"The system will pay for itself within a year or two," said Schulz, adding that it is easy to install with a screwdriver and a few other easily available tools. "Our product is such a no-brainer, I have to ask, why doesn't everybody with a lawn have one?"

The small company is venture backed, but Schulz declined to share any financial information. "Fund-raising has been a big part of my life for the past two years," said Schulz, who spends much of her time promoting the product to potential customers, mainly commercial landscapers and property managers.

Consumers can buy the Cyber-Rain system online at www.cyber-rain .com. Landscape contractors and owners of commercial buildings can purchase bigger systems through Ewing Irrigation, a Phoenix-based firm.

GREAT IDEA 86 — Build a Working Model of Your Product

Raising money to manufacture and market your great idea is almost impossible without a working model. Unfortunately, many entrepreneurs fall prey to invention scam artists who charge big fees and do absolutely nothing to bring your product to market.

So you need to find a reputable firm to build a working prototype. Most investors want to touch and feel the product before writing a check.

"People think that if they have a patent they are nine-tenths of the way there," said Henry C. Keck, the semiretired cofounder of Keck-Craig, the Pasadena, California, based firm. Keck has been designing products since the 1950s. "When the inventor says it's 90 percent complete, we say there's 90 percent more to go."

Keck's most famous design is the sleek metal-and-glass flip-top sugar dispenser sitting on millions of restaurant tables around the world. Based on the success of the sugar dispenser, he said everything they design for clients "has to be well styled and highly marketable."

In the 1980s and 1990s, the company's six engineers and model makers worked with many entrepreneurs to design everything from portable eye washers to battery-operated pesticide sprayers and a shrimp deveiner. Their tidy model shop is a tinkerer's dream, filled with rows of lathes, presses, mills, and saws. In recent years, the company has focused on building bigger, more expensive industrial prototypes and medical devices.

"We once designed a prototype for a head support used in neurological surgery," said Warren Haussler, president and owner. "We watched through the glass when they took it into the operating room and used to it stabilize a patient's head while they drilled holes into his skull."

The veteran industrial designer said too many inventors make the mistake of patenting their idea before they find out whether it can be mass produced in a cost-effective way. Haussler said the patent process is long and expensive, but having a working model can spell the difference between bringing a product to market and never seeing it built.

It can cost $30,000 to $50,000 or more to build a working model and make changes along the way.

"People suffer by being stuck to their patents," Keck added. "You can add things to a patent or make changes while it's being processed, but once it's issued, that's it."

Company officials said 2010 was a record year, especially in the medical products area. It is working with a Japanese company to design a tissue slicer for laboratories. The fees charged depend on the amount of time and work needed to design and build a model or prototype. Haussler said the company works with 10 to 20 clients at a time.

Jim Harris, who invented the Shrimp Pro 2000® shrimp deveiner, worked with Keck-Craig to bring his dream to reality in 1995.

Harris, who is now a commercial real estate developer in Los Angeles, said he came up with his idea when he was working as a seafood distributor. His mission was to reduce the time it took to prep seafood. When he shared his deveining concept to Keck-Craig's model makers and engineers, they spent four months, "yelling and screaming" throughout the design process.

"You have to agree to disagree," said Harris. "That's the most important part of the process. Engineers have a mind-set, and sometimes you have to bring creativity to their mind-set."

His machine, which he sold to Nemco Food Equipment Co., can devein 6,000 shrimp an hour and is used by restaurants around the world.

"Engineers are an absolute necessity for an entrepreneur," said Harris, who also invented the ProShucker® oyster shucker. "I was chief visionary officer. But, often, the best ideas come from people who are least capable of bringing them to fruition."

Harris advises other entrepreneurs looking for engineers and model makers to ask people with similar but noncompetitive products where they had theirs designed. "Check out their facilities and the company's resume. Look at what they've done," he said.

For information on filing for a patent, check the U.S. Patent and Trademark Office web site: www.uspto.gov.

GREAT

87

IDEA

Make a Model with 3-D Software

Matthew Blake has been playing guitar since he was 11, but he didn't make his first guitar until he got divorced for the second time.

"I decided to build a guitar as therapy," he said. "It was fun and people liked it."

A skilled carpenter and cabinet maker living in Delaware, Ohio, Blake said he originally bought a 3-D software program to help him design guitars, but it was very complicated and crashed often.

Frustrated, he started looking around for a better program and found software made by Alibre.com in Richardson, Texas. Blake paid about $200 (the program now costs about $99) and purchased an annual maintenance and tech support contract for an additional $99 a year.

"I was drawing stuff the first night, but it took me working at it one hour a night for three months to get the hang of it," said Blake, who now sells his hardwood-body, custom-made electric guitars for $1,500 to $2,500. It takes him between 40 and 60 hours to make one guitar. So far, he's been selling them through word-of-mouth and by attending guitar shows.

Nicknamed the "Caveman" for his rumpled appearance, Blake named his company Cavey's Clubs. It's a play on words because musicians call their guitars *axes* (www.caveysclubs.com).

The founder of Alibre said Blake is a typical customer.

"My vision from the beginning was to have a software product that lets individuals and small business owners turn their ideas into products," said Paul Grayson, CEO of Alibre. A veteran software guy, he founded and later sold for $100 million a company that made graphic software for personal computers.

He invested his own money to start Alibre, which posts annual revenues of about $10 million.

"We've lowered the bar so new companies can get their products to market," said Grayson. "We are part of the industrial revolution 2.0. . . . All you need is passion, persistence, and an idea you can turn into a product."

GREAT 88 IDEA
Serve the High and Low Ends of the Market

One of the most creative and savvy entrepreneurs I know built a lucrative frozen-pizza manufacturing business by serving all ends of the pizza market with targeted and price-specific products.

A former potato saleswoman, Kathy Taggares sold her condo, jewelry, and cashed in her insurance policies to buy an ailing salad dressing factory from Marriott Corp. in 1989. She named the company K.T.'s Kitchens. A few years later, she added pizza crust to her product line. She eventually added a full line of frozen-pizza products, selling them to Trader Joe's, club stores, schools, and the military.

With about 250 employees and 2010 sales around $45 million, she's doing something very right. Her most successful strategy relies on using the same basic ingredients—flour, sauce, and toppings—to make a variety of pizza products for the low, middle, and high end of the market.

At the low end of the market, she sells pizza in bulk to public schools and the military. K.T.'s produces a line of midpriced pizzas for club stores. At the high end, K.T.'s has made private-label gourmet pizza for Trader Joe's and Wolfgang Puck. In addition to pizza, she produces a line of salad dressings under the Bob's Big Boy™ brand.

Taggares said she saves thousands of dollars a year by buying flour, spices, sauce, and toppings by the container load. The bustling factory in Carson, California, features one of the biggest commercial freezers in southern California and the largest refrigerated U.S. Department of Agriculture (USDA) processing room on the West Coast. K.T.'s runs several production lines at once; some workers are making big, low-cost pizzas for club stores. Across the way, other crews are hand-stretching crusts for upscale lines.

Her advice to you is to find a way to tailor the same basic product to suit multiple customers and price points.

"The biggest benefit of a diversified product mix is to spread the risk," said Taggares, who started making private-label products because "I didn't have enough money to develop and market my own brand."

Maintaining multiple product lines has another strong advantage: "It helps even out the sales year-round," she explained. "During the summers, school business is down, but club store business is way up."

She cautions that her strategy of making the same basic product for different price points won't work for everyone. "It depends on the flexibility of your product line," she said. "We can serve pretty much every segment of the market with the same type of equipment. It wouldn't work if you needed different equipment to make different products."

Taggares is one of my closest friends. She personifies the American dream in so many ways. She started with virtually nothing and has built a successful business and a rewarding life. I've been chronicling her adventures since 1989, when I wrote a column about her buying the defunct Marriott food processing plant. In 2011, she was doing well by sticking to her core products. She told me she's no longer "chasing rainbows" by experimenting with branded products. A few years ago, she invested a lot of time and money to create a line of frozen pizza meals for kids featuring cartoon characters who were dogs. Shoppers were confused, thinking the pizza was for dogs, not kids. It was not a great idea. But, she moved on and now focuses on her core products.

Partner with a Big Company for Distribution

Doing a deal with a giant corporation is thrilling, intimidating, and scary. But the opportunities are out there. Big companies of all kinds are hungry for the nimble thinking and new products created by entrepreneurs.

The first challenge is making contact with someone at the big company who is interested in what you have to offer. Sometimes this takes weeks, but once in a while the big company finds you.

In the late 1990s, Santa Monica–based Roundhouse Products, which designed patented CD storage systems, signed a lucrative licensing and design agreement with office products giant Avery Dennison. (In 2000, Roundhouse was acquired by Targus.)

"When Avery came to us, we had a good, strong patent and something exciting to offer," recalled Howard Sherman, former CEO of Roundhouse and now an investor in several small ventures.

Jon Williamson, former senior product manager for new products at Avery, said the company was in the process of designing a CD storage system when he found Roundhouse's products and said, "This is it."

"They brought a freshness that I can't always get in a larger company," Williamson said. "I was constantly intrigued by their intelligence and how quickly they could get something to market."

The relationship, which lasted about eight years, greatly benefited both companies. Roundhouse leveraged Avery's tremendous retail distribution clout. Avery took advantage of Roundhouse's design talents and speed in executing new ideas. Neither company would disclose the financial details of the agreement, but both confirmed that it was positive.

At the time, CD storage options were in demand. Roundhouse's patented "Roladisc" system eliminated the need for the bulky plastic jewel cases by storing CDs in plastic sleeves.

Roundhouse also made a similar deal with a division of Sony to develop a line of customized CD storage products. "We didn't care about their company size," said Carl Walter, former senior vice president of operations for Sony Signatures in San Francisco. "What was important to us was that they were very creative and had a very innovative product that we liked."

How to Make a Distribution Deal with a Bigger Company

- Find the right person to contact.
- Sign a nondisclosure agreement before you share your idea.
- Present your concept in a clear, concise manner.
- Be well prepared for your first meeting so you make a positive impression.
- Surround yourself with experienced advisers, including your attorney and accountant.
- Be patient. Things take longer to be decided at big companies.
- Don't appear too anxious or naive, even when you are eager to do the deal. "It was very exciting for us when we first met with Avery," said Sherman. "But, we all had to wear our poker faces."

Sherman said you must be patient. Big companies move slowly. It took 10 months to sign a deal from the date they signed a letter of intent. "You also need to be flexible because the players often change within a corporation."

GREAT

90

IDEA

Take Advantage of an Online Technology Exchange

Licensing new technology to other companies is a win-win scenario for everyone involved. Licensing deals can create new opportunities to grow your business. One simple way to find a product to license or to expose your intellectual property to potential licensees is via an online technology marketplace.

That is how Frank Jaksch, former CEO of ChromaDex Inc., connected with German pharmaceutical giant, Bayer. ChromaDex is a small

Irvine, California–based company that sells high-purity chemicals isolated from plants to companies making "smart food" with vitamins and supplements.

ChromaDex connected with Bayer through yet2.com, a leading technology marketplace. At the time, ChromaDex had 12 employees and annual sales under $10 million. Making a deal with Bayer, which has 117,000 employees and operates 350 individual companies on all continents, would have been impossible without an intermediary.

Jaksch went online to find a test to detect minute amounts of bacteria in food and nutritional supplements. His searched yielded information about a bioluminescent toxicity screen made by Bayer. The test, developed by Bayer for internal use, was exactly what Jaksch needed.

"One of the ways to develop new products is to find out what other people have done, rather than creating things on your own," said Jaksch.

"We worked it out so we didn't have to outlay any cash and Bayer took a stake in our company," he explained. "We looked at the Bayer deal as a new method to raise capital."

Better yet, Bayer AG took a 10 percent stake in his company and a seat on his board of directors. "A company like Bayer is not going to take a deal like this lightly, so it says a lot about us and our credibility."

When we spoke a few years ago, Ralf Du Jardin, manager of new business development for Bayer AG, said posting information about its toxicity screen online "led us to a fast-growing innovative company, ready to extract the added-value from the R&D efforts we have pursued with our technology in the food market segment. . . . We agreed on an equity-based license so both of us could benefit from ChromaDex's product development and expanding portfolio of customers."

The company that made the match was founded by the late Chris De Bleser and Ben DuPont in 1999. Tim Bernstein, COO of yet2.com, said the entrepreneurs raised $1.5 million in private angel funds to get started. They've since raised money from Procter & Gamble, Siemens, Honeywell, DuPont, Caterpillar, and NTT Leasing. The privately held company has offices in the United States, Europe, and Japan.

The web site now has over 140,000 registered users, including many of the Fortune 500 and over 17,000 smaller technology companies. The company also works with 327 "broker partners" to help source deals.

"The partners help us find technology and help find buyers of technology," said Bernstein.

Bernstein said the network of brokers extends the reach of our core, full-time team of 25.

The company charges clients an up-front fee and a success fee. "Paying up-front fees demonstrates they are serious about the effort," said Bernstein. "It means there is a strategic priority for the effort."

He said companies pay fees ranging from $2,500 at the low end for basic services available mostly online and automated. Companies seeking personalized service pay $50,000 to $75,000 for the 25 executives to be calling their contacts. "Our success rates go up enormously at the higher end," said Bernstein.

Based in Needham, Massachusetts, the firm has relationships with open innovation organizations, technical expert networks, small and medium enterprise (SME) networks, technical magazines, and online technical communities, giving it access to new technologies in the United States, Russia, China, India, Korea, Brazil, South Africa, Japan, and the European Union.

The company has flourished for a couple of reasons. "There is a huge open innovation trend," he said. "More big companies are open to acquiring outside technology."

Three years ago, if yet2.com had brought a new technology to Sony, for example, it would have needed to become a $1 billion opportunity in three years.

"Now, there is a complete revolution based on a couple of underlying economic trends," he said. "Financial markets have less faith in trusting companies to invest their R&D dollars. Plus, everyone is cutting back on basic research, so the source of next generation products have to be these smaller players."

Bernstein said, "The pace of competition increases every year. There is less of a cushion for failed efforts. Companies need to find a quicker way to get new products to market."

With David and Goliath scenarios, Bernstein said they do what they can to "protect the little guy." Although they recommend that clients hire good attorneys, they have a library of templates available to craft technology transfer deals.

"About half the time, we are representing the little guys, other half of the time, we go out and find the technology on behalf of bigger companies."

DeBleser, who worked for Polaroid and Black & Decker developing new technologies, dreamed up the idea for the company based on personal experience.

"Both of us [he and DuPont] were frustrated over how hard it was to transfer technology," said DeBleser. "With our model, regardless of their size, companies are allowed to expose their intellectual assets to the world."

In 2010, the company signed a deal to work with ideaken.com, an India-based technology network.

"We look forward to a long partnership with ideaken," said DuPont. "Innovation is not regional. Developments from Bangalore or Delhi can easily find their way to the shelves of New York or Tokyo, just as innovations from Berlin or Johannesburg may help companies in Bangalore. Organizations like ideaken and yet2.com exist to make these connections happen."

"It makes a lot of sense to join forces and create a larger community of innovation seekers and innovation solvers—everybody wins," said Jayesh Badani, founder and CEO of ideaken. "This partnership is about applying this principle to ourselves."

Are you ready for a licensing deal?

Before posting your technology on a marketplace-type web site to attract interest, consider the following:

- Does something your company developed have value to another company?
- Have you filed for trademark, trade secret, or copyright protection?
- Have you established a value for licensing the technology to others?
- Is your company stable and prepared to make a deal with a bigger partner?
- If so, hire an experienced intellectual property attorney to draft contracts.
- Set a schedule that guarantees payments before you release all the technology to the buyer.

For more information, visit www.yet2.com or contact Tim Bernstein at (781) 972-0600.

GREAT

91

IDEA

Have Your Product Mandated for Use by the Government

Keeping clients who get their hair cut healthy and safe is the sole mission of King Research.

In the 1940s, Maurice King, founder of King Research Inc. in Brooklyn, cornered the market on a disinfectant used in barbershops and salons. King, who developed Barbicide, the bright-blue disinfectant for haircutters, traveled around the country with his younger brother, James, pitching state health officials on the virtues of his sanitizing liquid.

"Sure enough, state officials began to pass rules that there be a disinfectant [in barber shops] and in some cases, they said, 'Sure, Mr. King, but can you suggest a product?'" recalls Maurice's son, Ben King. "'Why, yes!' my father replied. 'Barbicide! It's germicidal and fungicidal.'"

When the product was mandated, sales took off, according to Ben King, who serves as chief executive officer and president of the business.

Barbicide sales soared when states required haircutters to soak their tools between customers. Although there are competitors now, Barbicide is still the industry standard.

The company celebrated its fiftieth anniversary in the late 1990s with a party at the Smithsonian Institution's National Museum of American History. The company presented the museum with a jar of Barbicide—and a donation. Maurice King, who died of a heart attack in 1988, would have gotten a big kick out of the ceremony, which included, of course, a performance by a barbershop quartet.

King's employees now make 20 different products, including talcs, hospital disinfectants, and creams. But bright, almost neon blue Barbicide is still the flagship brand.

"My father's secret joke was that he had a rash on his scalp and whenever barbers pricked him, it hurt like the devil," says Ben King. "When he developed Barbicide, he decided to name it as such because it translated into 'kill the barber.' I don't think he ever put that into his advertising."

GREAT

92

IDEA

Create a Business Based on a Personal Challenge

When Nellie Sutton was diagnosed with Alzheimer's disease in 1985, her son Joseph began searching for a place where she could live safely and comfortably. He visited several nursing homes and was not about to put his mother in any of them.

So, he rented a ranch-style house and hired a caregiver to take care of his mother. He found four other Alzheimer's patients to rent the extra bedrooms. That's how his business was born. Sutton has since sold the business, but his idea still has merit.

"I opened my first home to care for my mother—no other reason," said Sutton, who saw an opportunity to care for America's aging population.

About 30 million Americans have a family member suffering from the progressive, degenerative disease that affects memory. Many Alzheimer's patients require round-the-clock attention and supervision.

Gladys Thankachan, a gerontologist and hospital consultant, said small units of five to seven residents are more friendly and accommodating than large institutional facilities for people in the early stages of Alzheimer's, who often get confused and agitated. However, she said, independent "board and care" homes such as Sutton's can be difficult to regulate. Still, given the increasing geriatric population, she said, small group homes fill a need if we "can make sure the standard of care is appropriate."

By founding a company to provide a safe place for his mother to live, he's helped hundreds of other families. Although he is no longer involved, there are Sutton homes operating privately in Florida.

GREAT

93

IDEA

Sell Your Wares in a Farmers' Market

Americans have been shopping in farmers' markets for centuries. The first farmers' market opened in Alexandria, Virginia, in the 1750s. Today, the U.S. Department of Agriculture reports there are about 35,000 farmers' markets across the country. In addition, thousands of flea markets and other ventures sell everything from vintage or "junk" jewelry to jam.

Opening your business in an established market setting has tremendous advantages. The rent and utilities are usually more affordable than stand-alone retail space. Plus, the landlord takes on part of the responsibility for attracting customers through signage and advertising.

You can also find safety and encouragement in numbers. You won't feel so alone when you can wander next door and visit with your neighboring merchant, listen to live music, or munch on fresh-baked pastries.

Before you run out and rent space in a market, here are some tips:

- *Go shopping.* Visit all the markets in your area. Some are open every day; others open only on the weekends or every few weeks. For instance, the Norwich Crafts Markets and Winter Markets in Vermont are open once a month. There are weekly farmers' markets in Norwich, Woodstock, at Dartmouth College, and several towns in our area.
- *Make sure your merchandise fits the clientele.*
- *Check out the competition.* Make sure your product or service fills a need in that particular market. You don't want to be the fourth bakery in a market.
- *Speak with the other vendors.* Ask them how the landlord treats them and whether he or she keeps promises made to tenants.
- *Check out the appearance and maintenance.* Are the public areas and restrooms kept clean? Is there adequate, accessible parking for customers? Are there security guards? Will you have any storage space or will you be loading merchandise in and out every time?
- *Review all advertising materials or brochures.* Be clear about their marketing efforts and whether you can do your own advertising.
- *Find out how you will be charged for your space.* Some open-air markets charge by the running foot; others charge by the square foot. Make sure you understand exactly what you are paying for, including utilities.
- *Ask about insurance.* Will you need to buy liability insurance? Will you be paying a percentage of sales to the management?
- *Spend some time in the market to get a feel for the ambience.* You will be spending many days in the market, so be sure it feels right.

If you are in New York City, visit my favorite indoor market. The Chelsea Market features wonderful stores. Built in an old bakery, the architecture retains the best features of the factory. It's cool on a hot day and a fun place to wander around. The market is located at 75 9th Avenue at 15th Street. Go hungry and try the wonderful ice cream and pastries.

GREAT 94 IDEA

Set Up a Cart in a Shopping Mall

Boston's Quincy Market is credited with setting up the first kiosks and carts in 1976 as part of an effort by local developers to rejuvenate the city's ailing downtown area.

Today, about 80 percent of America's 1,800 enclosed and regional shopping malls and hundreds of airports have so-called "temporary tenants," according to industry experts.

Kiosks and carts have tremendous benefits for small business owners and mall operators. Entrepreneurs selling everything from sunglasses to colored rubber bands are able to display their wares in a prime, high-foot-traffic setting with a modest investment; malls benefit from a wider variety of interesting merchandise and extra rent.

"The mall doesn't have to take a risk on a long-term lease," said a spokesman for the International Council of Shopping Centers. "For the retailer, there's access to a lot of customers that they would not otherwise have."

Major mall developers rely on carts to add color and variety, as well as to generate income. Some cart operators move into a mall from May to December to capitalize on the busy holiday gift-buying and back-to-school shopping peaks, but many more remain year-round.

"The pushcarts act as incubators to test a potential market for a product," said Jennifer Ciotti, former manager of specialty retail for Boston's Faneuil Hall.

Unlike the rickety wooden pushcarts used at the turn of the century, today's carts, or retail merchandising units (RMUs), cost about $20,000 and feature phone lines, elaborate lighting, and computerized inventory systems.

"We have to approve the design, so our in-house designers help tenants design their carts," said Lisa Taylor, specialty leasing manager for the Mall of America in Bloomington, Minnesota.

Taylor said RMUs have to be designed to last for years, feature lots of storage space, and be able to be locked up when the mall closes.

Things to Consider When Looking for Mall Space

Locating your business in a shopping mall has certain advantages over renting space in a strip mall or in a downtown retail district. A mall has built-in foot traffic, good parking, and a mall-wide marketing budget.

But, you need to make sure your potential customers visit the mall. Spend time visiting stores, speaking to other tenants, and watching customers. It's best to work with an experienced real estate broker who represents many malls in your area. Shop for space carefully; leasing space is costly, and you don't want to be stuck in the wrong place. Before you start looking, consider the following:

- How much space will you need for your cart? Will you have access to a storage area?
- What kinds of businesses are operating around you? Are they competitive or complementary?
- How responsive is the management company to tenants? Speak to other small retailers in the mall to find out.
- What hours is the mall open on weekdays? Weekends? Holidays?
- Do you like the feeling of the place? Can you see yourself working here every day? Visit the mall at different times of the day and night to check foot traffic and parking availability.
- Find out how many shoplifting arrests were made in recent months. Any other crimes? Check with the local police department to determine the safety and security of the mall.
- Will you be paying for utilities? Do you have to pay for all interior improvements? Can you sublease the space to another business? Make sure you understand exactly what your lease includes and sign the shortest lease possible to give yourself an out if your business fails.

She said there are about 69 carts in America's biggest mall, which has 4.2 million square feet of space. Cart owners pay a premium for space at a consumer wonderland like the Mall of America. Rent for a cart in a high-traffic location can run $40,000 to $50,000 a year. That compares with rent of about $96,000 a year for a 1,200 square foot "in-line" store.

"When someone is operating a cart, they are right in the middle of the traffic," said Taylor.

A walk through the mall reveals companies selling sunglasses, jewelry, watches, and rubber bands in various shapes. "The sunglass guy has carts in four locations here."

Every year, about 40 million shoppers visit the mall. Tourists represent 40 percent of the traffic and spend an average of $162 per visit. Local hotels run free shuttles to and from the mall, which is a major tourist attraction. (Locals spend an average of $113, Taylor said.)

Smart retailers wait for years to get inside America's biggest mall. It is a major tourist attraction with an amusement park and Lego Land. Just wear comfortable shoes and bring a fat wallet.

Marketing Strategies

5

Your business will not flourish without a well-executed, multimedia marketing strategy.

Successful marketing campaigns depend on the message, timing, and tracking. Tracking is essential. Why spend money if you can't figure out whether something is working or not?

I love collecting cool marketing ideas—the nuttier the better. That's why this chapter includes the most great ideas.

The key to marketing is to set a goal and figure out how to reach it. Today, social media marketing is in fashion, but not everyone looks for information online.

Through the years, I've promoted my books by giving away wacky promotional items. My favorite premium was an acrylic fortune cookie key chain. The fortune inside mentioned the book. That promotion definitely boosted sales.

Glittery "magic" wands are still my most popular giveaways. They remind people of the magic wand I use in my presentations to vaporize toxic people.

Speaking professionally has certainly helped raise the profile of my business and it can help yours, too. Honing your personal presentation skills is essential, especially since you are a "walking brochure" for your business, according to Diane DiResta, a presentation skills coach and author of *Knockout Presentations,* published by Chandler House Press.

"You are your brand and speaking well is the new competitive weapon," said DiResta. "Speaking impacts every aspect of your life."

In addition to learning how to speak with coaching by former news anchor and psychologist Christen Brown, my professional success is due in large part to creating a clear vision backed by a strong marketing strategy. Brooke Halpin, a talented musician, author, and marketing consultant, changed my life with one phone call. I was happy writing my weekly small business column for the *Los Angeles Times* when he called and introduced himself.

"You could be the 'Dear Abby' for small business owners," he said.

I thought he was crazy, but he was persistent. I finally agreed to meet him for tea at a hotel restaurant to hear his vision and pitch. He was convinced Martha Stewart's "omni-media" model—which called for her content to be distributed on the radio, TV, print, and online—would work for me.

Although I loved writing my weekly, syndicated column for the *L.A. Times* syndicate, I dreamt of earning more money for my family. I was starting to envy all the entrepreneurs I was profiling every week. Most of them had no special degrees or talent—just moxie, stamina, and a great idea.

Brooke's five-year marketing plan required us to form a multimedia communications and consulting company, with my popular syndicated column as the foundation. We used a dual strategy: I would provide advice and practical information to help business owners succeed. Those efforts would be paid for by speaking and consulting with big companies to help them develop better products and services for entrepreneurs.

Thanks to Brooke and my tough, savvy entertainment lawyer, the late Jerry Gottlieb, we produced a syndicated small business radio report that aired on CBS stations for years. Top companies including American Express, Sprint, and Merrill Lynch signed on to sponsor my speaking tours.

A corny talk show pilot, directed by my wonderful ex-husband, Ron Stein, landed me a fantastic job at Bloomberg TV in 1996. It was there I met my dear friend Carla Ceasar. We developed and produced *Bloomberg Small Business* for the USA Network. I also served as the weekly show's national correspondent.

Since 1991, I've keynoted hundreds of business events across the United States and in France, Moscow, Canada, and Bermuda. IBM, AT&T, Canon, MasterCard, Microsoft, Hartford Life Insurance, Cox Communications, and Hewlett-Packard are among the companies that have supported my work.

In 1998, GTE Communications sponsored a 12-city book promotion tour, featuring an elaborate set transported in a moving van by a crew of roadies. After that, I hit the road for a 16-city speaking tour sponsored by

Sprint and the American City Business Journals. In 2011, I plan to visit at least 10 cities to promote the new edition of this book with support from Ladies Who Launch, an organization for entrepreneurial women and other business organizations and sponsors, including HubSpot.com and Elance.com.

In this chapter, you'll find great ideas on how to create cross-promotions, find a celebrity spokesperson, and try co-op advertising. You'll learn how to add pizzazz to your business card, and why you should send pizza to potential clients and market to callers waiting on hold. If you own a restaurant or bakery, you might consider working with StirandEnjoy .com, a Kansas City-based design firm that specializes in branding food businesses.

Read on to find out how to produce an infomercial, boost sales through coupons, and why *free* is the most powerful word in the English language.

I hope all these ideas inspire you to dream up a new marketing plan for your business. Don't forget to send your greatest marketing and promotional ideas to www.201greatideas.com. We'll be posting them and awarding cool prizes to the winners.

GREAT

95

IDEA

Strike a Deal with a Giant

The first step toward making a deal with a much bigger company is to target potential companies that are a good fit for your business. In our case, we target companies that serve business owners, including banks, credit card companies, and technology firms.

Get started by checking out web sites, magazines, and trade journals that serve your industry. Make a list of advertisers you see in those publications because those are the companies to contact.

Next, go online to scour the web site for contacts. Look for the top decision makers in the marketing department. Find out everything you can about the company's products, marketing campaigns, and other alliances. Find out which ad agency they work with by checking *Advertising Age*.

Once you determine who to contact, your challenge is to get through to them. Rather than sending an e-mail, call the main company number and ask to be put through to the marketing executive. You'll probably reach a busy assistant, so practice your pitch. You only have about 30 seconds to make a positive impression.

It's usually easy to figure out a company's e-mail format based on the media relations person's e-mail posted on the web site. Look for the public relations or media relations page of the site. If the media relations person's e-mail is: John.Doe@bigcompany.com, you can be pretty sure that's the style to use.

Try cutting through the clutter by sending an old-fashioned letter. Yes, a letter. Explain who you are, what you do, and how you can help the company beat its competition.

Don't get discouraged. It is very tough to connect with a big company. It took me years to build a reputation as a small business expert to leverage that into moneymaking deals. But you have nothing to lose by trying.

GREAT

96

IDEA

Look Bigger Online

One of the best things about the Web is that even though you may operate a tiny business, you can appear much bigger online. To do this, you need a professionally designed web site that you can update frequently. Your social media platforms should act as magnets, drawing traffic back to your site (see Great Ideas #63, #64, and #74).

There's no excuse not to have a dynamic and functional web site. It's critical to your success. Don't scrimp on site design and functionality. You want people to seek you out online and make a purchase, whether you sell high-tech components for airplanes or low-tech rubber stamps.

Here are some quick ways to raise your company's online profile:

- Customize your social media pages with logos, photos, and product information. My cool Facebook, Twitter, and YouTube pages were designed for around $200 by Brian Hanson. He can be reached via www.customtwit.com.

- Figure out something interesting to share and write a blog. Karen Caplan, president of Frieda's, a produce importer, posts a great blog on her site: www.friedas.com. Caplan comments on industry trends as well as her personal view on life and business.
- Promote discounts and special offers via Twitter and Facebook. Try Groupon, LiveSocial, and other group coupon platforms.
- Showcase your product on your home page. Hire a professional photographer and include multiple views (if appropriate). Consider hiring a professional copywriter. It will be worth it since bad copy can really dampen sales.
- Be creative but judicious with graphics. Make sure they tell a story, not just look cool.
- Display your company's name, phone number, and e-mail and street addresses on the home page and every other page so people can contact you immediately. Make sure someone answers the company phone 24/7 (easy to do with call forwarding).
- Hire an expert to optimize your site for search engines (see Great Idea #74).
- Monitor Google, Bing, and Chrome frequently to check your rankings.
- Tailor your site to appeal to your customers. If you sell auto parts, you probably don't want a lot of Flash animation on your site. Keep it simple and play to the masses.
- Update your web site at least once a week—on a schedule. Give customers a reason to return often.
- Publish a monthly e-newsletter with links back to specific landing pages on your site.

Take Advantage of Co-op Advertising

Do you ever wonder how local merchants get their name and address featured in the glossy magazine ads for a luxury car or watch? They do it through "co-op advertising," designed to draw customers into your store.

Ad agency executives tell me companies like Harry Winston, the high-end jeweler "tag" many of their print ads with local retail store information to boost sales.

"It's a mutual collaboration. Each one is building the brand of the other," said Erik Dochtermann, chief executive officer of KD&E, a Manhattan ad agency.

Dochtermann said retailers typically spend 3 to 10 percent of the total sales of an item on co-op advertising. (In most cases, money doesn't actually change hands. Small retailers get a discount on the merchandise when they participate in a co-op advertising program.) By working with a big manufacturer, small retailers not only get more bang for their marketing bucks, but garner exposure when ads appear in major publications or on billboards.

There is a catch: to qualify for inclusion in a co-op advertising program, retailers have to promise to stock enough of the product to be considered a major local sales outlet.

"They may need to take 5 to 30 pieces of a (watch or jewelry) collection," explained Dochtermann. "Then, the vendor will contribute more co-op dollars. In other words, if my expensive ads are driving customers into your store, I expect you to stock enough of my products to meet the demand."

For example, he said there are about 45 small retailers participating in the 2010 Harry Winston co-op program. The ads appear in regional editions, so local retailers benefit from the exposure.

If you sell clothes or video games, there are lots of co-op advertising programs designed to draw customers into your store. Dochtermann said the makers of the popular *Grand Theft Auto* video game buy in-store signage at the local level.

The more you do to promote the games, the more stock you'll receive, and the more money you'll make, Dochtermann explained.

"You can also sell space in your window and signage on your checkout counter. There is real estate available throughout your store," said Dochtermann.

He said his clients can spend $1 million or more with small retailers across the country when the company is promoting a new video game.

So, if you want to sell a hot product, you are going to have to pay for the privilege. "You might have to build a kiosk, create a shop within a shop, provide extra training for your employees, or help pay for ads saying the product is now available."

Check with your major vendors or suppliers to learn more about cooperative advertising programs. Even the biggest companies in the world look for ways to share advertising costs. For example, Intel promotes its processors in computer ads and on computers. My adorable Eee PC Netbook has an "Intel Atom" sticker attached.

GREAT 98 IDEA

Market to Callers on Hold

The average caller waits 45 seconds on hold before reaching a live customer service representative, so why not turn that annoying wait time into a marketing opportunity?

New York City–based Impressions on Hold (www.iohi.com) is an industry leader in the messages that are played while on hold. It started as a franchise about 15 years ago and now has about 30,000 big and small clients. Clients submit scripts to be recorded by voice-over professionals in Tulsa, Oklahoma. It costs about $1,200 a year for Impressions to record an unlimited number of scripts, which can be recorded in English or other languages.

"One of the beautiful and wonderful things is that we appeal to clients across the board," said Marissa Allen, who started out as a franchise owner and purchased the company with a partner in 2001. "We have major corporate clients, pizza companies, and funeral homes. We work with a single accountant working out of his home who wants to create a more professional image, all the way up to U.S. Cellular."

Unlike voice mail, which is limited to a short, outbound greeting, messages on hold are created to educate callers. The company creates the messages and e-mails digital files back to clients.

"I tell people: imagine I was able to fill Madison Square Garden with all of your clients and gave you the microphone for 30 seconds," said Allen. "What would you say to them?"

She said small business owners should take advantage of hold time to reach captive customers. "Messages on hold are like an employee who never calls in sick and is never in a bad mood."

Tips for Creating a Great Message on Hold

- Your message should encourage your captive audience to do more business with your company.
- Feature interesting topics including special offers or discounts, industry news, employee awards, or even a trivia game.
- Change the message every few weeks to keep it fresh.
- If you work with a company to produce messages, check their references and sign the shortest agreement possible.

GREAT 99 IDEA

Consider Multilevel Marketing: Send Out Cards

Kent Shields is a serial entrepreneur. He's owned a construction business and now owns a computer storage business.

He's also a part-time distributor for Send Out Cards, a multilevel marketing company based in Salt Lake City. (See page 149 for my exclusive interview with founder Kody Bateman.)

"I found out about the company through a friend who was a distributor," said Shields. "I knew I needed (the cards) because I can't remember people's birthdays or anniversaries."

He earns about $3,000 a year as a rep and spends most of that sending cards and gifts to clients. "Just the little bit I've done pays for the use of the system," he said. "You get a little percentage on what the people you sign up sell, but to make a living, you need to build a team underneath you."

It cost Shields about $400 to sign up as a rep. Best of all, he's received great feedback from the recipients of his cards and gifts.

"Sending cards is the biggest no-brainer for a small business person— it's a killer," said Shields. "People remember you, and they'll do business with you forever."

He said that once you enter your contacts into the database, it's easy to customize cards with company logos and images.

Exclusive Interview with Kody Bateman, Founder, Send Out Cards

The idea for Send Out Cards hit Kody Batemen after his brother died unexpectedly. Bateman said he always regretted that he didn't tell his brother how much he loved him the last time they were together.

"My original idea was to find a way to act on promptings to act in kindness and help others to do the same," said Bateman, in an exclusive interview. "It kind of evolved into a greeting card concept."

The cards were a natural extension of Bateman's first business, which sold Personal Touch Power Systems, a pre-Internet day planner with a greeting card holder in the back.

"Once the Internet came out and I saw how it worked, I could see the possibility of ordering greeting cards over the Internet," Bateman explained.

At first, he contracted with printers to produce cards. Then, he hired software developers to create the programs that let people customize the cards. Now, everything is handled in house.

Today, Salt Lake City–based Send Out Cards has 90 employees and about 85,000 independent distributors in the United States, United Kingdom, Canada, Australia, and Singapore. Bateman said about 200,000 customers have active accounts. He said his top sales rep earns $150,000 a month. Several reps earn about $40,000 a month. However, he said most reps work part time and earn $300 to $500 a month.

"I've always viewed this company as a billion-dollar household name," said Bateman, who started the company in June 2005. "We should do $80 to $85 million in sales this year (2011)."

He said his primary secret of success is staying true to the original objective. "We want to help millions of people act on their promptings, reach out in kindness to others, while providing a vehicle for financial freedom with a unique product."

To reinforce that message, Bateman leads dozens of "Treat 'Em Right" daylong, personal development seminars every year. Distributors are welcome to invite guests. "I thoroughly enjoy teaching the sessions," said Bateman.

His advice to business owners: "Find a resource for positivity. You must have a personal development plan. Read positive books, listen to CDs or tapes."

Motivational events are critical to maintaining dealer enthusiasm in the network marketing world. Send Out Card reps are expected to attend motivational seminars led by founder Kody Bateman. Shields said he's been to several "life-changing" sessions led by Bateman.

Although he's a salesman at heart, Shields said business owners should try network marketing to improve their sales skills.

"You pick up on the passion about a product," said Shields, who lives in Ouray, Colorado, near Telluride. "In network marketing, you end up meeting a lot of people with pizzazz."

Before you sign up for any network marketing opportunity, please speak with as many reps as possible to find out about their experiences and actual sales. Then, contact the Better Business Bureau to see if any complaints have been filed against the company.

GREAT
100
IDEA

Cross-Promote Your Products or Services

Ever tried a Blue Pearmain, Wolf River, Liberty, or 20-ounce Pippin apple? You would be munching away if you were a member of an apple CSA. CSA stands for community-supported agriculture.

For six weeks each fall, 55 members of the Out on a Limb heirloom apple CSA head over to the Rabelais cookbook store to pick up their apples. Members of a tomato CSA stop by to collect their bounty during the summer months.

"It's been a fabulous thing," said Samantha Lindgren, co-owner of the specialty bookstore located in downtown Portland, Maine. "It's a perfect fit and a great way to bring customers into the store who might not know about us."

Although she can't say exactly how much sales have increased, offering the store as a pick-up location has definitely attracted new customers. "This is the second year for the apples, and we'll certainly do the tomatoes again. It's been so popular we could have handled triple the (CSA) business."

John Bunker, a rare apple expert, author, and grower who runs the CSA, said dropping off apples at the cookbook store is a great idea. Bunker, who has spent the past 30 years studying and propagating apples, grows about 150 varieties of apples on his Super Chilly Farm in Palermo, Maine.

Growing heirloom apples is part of a growing consumer movement toward eating locally raised food and produce. CSA members like Stephen Berenson really enjoy trying new apples.

"My wife and I are fans of heirloom apples," said Berenson, who was interviewed by phone when he stopped by Rabelais to pick up his weekly supply of apples. "We came to an apple tasting last year and tried 30 to 35 varieties of apples. It was amazing."

Throughout the summer months, Portland-area tomato lovers also headed to Rabelais to collect tomatoes and basil grown on the Small Wonders Organic Farm. The four-acre farm is in Bowdoinham, Maine, north of Portland. During 2010, Sarah Trask and Pete Engler grew 30 different kinds of tomatoes, including rare ones like Costaluto Fiorentino and Paul Robeson.

Trask said about 25 CSA members paid $100 for six weeks' worth of tomatoes. "This was our first year farming and we planted a ton of tomatoes," said Trask. "We needed another way to sell all our tomatoes, other than selling at farmer's markets. It was such a good idea to have people pick them up at the cookbook store in Portland."

The CSA movement is growing every year, according to Local Harvest, a group that promotes local agriculture. Tens of thousands of people belong to CSAs. While no agency keeps track of how many CSAs exist, Local Harvest (www.localharvest.org/csa) estimates there are at least 2,500 around the United States, and the number is increasing every year.

Tips for creating your own cross-promotion:

- Look around for businesses in your area that also serve your customers.
- Contact the owner to discuss ideas. If you own a clothing boutique, how about offering discount coupons to a local dry cleaner? The dry cleaner can offer discounts for purchases at your store.
- Start small and test your idea before expanding.
- Ask your customers to recommend local businesses to connect with.

Sell through a Dealer Network

We are used to buying tires, cars, and computers through authorized dealers. Other businesses may benefit from a similar sales model.

David Usher founded Greenwich Workshop in 1972. Usher, who died in a kayaking accident in 1997, believed direct distribution was the best way to sell high-end prints. He traveled around the United States, establishing close relationships with the owners of galleries and framing shops. His son, Scott Usher, is now running the company.

Scott Usher told me that one secret of the company's success is treating every dealer like part of the family. Howard Terpning, James Christensen, Bonnie Marris, Z. S. Liang, and Steve Hanks are some of the top artists whose paintings are turned into high-quality prints.

"The past two years have been interesting because we are selling art, which is a luxury item," said Usher.

Ten years ago, the average price of a print was $150; now it's over $500. Most Greenwich prints are giclee prints on canvas. Greenwich dealers buy the art outright at wholesale prices (50 percent of the retail price), but they can return unsold prints for credit if it means preventing it from being sold at a discount.

"Our galleries today are beginning to offer original artwork as well," said Usher. "The framing component is still a big part of their business. But, they are not just a frame shop."

Usher said giving a dealer a geographical territory doesn't work anymore, especially with so many consumers buying art online.

"The concept of what an authorized dealer is, is in significant flux," he admits. "We still depend upon it and are working on ways to enhance the opportunity for a local dealer to hang on to their customers."

Greenwich is in the process of putting together a universal shopping cart that can be personalized for each dealership.

"The outlook is positive, a little bit of last man standing scenario," said Usher. "We don't have a highly capitalized group of folks out there. We have lost a good number of dealers in the last two years."

In 1998, the Seymour, Connecticut–based company was purchased in a stock deal by Hallmark. In 2002, when Hallmark planned to spin it off, Usher decided to buy back the company. He now has about 30 employees.

Tips for a Dealer Network

A successful dealer network depends on good communication and support from the home office.

Here are some ways to support the people who sell your products and services:

- Keep them well informed via weekly e-mails and by posting confidential information on a password-protected area of your web site.

- Create a monthly e-newsletter to share sales tips, success stories, and company news with your dealers.

- Limit the number of dealers you sign up in each geographic area. This honors the relationships you have and offers dealers a better shot at making more money.

- Ask veteran dealers to mentor new dealers in other areas of the country. Suggest that veteran and novice dealers schedule a phone call once a month to share information.

- Ask your dealers to tell you what you can do to make things work better. Keep the lines of communication open, and let them know you really value their opinions and suggestions.

Despite the challenges, Usher said Greenwich will continue relying on independent dealers to sell art. Several dealers I interviewed said they like working with the company and plan to continue their long-term relationships.

GREAT
102
IDEA

Create a Cool Business Card

C lifton Alexander, co-owner of Reactor Design Studio, in Kansas City, Missouri, decided to limit web design projects in early 2010. Now, he focuses on creating expensive, eye-catching, "amazing and ridiculous" business cards—some cost $8 apiece.

"A good card is a great way to break through the clutter," said Alexander, whose cards have won design competitions and have been featured in *Inc.* magazine.

His personal card is intricately layered with multicolored papers and complex cutouts.

"The more creative your card is, the more oohs and ahhs you'll get from people you hand it to," said Alexander. "One glance tells people right away how you think."

Although everyone thinks online marketing dominates, Alexander said he heard that Twitter employees were handing out paper business cards at last year's South by Southwest (SXSW) music, film, and digital media festival.

"I'm not saying down with digital—we use everything digital in our daily work," he explained. But in this super high-tech world, Alexander sees great value in a well-designed, fun, and informative business card.

Here are some tips for coming up with the perfect card:

- See what's out there and figure out which cards resonate with you.
- Save business cards that you like to share with the designer.
- Ask people whose cards you like to refer you to their designer.
- Contact an art school to see if you can work with a promising design student. Students are often looking for real-world experience, and their rates are generally lower than a professional's.

GREAT
103
IDEA

Create a Dynamic Database

If you look at the piles of business cards on your desk and just see a mess—look again. You are looking at potential income. No matter how small your business is, you need a dynamic database. It's easy to create one with a card scanner and simple software. Once you have a good list, you can send all sorts of information to customers.

Add telephone numbers to your database, and you are ready to kick off a telemarketing campaign.

Building a database is easier than you think. All your e-mail and online contacts form the basis for your list. Next, add in names from business cards, vendor invoices, catalogs, and directories. Note names you see in magazine and newspaper articles and find those people, too.

Business magazines such as *Entrepreneur* usually include contact information and web sites in their articles.

There are many affordable programs that help you enter and keep track of the information. A database also lets you cross-reference and access information in various ways. Many people rely on Microsoft Outlook to keep track of contacts.

More complex customer management programs can organize your daily appointments and remind you when to make calls. The biggest job is entering the data into the program. You can ask a staffer to do it or hire a temporary worker. Be sure you sort out the contacts and discard ones you don't need.

Also, figure out what information you want to appear in each field. And remember, your database has to be updated frequently. People move and change jobs all the time.

Once your database is complete, use it. Check into sending out a monthly newsletter with Constant Contact or another online service. HubSpot.com also has an e-mail marketing program that we use. As part of its national book tour sponsorship, HubSpot also built and designed my site, so check it out: 201greatideas.com.

Package Your Products for Success

Provocative or practical, packaging your products well is critical to your success. Without great packaging, the best product in the world is destined to sit on the shelf or arrive in a zillion pieces.

"A product properly packaged is half sold," said Tara Abraham, one of the nation's leading commercial packaging design experts. Abraham, who began her merchandising career at Bath and Body Works, left her job 15 years ago to open a small "pick and pack" operation.

Today, Accel Inc., based in Lewis Center, Ohio, creates turnkey packaging solutions for big and small companies, including The Limited, Victoria's Secret Beauty, and Bath and Body Works. Accel posted annual revenues in excess of $20 million in 2010. It operates out of a 580,000-square-foot facility. From July to January, during the pre-holiday and busy holiday gift season, the staff expands from 260 to 1,100.

The company's minimum order is usually 5,000 units, but Abraham said if she thinks a new product has promise, she will work with a small business owner on a budget to create the right packaging solution.

"A great package has clean, sleek lines and colors that pop," said Abraham.

No matter what you sell, the package is the first thing you notice about any product, according to Glenn Tatem, a development engineer. Tatem, who specializes in designing packages for celebrity fragrances, works for The Maesa Group, an award-winning global design firm.

"A package needs to look good and function well," said Tatem. "You don't want the product breaking or shattering in your purse."

No matter what you make, the package has to fit the product. For example, if you sell a small, valuable item to a big box store, you'll probably need to protect it with a tough plastic "clam shell" (you know, the frustrating bulletproof package you can only open with a hacksaw when you get home).

Branding experts believe a great package design can set you apart from the competition.

"A good package has to differentiate your company and product from the marketplace, but not be so crazy looking that it turns your customers off," advises Julia Reich, a graphic designer who works with many small companies, including several wineries in upstate New York.

Reich said winemakers are especially savvy when it comes to great label design. She points to the success of Yellow Tail, an Australian wine known for its bright yellow label.

Her advice: never let a customer walk out the door with a plain bag. "Even if you are on a budget, putting your product in a beautiful bag goes a long way," said Reich.

GREAT

105 Give to Charity

IDEA

Small business owners can raise their community profile by making personal contributions of goods or services to charities. In addition to benefiting others, your contribution could lead to more positive customer and employee relationships.

One business in Kansas has seen great value come from its charitable efforts.

ICOP makes digital video cameras for police cars. President and COO, Laura Owen, said donating money and time to charities that support law enforcement officials and agencies makes sense for her company. The publicly traded company has about 52 employees and annual revenues of $12 million. Owen declined to disclose exactly how much money the company donates to various charities, including the Special Olympics.

For example, ICOP supports a variety of long-distance charity rides that benefit the families of fallen officers. In 2010, the cross-country Law Ride provided an opportunity for the company to stream live video from cameras attached to officers' bikes. (ICOPS' police car video systems cost about $5,000 per vehicle.)

"Our charity activities provide a business benefit as well as an intangible benefit," said Owen, who also encourages her employees to volunteer their time.

Even if you can't afford to write a big check during the busy start-up phase of your business, contribute something to one or two local nonprofit groups or buy raffle tickets for a fund-raiser.

Encourage your employees to volunteer by giving them a paid day off once a month or quarter. Sending them out into the community to do good work is a great way to generate positive buzz about your business.

Tips for doing good work:

- If you have a retail store, collect food or clothing for the homeless or for a favorite local charity.
- Ask your employees and their families to participate in a blood drive for the Red Cross or a local hospital.
- Donate some of your products or services. A dry cleaner in Ohio, for example, offered free dry cleaning to unemployed customers who needed clean clothes for job interviews. When someone landed a job, of course, he or she became a steady, loyal customer for life.
- Join with other business owners to sponsor a trash pickup or graffiti cleanup campaign. Ask a local paint store to donate paint and brushes.
- Ask city officials if you can plant trees in a blighted area or start a community garden.

- Ask your accountant about the tax advantages of donating excess inventory to a charitable organization.
- If you own a restaurant, host a fund-raising dinner for a local charity. A small Greek restaurant in Maryland hosted a dinner and gave away a free trip to Greece donated by a local travel agency. The local TV station and newspaper covered the event.
- Create an apprenticeship program. Hire high school students or welfare recipients to work part time at your company.
- Once you've chosen a project, send a press release to your local newspapers, radio, and television stations. Reporters love upbeat, local feature stories.
- If you have a conference room, offer the space to a community group. They can meet there after hours and expose new customers to your business. (One of the women's groups that my mother heads meets at Montecito Bank in Westlake Village, California.)

Use Coupons to Attract Customers

One balmy summer evening, I took myself on a date to the local movie theater. A young man wearing a Häagen-Dazs apron was passing out coupons offering a "double feature"—a free scoop of ice cream when you bought one scoop at the regular price.

As soon as the movie ended, I trotted down the block, ticket stub in hand. For under $2, I savored my calorie-laden pralines-and-cream and coffee-chip double scoop. The kid in the apron even let me keep the coupon for a repeat performance. Talk about generating goodwill!

That free extra scoop of ice cream brought me into the store for the first time. And, of course, it wasn't the last. It also proved to me that a coupon is a low-cost way to attract new and repeat customers.

Coupons are great because they are cheap to print and easy to distribute. You can print them yourself or buy space in a value package. You can pay to have coupons stuffed into the local newspaper.

Before printing anything, add codes to track response. For example, put an "N" if they were stuffed in a newspaper, "M" if they were mailed, or "W" for a downloadable Web coupon.

Don't forget to check out the new social marketing discount platforms, including Groupon and LiveSocial. Just be sure to crunch the numbers so you will make and not lose money on the deal. I've spoken with many small business owners who have had less-than-positive experiences with the concept, especially when long-standing customers don't participate in the deal. You don't want to alienate your loyal customers for a one-time hit.

No matter what you do, dream up a compelling offer. Anything "free" works if you have some sort of retail operation. It doesn't matter what you offer as long as it has a high perceived value. Think of all the makeup samples and bags you've collected through the years just because it was free with a purchase.

GREAT
107
IDEA

Use Food as a Selling Tool

Since everyone eats, food is a cheap and effective marketing tool. Most banks offer customers free coffee and tea, as well as bowls filled with lollipops. They also host barbecues for their customers and employees throughout the summer. The barbecues not only give people a chance to socialize, but also help the bank's management keep up with what's going on in their offices.

Food is often the most appropriate gift for business purposes. Holiday gift baskets filled with southern delicacies, including divinity, pecan rolls, and miniature pecan pies, were a huge hit among our clients and associates—so much so that I sent the same basket two years in a row, then switched back to Harry & David fruit baskets the following season.

One of the nicest presents we've received from a client was an attractive wicker basket filled with wine, goblets, coffee, chocolate, and gourmet snacks. Try sending gifts at Thanksgiving to beat the holiday rush.

Food gifts have another advantage: they are appreciated by everyone, no matter how affluent they may be.

Set Up a Strong Referral Network

Successful entrepreneurs know "what goes around comes around." While many referrals are made informally by word-of-mouth, smart entrepreneurs take it a step further.

Dana Adkinson, owner of Keepsake Floral Inc. in Orlando, Florida, runs a successful floral preservation service. She relies on referrals from florists and wedding consultants to keep her 12 employees busy. Every year, Keepsake preserves between 1,000 and 1,500 bouquets. Adkinson said she started the business in 1994 at her mother's suggestion.

"While we were on our honeymoon, my mother took my bouquet and one from my maid of honor and went looking for some way to preserve them," said Adkinson. "She couldn't find anyone to do it. So, when we came home, she said, 'This is the business you need to start.'"

"We have two different referral programs," Adkinson explained. "If you are a florist or a wedding consultant and refer a client, we send you a $30 check."

For florists and wedding professionals who want to be a bit more aggressive, she offers a "preservation partner" program. "They pay us about $100 for an actual sample of a preserved bouquet," she said. "They have all our promotional materials to help explain the process. When they take the deposit from the bride, they keep a $50 referral fee."

Adkinson offers referral programs to extend her marketing reach and bring in new business. About 40 percent of her business comes from florists and preservation partners. About 20 percent comes in over the Internet. She also does some telemarketing.

Although Adkinson says she hopes brides decide to preserve their bouquet before the wedding, most orders come in afterward, "when they have fallen in love with their bouquet."

The actual preservation costs between $200 and $600, depending on the keepsake display they choose and the size of the bouquet. Brides are asked to send the bouquets in within two weeks of their wedding. When the bouquet arrives in Orlando, it is photographed. Then, Keepsake Floral employees carefully take apart the bouquet so each flower can be individually preserved by freeze-drying or with a chemical drying agent.

The Power of Referrals

Word of mouth is the most powerful marketing tool, but incentives can help.

- Establish a "best customer" program. Reward referrals with cash, free shipping, two-for-one and early-bird specials, or extra discounts on products they buy frequently.
- Ask customers to refer new business to you.
- Publicize referrals on your web site or newsletter. People love to be recognized for helping you succeed.
- Offer incentives to your employees who refer new business. A half-day off with pay is a great way to say thank you for landing a new client or customer.
- Thank customers for referrals by sending flowers, a fruit basket, a gift certificate for a restaurant, or movie tickets.

Depending on what the customer wants, bouquets are reassembled and arranged inside an airtight shadow box or picture frame. The flowers are expected to last for decades.

Business has been steady, despite the economic downturn. "You do have to work harder for the same dollars," said Adkinson, who often gets new business from the wedding planners at Disney's Fairy Tale Weddings. Check out her company at www.keepsakefloral.com.

GREAT

109

IDEA

Give It Away

Free is the most powerful word in the English language. Offering potential clients or customers something for free is an excellent way to bring in new business and build customer loyalty.

"Sprint once gave me a deal that covered all my local telephone service for two years, free calling on Fridays, plus free 800-line pagers for my employees," said Bob Dudley, president of a San Diego commercial satellite-dish provider.

It doesn't matter what you do or sell. If you provide consulting services, offer a free breakfast session as a way to share your expertise and prequalify clients.

If you sell clothing, position yourself as a personal shopper. Provide a free fashion consultation. Image consultants can organize a free "dress for success" seminar to local businesses. Business owners will welcome your advice, and you'll probably attract a few paid clients.

Follow the lead of major cosmetic companies, such as Clinique and Estee Lauder. They often offer great gifts with purchases.

Offering free samples is an inexpensive and effective way to put products into the mouths of consumers. Big and small food companies rely on in-store demonstrations to test-market products.

A few years ago, I was browsing through the aisles of a gourmet food store when a demonstrator stuffed a morsel of plum pudding in my mouth. I admit, I never would have tasted the dark, dense substance otherwise. It was so delicious, though, I ended up buying one for a gift—and interviewing her for my syndicated column.

GREAT
110
IDEA

Design a Great Sign for Your Business

Your sign is a big magnet for business, especially if you are located on a busy road or in a strip mall. Before he retired, Lloyd Miller owned a travel agency in Winter Park, Florida. "My agency was on a high-visibility corner," said Miller. "We put our cruise price specials on a dry-marker board labeled 'Cruise Catch of the Day.'"

He said the big, eye-catching sign prompted people to call from their cars while driving by.

You don't need a big budget to design an attractive sign for your business. Many sign makers rely on computer technology to design affordable signs. Or hire a sign painter for something more unique.

Put contact information and hours of operation on the edge of an awning. No matter what kind of sign you order, try to include your phone number, hours of operation, and Web address.

I love brilliant neon signs, but not everyone does. Remember, before you order a sign, check with local officials to make sure you meet local sign regulations.

GREAT
111
IDEA

Produce an Infomercial

If you think marketing your product via an infomercial is a quick and easy way to make millions—think again. Industry experts say only 1 product in 20 actually hits the big time.

Although consumers buy more than a billion dollars' worth of goods a year, producing an effective infomercial remains an "imprecise science," according to a spokesman for the Electronic Retailing Association (ERA).

Infomercials first hit the airwaves in 1984, when Congress deregulated the television industry. Most fall into a few broad categories: health and beauty products, exercise equipment, motivational programs, and household products.

One big success on the housewares front was the Smart Mop, designed and manufactured by Santa Monica–based Smart Inventions Inc. Cofounder and president Jon Nokes, a former biology teacher from England, began selling his super-absorbent rayon mop on the county fair and home-show circuit about seven years ago.

Although retailers expressed strong interest in the mop, Nokes decided to market it directly to the public. When three established infomercial producers turned him down, he and a team of out-of-work actors and models hit the home show circuit, selling enough $29 mops to raise the $65,000 needed to shoot their first infomercial. Then, they bought about $15,000 worth of air time on a few stations to test consumer response. The mops took off. They've sold more than five million mops to date.

Nokes, who started the company in a tiny apartment and stored the mops in rented garages, said the secret of making money is to make

Tips from the Electronic Retailing Association

- Do your homework. Find out what worked for successful infomercial producers.
- Pick the right stations, market, and time to air your infomercial.
- Offer strong money-back guarantees to boost consumer confidence.
- Believe in your product.
- Contact the ERA at www.retailing.org.

Smart Inventions Tips for Selling Products on TV

- Have something that makes consumers say, "Wow, what a great idea!"
- Your product has to be unique, innovative, and of good quality.
- Your product should be easy to demonstrate.
- Your product should solve a common problem and be easy to use.
- Your product should appeal to a mass audience. Niche markets are difficult to make profitable.
- Not currently available to the public.
- Have a retail markup with enough of a margin to still make a profit after production and media costs.
- If it is an infomercial product, it should sell for $29.95 or more.
- If it is a DR (direct response) spot product, it should sell for $19.95.
- Make a prototype of your product.
- Prevention products don't sell well on TV (i.e., fire extinguishers, burglar alarms).

something easy enough for an eight-year-old to use. It has to be cheap to make but have a high perceived value. In his case, the mops cost under $5 to manufacture, but they sold for six times that much (including refills) on the air.

Nokes said a successful infomercial sets the stage for huge retail sales. "We went into retail stores, and during the first three months we sold one million mops a month," he said. "The following year we sold almost four million units."

His company has sold five million Smart Choppers, five million Tap Lights, and millions of Quick Sand easy-cleaning cat boxes. He believes infomercials are a great way for entrepreneurs to introduce new household products.

"It doesn't matter how good the product is if the public doesn't know about it," he said. "When you have a new product, you need to educate the public."

GREAT
112
IDEA

Put a Pig in Your Window

Veteran retailer Iris Fuller told me she cried for two hours after attending a retailing seminar by the late Peter Glen. They were tears of joy and inspiration. "He made such a difference in the way we did what we did," said Fuller, who owned Fillamento, a San Francisco boutique that closed a few years ago.

Fuller ultimately hired Glen, a former actor turned retail guru, to meet with her staff and teach them the secrets of visual merchandising. At his suggestion, she took all her employees to Las Vegas so they could steal ideas from Cirque du Soleil's magical performance.

Thousands of small retailers relied on Glen's advice and zany ideas to get them out of a slump. He urged retailers to set themselves apart from their competition by creating "cheap miracles" to attract shoppers.

For example, Glen suggested tying a big ribbon around your retail store. Put a stuffed pig in the window or a bull in your china shop—as one New Zealand shop owner did. Do whatever you can to create a visual stir.

"The retail business is routine and can kill you one day at a time," Glen told me. "Retailers have to face the competition instead of whining about it," he said. "Most are waiting for Walmart to kill them."

He also told clients not to offer deep discounts. "Don't discount it, and don't give it away," he said. "You have the unique ability to provide real customer service and keep a customer for life."

No matter what you are selling, you need to work hard to "love your business again."

"Retailing is a terrible job—nobody is in it for the hours or the money," said Glen. "Concentrate on what you do best and go in that direction—furiously."

My friend Victoria Wallins is a veteran retailer. She works with a professional window dresser to draw customers into Essentia, her wonderful boutique in Wellesley, Massachusetts. You'll never see snowflakes or fake presents in her holiday window. Just beautiful merchandise displayed in extremely creative ways.

GREAT IDEA 113

Put Your Company Name on Everything

It sounds so simple, but too many small companies neglect to put their name and phone number on their products.

One small Arizona company, Tessita's Secret, was smart to print their contact information on the label. After just one sniff, I fell in love with their deliciously fragrant lotion made with cactus extracts and aloe vera. Before I used the last dab, I called the number on the bottom of the jar and ordered more.

Your package should be a tiny billboard to attract repeat sales. Always include your address, phone number, and web site. If people liked your products, you want to make sure they know how to buy more.

Free Up Your Sales Team to Sell

"**M**ost salespeople love to sell but hate to generate their own leads," said the co-owner of a financial planning firm in Orlando. "So we invest a great deal of time and money for telemarketers to generate leads. This frees the salesmen to do what they love to do the most—sell."

It seems odd, but sometimes the most aggressive salespeople are reluctant to find their own leads. That's why it is a good idea to rely on someone else to do the prospecting. This would be a good project for a freelance marketing person.

Taking a two-pronged approach works especially well when you are selling a high-end product or service, such as financial products.

Making a sales appointment is critical to success. People hate to be interrupted in the middle of dinner by an unsolicited phone call. I started

How to Hold Your Salespeople Accountable

Colleen Stanley is one of America's top sales trainers, an author, and founder of Sales Leadership Inc. based in Lakewood, Colorado.

Stanley says a successful sales effort depends on sticking to a sales activity plan and setting key performance indicators (KPI). "You also have to spend at least 90 minutes a week making prospecting calls," said Stanley.

Her staff not only has to make cold and warm calls, but attend networking events, produce video clips for her web site, book Stanley to speak at events, update the company's social media sites, and write blog posts. They also send gifts, cards, and books to thank clients for their business.

"We set 'give goals' at sales meetings," said Stanley, whom I met on a speaking tour. "I ask everyone, 'who did you help out last week? Was it your client?' You have to always be making deposits in the relationship account. It's all about reciprocity."

working with an independent insurance broker because he responded to a card I sent and then scheduled a time to talk.

You might have great salespeople, but often they dislike and resist filling out the after-sale paperwork. And when they mess it up, it creates more problems down the line. So consider hiring an assistant to take care of the after-sale details. This expedites orders and frees the salesperson to move on to the next sale.

Smart managers know exactly what everyone's time is worth and provide all the necessary tools and support to maximize productivity.

Hire a Celebrity Spokesperson

About 15 years ago, David Blumenthal, president of Lion Brand Yarn Co. in Manhattan, heard that *Wheel of Fortune* hostess, Vanna White, loved to crochet.

He immediately contacted her agent to ask if White would be interested in becoming the spokesperson for a line of yarns and crochet patterns.

She said yes and they crafted a deal that has endured through the years. White works with Lion to write illustrated pattern books. She appears at trade shows on behalf of Lion Brand Yarns, demonstrating her crocheting skills and emceeing a fashion show of crocheted creations.

Not everyone can land a major celebrity like Vanna White, but you might benefit from the third-party endorsement of a spokesperson. For example, when companies sponsor my speaking engagements or other project, I always mention their products and services, which is an endorsement.

Remember, connecting your product with an expert or celebrity provides a great cobranding opportunity and can attract some media attention. Look around to see which well-known celebrities might be a good fit for your business.

You can also work with product placement companies that charge a fee to get your product into the hands of a famous person. There are also companies that put together celebrity "swag bags" for high-profile events like the Oscars®.

Product placement firms can also present your products to producers of films and television shows. It's expensive, but if you want to reach a mass audience, consider it.

GREAT

116

IDEA

Publish a Newsletter or Blog

In this age of instant access to information, it's comforting to know that there is still a demand for newsletters, especially industry-specific e-newsletters. Your challenge is finding people willing to pay for exclusive or insider information. Unless you are truly an expert, you may find it tough to attract subscribers or advertisers.

Every morning, I look forward to reading the *Morning Stretch*, a lively, one-page, free e-newsletter featuring tips, recipes, and inspirational messages from Denise Austin, my fitness guru. I love Denise Austin. I work out with her DVDs at home almost every day. Her newsletter is free, but I've purchased products featured in the ads.

If your business lends itself to an e-mail newsletter, go for it. My friend Diane DiResta has a great newsletter with links to video clips (subscribe at www.diresta.com). By the time you read this, we'll have a 201greatideas .com newsletter available by subscription on the web site.

Start with one or two editions and track the response. If more people opt out than opt in, you need to fine-tune your content.

Tips for e-newsletters:

- Concentrate on a topic you know really well.
- Develop content of interest to customers or clients.
- Subscribe to competitor's newsletters to see what they are saying.
- Ask industry leaders to contribute articles and then ask them to send out the newsletter to all their contacts.
- If the newsletter is a success, issue special reports or white papers or consider writing a book.

Market Your Consulting Services

Selling your expertise—an intangible product—requires a different approach than selling a product that sits on the shelf. Some professionals, like doctors and lawyers, are limited by professional ethics to marketing their services through specific channels. If you're a business coach or consultant, you have more options.

One of the best ways to market your professional services is to become recognized as an expert in your field. This can be accomplished by writing articles for trade publications or general interest magazines—or by being quoted in newspapers and making guest appearances on radio or television shows. You may think that you could never attract a reporter's attention, but it's easier than you think.

Reporters are always looking for a good story and need new sources, but they are often too busy or stressed to find you, so you need to do the legwork. So here's how to make contact: First, find out who covers your particular industry at the local newspaper, business journal, or radio or television station. Never send a blind letter to a reporter or editor.

Once you have the reporter's name, send a short introductory letter (not e-mail). Tell them who you are and offer to provide background information, resources, or insights on a particular subject or industry. Be specific.

Attach your business card and a company brochure. Wait about a week and then make a follow-up telephone call. But, first, find out when that particular news organization is on deadline. Most morning papers are editing the paper in the late afternoon. Television producers are more likely to pick up the phone between 10 AM and noon. Just call the news outlet and ask for the assignment or news desk. Whoever answers the phone should be able to tell you who to contact or put you into someone's voice mail to leave a detailed message.

Even if you get no response, every month or so send clippings and items of interest. Once you are interviewed by a reporter, other reporters are more likely to call you. If a reporter calls, drop everything to take the call. You only get one chance when a busy reporter or producer is on a deadline.

Another good way to raise your profile and impress potential clients is to offer them a taste of your expertise. Invite current and potential clients to a free breakfast or one-hour workshop. Give a brief presentation to whet everyone's appetite, and then take questions from the audience. Ask your existing clients to invite one or two guests to expand your circle of contacts. For example, my friend Suzanne Dudley Schon is a life coach. She's promoting herself by offering a free telephone session to the winner of one of my "Great Ideas" contests conducted on our site.

Remember, your current clients are always your best source of new business. It may seem like a chore, but you need to spend at least one hour a day soliciting referrals; sending out e-mails, letters, or brochures; or making cold calls.

GREAT 118 IDEA

Host an Open House

One of the best ways to acquaint customers and clients with your business is to host an open house. An open house provides you with the opportunity to do some serious one-to-one marketing. It is also a good way to show your appreciation for good clients and customers.

Of course, if you deal with toxic chemicals or dangerous machinery, you might have to host a party at a local hotel or private club.

Visiting a business can be memorable. One of my strongest and fondest memories was touring the Pepperidge Farm bakery on a third-grade field trip. I'll never forget the sweet, yeasty smell of the bakery and the freshly baked loaf of white bread the tour guide handed each of us to take home. A whole loaf of bread just for me! I've been a loyal Pepperidge Farm customer since then (Mint Milano cookies rock).

Hershey Foods draws thousands of visitors into their factories each year. That open-door policy has turned Hershey, Pennsylvania, into a major American tourist mecca, complete with an amusement park.

Even if you rarely have visitors, think of the things people might want to know about your business. Everyone likes to go behind the scenes, especially since very few people have the opportunity to see how things are made and packaged.

You may not have a glitzy office, but even a small-scale open house can draw people to your door.

Here are some tips for planning an open house:

- Appoint a committee to plan the party.
- Figure out whether you'll give organized tours or let people wander around on their own.
- Plan a menu of easy-to-eat finger foods and simple beverages. Restrict eating to the lunchroom or other suitable area.
- Pick a time of year when your business looks its best and weather won't jeopardize attendance.
- Send out invitations via e-mail or hard copy at least a month in advance.
- Ask people to RSVP via telephone or e-mail. Schedule the event to last no more than two or three hours.
- Ask all your employees to tidy up their work space.
- Lock up any valuables before the open house.
- When guests arrive, give them a one-page flyer with basic information about your company.
- Assign plenty of staffers to act as hosts and guides.
- Buy flowers or plants to decorate the reception area.
- Rest up the night before so you are ready to meet and greet people.
- Try to have fun.

GREAT

119

IDEA

Use Great Public Relations to Promote Your Business

One of the best ways to generate publicity for your company is to do something positive for the community. You might consider inviting your local radio or television station or paper to participate in your event as a media sponsor. News outlets often support community events as well as cover them.

The Whistle Stop Restaurant & Bakery in Birmingham, Michigan, needed help publicizing a "Name Your Price for Dinner" week in 2009.

The restaurant owner hired Jason Brown, founder of PublicCity PR, to build the buzz surrounding the community focused event.

PublicCity attracted media exposure for the Whistle Stop by taking a local feel-good story and bringing it to the national spotlight. The story had great appeal, especially in Michigan during the depths of the Great Recession when unemployment and foreclosure rates were the highest in the country.

"The campaign garnered reports on WXYZ, WDIV, and WJBK, including an in-studio WJBK cooking segment, plus radio reporters and interviews on seven other stations," said Brown.

His efforts led to front-page stories in the *Detroit Free Press* and the *Birmingham Eccentric*, plus additional coverage in the *Detroit News, Oakland Press*, and *Metro Times*. "Because of the tremendous local press that PublicCity was able to garner for the Whistle Stop, the national media started to take notice and wanted to know more about restaurant owner Matt Rafferty's generous offer to the community," said Brown.

Best of all, the feel-good story made *Inside Edition,* CBS's *The Early Show,* and *NBC Nightly News* with Brian Williams.

This is a great example of how good PR can generate enormous attention for a small business. Yet too many entrepreneurs use a scattershot approach to public relations, primarily because they don't understand how PR works.

Public relations is not marketing. PR is not advertising.

You pay for advertising space on a web site, newspaper, or magazine. You buy time on radio or television stations. If you pay for the time, you control the message.

You can't control the outcome of PR efforts. They are based on securing third-party endorsements for your product or service, primarily when a member of the press writes a story or produces a report about you or your company. The most important thing to remember is you cannot control the message or timing.

Before your hire a PR person, find out what your competition is doing to promote itself. Use this information to develop a strategy and a reasonable budget. Then, it's time to find the talent needed to execute your strategy.

"An effective PR program can bring valuable recognition to your company if your product or service is mentioned in the media," explained Christine Soderbergh, a veteran PR consultant based in Los Angeles.

Tips from Stefan Pollack for Achieving PR Results

Maximizing the effectiveness of a PR agency is largely dependent on an understanding of a working relationship. Be sure to ask a PR agency the following critical questions:

- How long will it take to get up to speed on my account?
- What reporting and ROI (return on investment) methods are used?
- What accountability measurements will be in place?

Pollack said clients must do more than pay for the services of a PR company. "The relationship must be approached as a partnership," said Pollack. "The agency should become a satellite office of a company's business, part of the management team, and extension of their in-house capabilities."

Contact StefanPollack at spollack@ppmgcorp.com.

The key difference between advertising and PR is that when you pay for an ad, you can, within reason, say anything you want to about your product or service. With PR, you don't have a say over the editorial process.

"Don't ever ask a reporter if you can see the copy before it appears," advises Soderbergh. "And if you call an editor or reporter cold, always ask if they have a minute to talk or if they are on a deadline."

Another tip: match your story pitch to the right reporter. Learn to look for bylines and see which reporters are assigned to cover stories about your industry. Make sure they are still on that beat by calling the news organization before you call or e-mail a pitch.

Reputable PR people charge by the project or ask for a monthly retainer and are not paid for the placement or "hit." Larger PR agencies usually want a retainer, usually $3,000 to $5,000 a month or more, plus all expenses.

Stefan Pollack, president of the Pollack PR Marketing Group in Los Angeles, said that now, more than ever, social and online media are blurring the lines between public relations and marketing.

"Still, PR has taken front and center stage with the new formats for very good reason," said Pollack. "Communicating with a company's many publics has always been at the core of public relations. In the past, PR activities centered on communicating through mainstream media. Now it has expanded to communicating directly to a company's audience through the new added format—social media platforms."

If you can afford to hire a PR professional, here is what they can do, according to Pollack:

- Develop/unify messaging and positioning for the company.
- Manage interactive communications on behalf of a company, monitor industry news and mainstream media to evaluate communication opportunities, and create online programming geared to reaching target audiences.
- Implement an online media strategy. Distribute news releases with a focus on company news and industry news to fit a specific news cycle.

GREAT
120
IDEA

Coproduce a Seminar

Karen Tate, president of the Griffin Tate Group in Cincinnati, teaches employees of big and small companies how to manage complex projects. Project management professionals (PMPs) are highly trained and function like a certified public accountant (CPA) for project managers.

To promote her seminar business, Tate often partners with a local chapter of her professional organization, the Project Management Institute (PMI). PMI has over 200 chapters all over the world and over 300,000 members. Worldwide, there are about 400,000 certified PMPs, which is a designation similar to a CPA.

"The local PMI chapters like to offer seminars to their members," said Tate. "I offer to teach one for them and we split the profits, I get exposure, the chapter gets a high-quality seminar, their members get the credits they need to maintain their PMP certification—it's a win-win-win. They market it and sponsor it, we share the work, and we both get paid."

Tate is an accomplished author with several books, including:

- *Project Management Memory Jogger*™ (Goal/QPC, 2010) A Project Management Institute best seller.

- *The Advanced Project Management Memory Jogger*™ (Goal/QPC, 2006).
- *The McGraw-Hill 36-Hour Course in Project Management* (McGraw-Hill, 2010).
- *Getting Started in Project Management* (John Wiley & Sons: 2001).

For more information, visit www.griffintate.com or call (877) 984-8150.

Ask for Two Business Cards

When you meet an interesting new person, always ask for two business cards. Why? Because you can keep one and look to pass the second one to someone else who might benefit from this person's products or services.

I learned this tip from a veteran networker who attended many networking breakfasts. Asking someone for two cards is also a great icebreaker and is very flattering. Chances are, you will more likely be remembered by the person you just met.

Here is another great business card tip: When you attend a trade show, meeting or conference, always wear a jacket with two pockets. Use one pocket to hold the cards collected from the people you meet and the other to store your cards.

This two-pocket system eliminates fumbling in your purse or wallet to dig out a business card when people are on the move. Don't forget to sit down and sort through the cards at the end of the day. Make notes on the back so you'll remember how to follow up with new contacts.

Treat Your Best Clients Well

Treating your best clients well seems like a no brainer, but too often, we take them for granted.

When my clients call, I drop everything to respond to their requests. One time, one of my best clients was asked to moderate a small business panel on short notice.

His secretary sent me the background information and a slide template. I got busy. I did the research and prepared slides for his presentation—all within a day.

They were so impressed that my contract was extended and I was asked to work on an even bigger, long-term project.

Never take your clients or customers for granted. And, don't be shy about asking them what else you can do for them. Remember, most new business comes from your existing customers and clients.

GREAT 123 IDEA

Invite Associates to a Trade Show

If attending a trade show is on your calendar this year, make the trip more valuable by inviting clients, potential customers, or business associates to meet you at or near the show.

As soon as you register to attend, go through your database to make a list of everyone you know who lives within 100 miles of the show.

Meeting people at a national conference or trade show has several advantages. It saves you a subsequent trip to their city. If you can afford it, pay the registration fee so they can visit the exhibit floor. If you have a booth, they'll see you in action. They'll meet your best salespeople and watch you interact with the public.

If you can wangle an invitation to participate in a panel discussion, better yet. What a great way to position yourself as a leader in your industry.

Even if you aren't an exhibitor, it's still great to walk around the show with a good customer at your side.

If your clients accept your invitation to meet at a show, rent a hotel suite and plan a party. Or take them out for a meal. Make reservations early because nearby restaurants may be overrun with convention attendees.

Attending a trade show, with or without guests, is essential to your success. It's the place to check out your competition and let them know you are coming after them. It's also the easiest way to connect with industry movers and shakers.

Tips for Really Working a Trade Show

Hedy Ratner, cofounder of the Women's Business Development Center (WBDC) in Chicago, really knows how to work a room. A consummate networker, she has devoted years to helping women entrepreneurs start and grow their businesses.

Here are some of her great tips for making the most of a trade show:

- Set goals before you go. Are you there to find new suppliers or customers or to study the competition?
- Dress for success and comfort. "First impressions are important, so dress businesslike," Ratner advises.
- Wear comfortable shoes because you will be on your feet all day and walk for miles.
- Plan your schedule the night before to decide which booths to visit and which seminars to attend.
- Make notes as you walk the show, either in a notebook or with a digital recorder.
- Plan to attend key seminars, workshops, and parties.
- Bring lots of business cards and brochures. Toss out the stuff you collected that you don't need before you pack up to go home.
- Be flexible and be open to spontaneous meetings with people you meet. "Trust your instincts to lead you to mentors, key contacts, and resources," said Ratner.
- Follow up immediately after the show. People forget who they meet at shows, so get back in touch right away.

GREAT
124
IDEA

Know Your Competition

Entrepreneurs love to brag about beating their competition, but the truth is that most small business owners are too busy to know what their competition is up to. But remember, operating your business in a vacuum can lead to its demise.

"You need to know what your competition is doing," said Guy Kawasaki, author of *Reality Check* (Portfolio, 2008) and *Enchantment* (Portfolio, 2011), among many other best-selling books.

"You need to shut off the phone, close the door, and figure out what you stand for, what your competition is doing, and what they stand for."

Kawasaki, who founded www.alltop.com, a popular and innovative site for news junkies, says there's no excuse not to know everything about your competitors. You can find out so much by tapping into Google and other online sources.

After you fully understand what your competition is doing, figure out where they are vulnerable. "You're looking for chinks in the armor," said Kawasaki. "You're looking for dissatisfied customers that you can steal from them."

Seena Sharp, author of *Competitive Intelligence Advantage: How to Minimize Risk, Avoid Surprises and Grow Your Business in a Changing World* (John Wiley & Sons, 2009) said business owners need to understand the current state of the market before making any big changes.

"Ask yourself, is the market changing? Where is it changing?" said Sharp. "Where are the gaps and how can you fill a niche?"

Sharp said it's important to know that competitive intelligence complements, not replaces, market research. "For example, when we are doing competitive intelligence, we'd be interested in understanding the pricing strategy. We want to know how a company comes up with the price and what relevance it has to the end user."

One low-cost way to do competitive intelligence is to read trade publications and newsletters. "Talk to people in your industry, your suppliers, distributors, even the repair people."

It's also important to explore what strategies have been successful in other industries. For example, American Airlines launched one of the first frequent flier programs in 1981. Now, all sorts of companies, including hotels, office supply stores, and car rental agencies, rely on frequent buyer programs to build customer loyalty.

"Pay attention to what is successful and figure out how to make it work in your business," Sharp advises. If you are new to your industry, go online or visit a library to look through the *Encyclopedia of Associations*. There are also hundreds of industry-specific publications providing a wealth of information.

Sharp said companies often make poor decisions because they ask only employees and executives for feedback. "Warren Buffett said you should speak to 90 percent external and 10 percent internal people before making a decision."

For more information on Sharp's company and her book, visit www .competitiveintelligenceadvantage.com.

Here's how to check out your competition without spending a lot of money:

- *Go shopping.* If you make or sell a retail product, get out to stores at least once a week. One of the most successful entrepreneurs I know, Kathy Taggares, president and founder of K.T.'s Kitchens, prowls supermarket aisles checking out the placement of her private-label frozen pizzas and Bob's Big Boy salad dressings. (For more about her company, see Great Idea #88.)
- *Subscribe to your industry's trade magazine or e-newsletter.* Read it from cover to cover when it arrives.
- *Attend a professional meeting at least once a month.* Getting out of your office and meeting competitors face to face is invaluable. People love to brag about what they are doing and often say too much about their upcoming products or services.
- *Go to a major trade show at least once a year* (see Great Idea #123). You may associate trade shows with exhaustion and aching feet, but walking the aisles at an industry show can revitalize or even save your business. Eavesdrop shamelessly during cocktail hour.
- *Survey your customers.* Ask them what they like and don't like about doing business with you. Try SurveyMonkey.com.
- *Assign a staff member to order your competitor's materials*—brochures, catalogs, annual reports, price lists, and so forth. Check out their pricing and return policies.
- *Order your competitor's products every few months.* This is the best way to find out what they sell and how they treat customers. If what they sell is too big or too expensive to buy, visit their showroom.
- *Organize an informal focus group* at your church, book club or synagogue, or with members of an organization. Ask people what they like and don't like about your products and your competitor's.

- *Follow industry analysts or consultants who serve your industry.* Read annual reports and other public information. Follow analysts' blogs, and read articles about your industry.
- *Read a daily newspaper and newsmagazines. Bloomberg Businessweek* is a terrific magazine. Their investigative reports are great.

GREAT
125
IDEA

Tap the Growing Hispanic Market

The U.S. Hispanic community is growing stronger every day. "Best of all," says George Herrera, former president and CEO of the United States Hispanic Chamber of Commerce, "it's a young population, which means it's a population of consumers who will be here for a long time. We are offering corporate America a very young and very long-term consumer base."

By 2011, Hispanic purchasing power will be at $1 trillion, with 71 million children under 18 years living in households.

A young and growing population represents an increasingly significant economic force, Herrera says. Corporations on the ball already are moving to serve this market. Others will follow. One way to test sales in the Hispanic market is to partner with a Hispanic-owned or -managed company.

Another way is to repackage your products to appeal to Hispanic tastes. But this takes an investment and careful planning.

Savvy business owners wanting to expand sales into the Hispanic market should always rely on a competent translator. One Los Angeles bank had egg on its face a few years ago when a loan campaign aimed at Spanish-speaking clients went awry. When translated into Spanish, the ad copy said something like: "Remember when your mom used to steal money from you? Think of us as your mom."

A mortified bank representative blamed the advertising salesperson for the bad translation. So never trust an amateur to translate your copy. Hire someone familiar with the local dialects and who knows the cultural nuances of the specific Latin consumers. Mexicans speak a different style of Spanish and have a far different culture than Salvadoreans or Panamanians.

Many ad agencies now specialize in ethnic marketing, so find a good one and try test-marketing one product or service at a time.

GREAT

126

IDEA

Make Your 800 Number Ring

If you serve customers in a wide area, you should have an 800, 888, 866, or 877 toll-free number. It is a good way to generate goodwill. I'm not happy when I have to pay for a call to order products. Toll-free 800 numbers can be assigned at www.tollfreenumber .org/.

The cost is often determined based on where the call is forwarded to—the entrepreneur's cell/home, virtual assistant, or the like.

Most long distance providers can set up a toll-free number, so check around. Visit www.tollfreenumber.org/low-toll-free-rates.html ?referralsource=fp-signup to compare rates.

You can also visit www.tollfreenumber.org/products-services/ to explore various packages, including "The Business Toll Free Saver" and "The Virtual Telecenter."

Here is some basic information from that site.

The Business Toll Free Saver

Forwards to your phone
Monthly cost: None
Maintenance and recovery fees: $7.99/mo.
Nationwide per-minute cost: $.039/min.

The Virtual Telecenter

Toll-Free Ring—to auto attendant
Monthly cost: $49.99
Maintenance and recovery fees: None
Nationwide per-minute cost: None

Five Tips to Generate More Calls

1. Put your 800 number on everything you post online, publish, or sell.
2. Buy a rubber stamp or colored stickers that say, "Call us toll-free at ..."
3. Add your 800 number to labels, invoices, and wall or magnetic signs.
4. Send an e-mail blast featuring the 800 number.
5. Add your 800 number to voice mail greetings.

GREAT

127

IDEA

Attend Charity Events to Make Contacts

A great way to meet the "who's who" in your area is to buy a ticket to a local charity event where you can mingle and schmooze your way through the cocktail hour. Then, look for an empty seat at a corporate-sponsored table and boldly ask if you can sit there.

Volunteering at a glitzy social event is also a great idea. A friend, who was making a transition from selling shoes to high-end real estate, signed up to work at the registration table for an event with a $1,500 ticket price. Since she was beautifully dressed and gorgeous, she was asked to pin carnations on the lapels of all the men.

She bantered and flirted for an hour with the most interesting men in New York City, including a billionaire she ended up dating. The contacts she made that night also launched her real estate career.

It's easy to find out about charity events by reading the newspaper or checking online.

If you can't volunteer, break down and buy a ticket if you think you will made good connections. Focus on events that will attract industry leaders.

For example, if you are promoting a band, attend the annual MTV benefit that raises money for music education.

Since most people don't bring business cards to a formal event, bring a tiny notebook and make notes. Make follow-up calls or send an e-mail right after the event. You don't want them to forget who you are. Here's a great idea: contact someone you saw but didn't meet. Pretend you met anyway. You can probably get away with it, especially if there was a long cocktail hour and everyone was tipsy.

GREAT
128
IDEA

Publicize Your Specialty Food Business

When it comes to driving sales of offbeat specialty foods, positive publicity counts. Americans buy an estimated $700 million worth of specialty foods a year, mostly by mail, according to the National Association for the Specialty Food Trade in New York City (www.specialtyfood.com).

Americans love specialty foods. Despite the recession, retail sales rose 8.4 percent in 2008 to reach $48 billion. According to the association's web site, specialty food sales in natural food stores grew 17.4 percent in 2008 versus 2007. Cheese and cheese alternative are the largest specialty food category, with $3.4 billion in sales in 2008.

There are about 2,500 new products introduced a year, with significant growth in chocolate, confectionery products, desserts, ice cream, and alcoholic beverages. Many small companies are in the food business because the start-up costs can be low.

A short blurb by a noted food writer, critic, or author often means the difference between success and failure for a startup. For example, a few years ago, a short mention in Florence Fabricant's *New York Times* column launched Matt and Ted Lee's boiled-peanuts-by-mail business. Today, the company sells a variety of Southern foods, in addition to peanuts.

"The reason I went for the boiled peanuts was because it was a regional specialty," said Fabricant, who is always looking out for unique and unusual foods. "Before the Lee Brothers offered them, boiled peanuts were not available outside a certain region in the South."

Fabricant told me she receives dozens of pitches a week from small, specialty food product makers hoping for her attention.

The Lee brothers told me they owe their success to journalists like Fabricant. "Publicity is crucial," said Ted Lee. "We've never paid a dime for advertising." Check out their products at www.boiledpeanuts.com.

When Ted and Wendy Eidson, founders of Mo Hotta Mo Betta, started their San Luis Obispo, California–based spicy food catalog in 1989, they relied on the public library to find the addresses of 200 regional newspapers. They attached samples of spicy wasabi chips to tempt the palates of the food editors. The Eidsons said 30 to 40 percent of the editors they contact do something with it.

In addition to selling all sorts of hot sauces and marinades, the company sells "Ass Kickin'" snacks, candies, and spicy chips.

About 30 years ago, an article in Delta Airline's *Sky* magazine drew customers from all over the country to Nathalie Dupree's tiny Georgia restaurant. Dupree, an Atlanta-based author of 10 cookbooks and a cooking expert, has produced more than 300 shows for PBS and the Food Network. "When an article is written about me, I may get calls for up to five years afterwards," said Dupree, who said if she mentions a new food business, it can really boost sales. "I don't mention anyone unless I think they can handle the business," Dupree said.

If you are interested in getting into the specialty food business, join the National Association for the Specialty Food Trade (NASFT), read their publications, visit their web site, and attend their fancy food shows.

GREAT

129

IDEA

Market to Uncle Sam and Other Agencies

There is no recession when it comes to Uncle Sam. The federal government is the largest purchaser of goods and services, so why not get in line?

"Almost all large contractors have a mandate to reach out to work with smaller contractors," said Vicki Garcia, a marketing consultant who has a contract with the airport authority to help small businesses become subcontractors on the San Diego airport expansion project.

Garcia helps business owners understand the somewhat complicated process. First, she said, you have to be certified as a historically underserved business enterprise (HUBE). Most minority, veteran, or woman-owned businesses will qualify for this designation, so check with your city and county to learn how to get certified. Once you are certified, you will be put on a list and authorized to submit bids for jobs.

"If you are interested in a project, you have to go to the prebid meeting, or you can't bid," said Garcia. That meeting is a great place to meet the big contractors and find out what they need.

The Federal Marketplace should be your first stop. To get started, check out www.fedmarket.com. The site is rich with information on how to market and sell products and services to Uncle Sam (really the General Services Administration).

There are dozens of interesting articles on the site, including one that wonders why there are only 20,000 companies qualified to bid on contracts because the requirements are so tough for new businesses to meet. If you want to get in line for federal contracts, the first step is to find a Procurement Technical Assistance Center, which helps small companies navigate the procurement maze to get to the Department of Defense and other agencies.

There are a variety of programs that are supposed to help minority-owned small businesses receive federal contracts on a sole-source or limited competition basis.

The Procurement Automated Service System (PASS) is a database with more than 200,000 small companies interested in doing business with the government. PASS provides companies with a quick way to find small suppliers.

Most government agencies have a special department dedicated to helping you do business with them. Ask for the Office of Small and Disadvantaged Business at any federal agency. The Small Business Administration (SBA) also has special programs for veterans, including loan guarantees.

130

Get Certified as a Woman- or Minority-Owned Business

Big companies get brownie points for buying goods and services from small businesses, but in many cases, only if the small business is certified by a legitimate third-party certification group.

One such organization is the National Minority Supplier Development Council (NMSDC), which works closely with 43 regional supplier councils to match up 25,000 certified minority business owners with 3,500 corporations.

Most big U.S. companies actively seek to do business with minority firms in order to meet various government and corporate supplier diversity goals. Corporate marketers also understand the economic advantage of catering to minority consumers.

"The buying power of minority groups is billions of dollars a year, and that is a huge opportunity we have to pay attention to," said John Edwardson, former president and chief executive officer of United Airlines.

Small, minority-owned companies provide a variety of services and products to large companies. For example, H. K. Enterprises, a small New Jersey firm, developed "Undeniable," one of Avon's best-selling fragrances. "We see minority business development today as an investment in our own future," said James Preston, former chairman of Avon Products.

When he was in charge, Avon contracted with 400 minority-owned suppliers, accounting for 12 percent of the cosmetic company's annual purchases. The 12 percent was about three times the national average for corporate purchases from minority suppliers.

Avon is committed to buying from minority-owned firms because Avon products, sold by independent representatives, are extremely popular among women of color and their families. Preston said his minority suppliers also provide Avon with insight into the marketplace.

Dealing with minority-owned companies makes good economic sense for any company. Census data indicates that by the year 2050 two of every five Americans will be of minority descent.

The SBA and the Commerce Department's Minority Business Development Agency have programs for minority business owners. For more information, contact NMSDC.org.

Women-owned businesses should apply for certification through the Women's Business Enterprise National Council (http://wbenc.org). The group has about 250 corporate members who seek out certified women-owned businesses. The WBENC annual conference is a great place to meet with potential clients and customers.

GREAT IDEA 131

Don't Forsake the Yellow Pages

The printed telephone directory may soon be just a doorstop or fodder for recycling. Many companies are forsaking printed directories in favor of promoting online access to business and consumer information.

Yellow Pages, once a $31 billion a year industry, is in a state of flux. Print ads declined about 7 percent in 2009, according to the Yellow Pages Association.

But, don't count the Yellow Pages out yet. Last year, the print version yielded 12 billion references, versus 4.9 million for the Internet Yellow Pages. In the month they participated in an industry survey, 65 percent of consumers said they still look for information in the Yellow Pages.

Some companies, including Super Media, are integrating print, direct mail, and online advertising efforts. One tactic is to print bar codes on ads and direct mail campaigns. Smartphones can scan the code to download a free SuperPages phone app designed to help users search for listings.

Many small business owners still depend on the Yellow Pages to attract business. Daniel Crowe, owner of Freelancer Video, in Hartford, Vermont, told me he considered dropping his Yellow Pages ads, but decided against it. Instead, he reduced his spending from $7,000 to $4,000 last year.

"Instead of canceling ads, I took out smaller ads in three Yellow Pages directories," said Crowe, who shoots and edits video for clients. (He is my go-to guy for making DVDs.)

"I decided that I still needed to be there (in the Yellow Pages) for the 40-year-old and older demographic I serve," he said.

One thing that really bugs him is when he sees stacks of undelivered Yellow Pages directories collecting dust in the local post office. That's when he calls his Yellow Pages' ad rep to complain.

Send Pizza to Potential Clients

P izza is hot, gooey, and delicious—it's also a great way to generate new business, especially if you are in the advertising or marketing business.

Here's a great, slightly crazy idea I heard from a Florida advertising guy:

Order a pizza and personally deliver it right before lunchtime to a client you are wooing. Remove one slice from the box and replace it with a message such as: "For a larger slice of your market, call us," or "We want a piece of your business."

A couple of other food-related marketing ideas: Send a pair of chocolate shoes or cowboy boots to a prospect with a note: "I'd love to get a foot in the door."

A few years ago, marketing expert and author, Nancy Michaels, sent one flip-flop sandal to an executive she was trying to connect with. Her quirky gift—with a note saying she wanted to get a foot in the door—worked, and he invited her to meet him.

She also bid on a game-changing lunch with the CEO of Office Depot at a women's conference sponsored by the company. He was so impressed by what she had to say, he hired her to be their small business marketing expert.

So think of a tasty promotion and give it a try.

Think BIG—Why Not?

A ll the entrepreneurs I've profiled for my columns and books have taught me one thing: *it doesn't cost any more to think big than it does to think small.*

Long ago, when I was working in the remodeled garage behind my Sun Valley, California, home, I bought some big vinyl letters at the hardware store. Then, I spelled out: "THINK BIG" on the battered file cabinet beside my desk.

That message inspired me to work seven days a week to create a successful multimedia and consulting company. Some years have been bigger than others, but I've never given up.

No matter what kind of business you have, strive to land the biggest accounts and make the biggest deals. Thinking big motivates you to operate at the highest professional level. There isn't much science to prove it, but I know success depends on your attitude, and a positive attitude leads to action. If you feel and act confident, you will be more successful in life and in business.

Looking back, it was pretty audacious to think I could provide custom small business–oriented content and event production services to the biggest companies in the world. But my entertainment attorney, the late Jerry Gottlieb, treated me and my projects the same way he treated his celebrity clients, which included Jane Fonda and Quincy Jones. Gottlieb said he kept the first commission check I sent him because it was in the "four figures"— probably $43.44.

He believed in me. After he negotiated a lucrative contract with American Express to produce and syndicate my own small business radio report, I was asked to join the American Express Small Business advisory board. I've been working with Amex ever since, most recently writing a bimonthly column for the company's Open Forum site.

Thinking big after the terrorist attacks on September 11, 2001, prompted me to create Back on Track America™, a national coalition designed to revive the small business economy. This huge idea hit me a few weeks after 9/11.

On that horrible day, my friend Vanessa Freytag was visiting me in my office before she was scheduled to fly home to Cincinnati.

We were watching CNN when the second plane hit the World Trade Center. I remember thinking, "Why are they showing a disaster movie in the morning on CNN?"

Once we realized what had happened, Vanessa became hysterical. She was insisting that she had to leave right away. Of course, the airports were closed and, within an hour, there were no more rental cars anywhere near

Manhattan. A long-time fan of Amtrak, I called the 800 number, believing the trains would probably start running before the airports would reopen.

I stayed on hold for almost an hour and finally booked her a ticket on a train heading from New York to Boston two days later. She slowly made her way west, eventually returning home to Cincinnati.

A few nights later, I woke up with a brainstorm. I had spent the day speaking with clients who were canceling all upcoming meetings and conferences. Not good for us, since we were planning events and I was booked to speak at several.

My crazy idea was this: if Amtrak would give me a train (or at least free tickets), I could take a faculty of small business experts around the country to boost the morale of small business owners already suffering from a recession before the terrorist attacks.

The "back on track" phrase came to me that night, but it was our CPA, John D'Aquila, who suggested adding "America." With the perfect name and a simple premise, I went into a manic phase that lasted three weeks. I called every person I knew and asked them to join what soon became a coalition of big and small companies, business associations, and business experts willing to volunteer their time and brainpower to get the nation's business owners back on track.

A dozen speakers signed on to speak and waived their fees. Event and video producers cut their day rates. My dearest friend and colleague, Linda Denny, started calling her contacts. She was working for ING and contributed some cash. Then, she got on the phone to round up complimentary hotel rooms at Wyndham Hotels and signed up Club Corp. to host VIP receptions at their clubs across the country.

Our biggest client at the time, America Online, provided online marketing and public relations support for six stops on the tour. They also paid for a lively kickoff and press party in Union Station in Washington, DC.

The "Back on Track America" tour opened on Broadway. Fleet Bank rented the Hudson Theatre in Times Square. The next day, we produced an event at the New Jersey Performing Arts Center in Newark.

The Small Business Administration endorsed the effort. Service Corps of Retired Executives (SCORE) counselors set up shop at every event. Every Back on Track event included free workshops, a networking reception, and a community Town Hall–style meeting, with me as the moderator.

How to Think Big

- Once you perfect your idea on a small scale, figure out how to grow it fast.
- Engage other big thinkers to help you. Ask successful industry leaders to serve on your advisory board or act as informal mentors.
- Enroll your employees in the concept by sharing your vision frequently.
- Tell your story. Once someone reports on your idea, it's much easier to attract new investors and supporters.
- Don't be afraid to regroup and change direction if necessary.

Everyone I knew got on board. Singer-songwriter Carmin Turco wrote a theme song. My friend Ian Jack, a gifted singer-songwriter, produced "Back on Track." He and Carmin recorded the song in Hollywood and distributed it to radio stations.

My wonderful friend Yves Kamioner, a talented custom jewelry designer, designed a precious lapel pin in the shape of a tiny railroad track. We presented gold and silver pins to sponsors.

I'm still paying off some expenses from that tour, but I don't regret it. I know Back on Track America helped thousands of business owners across the country get back to running their business.

Everyone loved our message: "Bringing Spirit, Strength, and Prosperity Back to America's Entrepreneurs."

People

People can make your life magical or miserable. If it's magic you want, surround yourself with talented, confident, and resourceful people.

Your challenge is to find the right mix of people. The good news is that the Great Recession has been a blessing for small business owners. And, there are millions of talented people still out there looking for work.

Based on experience, I beseech you to be picky about hiring. Don't hire your nephew's son just because he needs a job. It's incredibly tough to get rid of a bad employee. If you don't follow the rules when it comes to terminating an employee, you may face a labor department complaint, or even worse, a lawsuit.

I've learned the hard way how to deal with employees. I hired my first employee in 1992. He was the top graduate of a prestigious MBA program. He hated working for a small business and we parted company a few weeks later. Through the years, I've dealt with a disruptive office romance, a drug-addicted assistant, and a parade of other wackos. And all this grief happened after interviewing lots of people and checking their references!

At times, when my head is about to explode, I dream about the early days when it was just me, my cat, and my computer in a cozy corner of my den in Sun Valley, California. But, of course, you can't look back. You have to learn to manage yourself and then manage the people working around you.

Above all, I've found that good communication is critical to managing people. Sounds simple, but it's not. The key is to be clear about your expectations. No one is a mind reader. So write down exactly what you expect people to do and when you need to have it done.

Everyone communicates differently. Being a writer, I write endless notes. My husband, Joe, and our kids, Jeanne and Evan, hate them.

"Just *tell* me what you want me to do," admonished my daughter, Jeanne, before she moved out to attend college. "Don't write it down." The problem is that she ignored my verbal requests all through high school.

"You'll be leaving notes on our graves," quipped Joe, my husband. He's probably right.

No matter what communication style you embrace, stick to it. Then, move on to master the art of motivation, appreciation, and delegation. It's a fact that when people feel truly appreciated, they work harder.

You might be surprised to learn that money is not the best motivator. In fact, Dr. Bob Nelson, my favorite human resources guru, said thanking people and providing the tools they need to do their job well are more effective. We love hearing the sound of our name more than anything else.

So call a person by their name and say something positive. Sometimes a simple "thanks, good job" is all you need to say. Try it.

If you want to acknowledge extra effort, give people a day off with pay.

For some great hiring tips, I turned to Chris Gorog, a good friend who is a respected entertainment industry executive. Gorog has headed several successful companies, including the House of Blues, Roxio, and Napster. Before taking a break to consider new opportunities, he orchestrated the sale of Napster, the revived music sharing company, to Best Buy for more than $130 million.

"I always like to find someone who really wants the job," said Gorog, "Someone who is emotionally connected and will just die if they don't get it."

Knowing everything about the company and the management team, especially the CEO, is essential for any job applicant, he said. Anyone who doesn't do their homework is immediately dismissed by Gorog. He also looks at how long the applicant has worked at their previous jobs. People who hop around show a "lack of loyalty and respect," he said.

He urges employers to carefully check references, but not by calling the human resources department, which can often just confirm dates of employment. "Check references at the senior level," advises Gorog. "Executives will talk to you about a person."

Finally, he said it is essential to "pay attention to the chemistry" when hiring. "If the chemical reaction isn't right, the person will not be good for the job."

Read on to learn how to include your best clients in the hiring process and whether you should hire an interim executive. I also have some great ideas about training and teaching English to your employees who need to improve their language skills.

I'll never forget when I was a cub reporter and a top executive said to me, "business is great, except for the people." Pretty funny, but so true: A successful business is all about the people.

GREAT

134

IDEA

Cast a Wide Net to Attract Good Employees

It's very tough for a small company, especially in the start-up phase, to compete with bigger companies when it comes to offering competitive salaries and attractive benefits. But it's essential to hire the best people from the very beginning. Hiring mistakes are costly. A big company can afford a few duds on the payroll, but a small business doesn't have the time or financial resources to waste on a poor hire.

Here are some low-cost ways to recruit good workers:

- *Tell your customers and vendors that you're hiring.* They know your business and can refer people they would like to work with.
- *Call other small business owners and ask if they've interviewed any talented people they weren't able to hire.* This isn't as strange as it sounds. Many times colleagues wish they could hire someone, but the timing wasn't right.

- *Consider hiring older and younger workers.* Students and retired people are a tremendous resource for small businesses (see Great Ideas #140 and #141). Contact your local business school, community college, or high school to find students.
- *Advertise in the local newspaper or in trade publications* before you spend a lot of money on advertising in major papers. Place an online ad in trade journals or weeklies serving your industry.
- *Contact your state employment development department.* The state can help you find job candidates in many fields. The state also offers training programs and tax incentives for hiring new workers, so check out what's available in your state.

I've found great research assistants at the nearby journalism school. Inquire about internship programs that offer students class credit for work experience.

Contact your trade or professional association or local chamber of commerce.

GREAT 135 IDEA Write Clear Job Descriptions

Big companies always prepare extremely detailed job descriptions. You should, too. Putting everything in writing avoids confusion and boosts productivity. It also helps when it's time to cross-train your employees to cover for each other. (Cross-training is essential for a small business.) Be sure to update your job descriptions every six months and also whenever you hire new people or retain consultants.

If you think writing down job descriptions is a waste of time, try this: Walk around the office asking people to tell you exactly what they do every day. They may think you are crazy, but I bet you will be very surprised at what they tell you. What you hired them to do and what they are actually doing at work may be very different. Why? Because people always morph their jobs into what fits their interests or skills. It's human nature to avoid doing what we don't want to do.

Take this opportunity to realign work flow and redefine what people are supposed to be doing every day.

GREAT
136
IDEA

Know What *Not* to Ask Job Applicants

When 100 small business owners were asked if they had ever asked a job applicant any of the following questions during an interview, all of them said "yes."

* Have you ever filed a workers' compensation claim?
* Do you have any physical problems or injuries?
* How many sick days did you take off last year?
* Are you currently taking any medication?
* Have you ever been treated for drug abuse?

Actually, it's *illegal* to ask applicants any of these questions, according to my legal experts.

In addition to asking the wrong questions, small business owners are also at risk when it comes to complying with the Americans with Disabilities Act (ADA) and a zillion other employment-related laws. It doesn't matter that you are too busy to keep up with current regulations. Ignorance of the law is no defense if a prospective employee decides to file a complaint or sue you.

The best way to stay out of trouble during an interview is to stick to questions relevant to the prospective employee's ability to perform the essential functions of the job—nothing more. You can ask about their proficiency in a specific software program or whether they like to write proposals.

Take a minute to ask your attorney to review your interview questions. And if you don't have a written employee manual outlining policies and procedures, get busy. There are lots of fill-in-the-blank templates you can buy to get you started.

Recruit Great Employees

A small business can't afford to make poor hiring choices. Yet small business owners too often hire the first person who drifts through the door, even for key jobs. Casting the widest net possible before hiring anyone makes sense (see Great Idea #138). For a key hire, it may pay to retain a search firm.

Executive recruiters, often retained by big companies to find just the right person, also work with many smaller firms. Their fee—traditionally 33⅓ percent of the total first year's salary plus all expenses—may be steep, but think of it as an investment in your success.

"We create a strategy for the hunt," said Brad Marks, chairman and chief executive officer of Brad Marks International in Century City, California (www.bradmarks.com).

Most recruiters specialize in an industry. He's known for placing many top executives in the entertainment industry. A former executive at Walt Disney Co. and ABC, he's been helping companies find the right people since 1982.

He was a pioneer when it came to placing high-level women in traditionally male-dominated jobs in the entertainment industry. "I have a distinct desire on my part to find the best executive for the position, and in many cases that turns out to be a woman," said Marks.

Hollywood studios, primarily family owned, became more open to hiring women when the leveraged buyouts of the 1980s gave control to major corporations.

Marks made headlines when he placed Dawn Tarnofsky at Lifetime Television. It later was acquired by A&E Networks. Now known as Dawn Ostroff, she is president of the CW Network.

His type of high-level recruiting is very "cloak and dagger," especially when he is hired to replace people who don't know they are about to lose their jobs.

The executive search process is complex. After meeting with clients to determine exactly what kind of person they need, the recruiter begins searching for suitable candidates.

It can often take up to 10 weeks to track down and interview candidates. In Marks's case, he narrows the field to about 20 people, who are interviewed by him and his associates. After careful evaluation, the top five people are scheduled to meet with the client.

Hopefully, one candidate will be a good fit. If not, the recruiter keeps looking.

Look Far and Wide for the Best Person

Finding the right person to help grow your business may mean hiring an out-of-towner and paying to relocate that person. Relocation involves a myriad of financial and emotional issues for both you and your employee. It's a complex and expensive process.

A comfortable place to live is important, but a positive relocation depends on many more factors, according to Maryanne Rainone, senior vice president of Heyman Associates, a Manhattan executive search firm. "We talk to thousands of job candidates and know what kind of things are red lights for a prospective employee," said Rainone.

During the first call, it's important to ask job candidates if they've thought about relocation. If moving isn't an option, don't waste your time. If their resumes show they've gone to school and worked in only one state, they are probably not interested in a cross-country move.

"Make sure the candidate is open to moving before you get too interested, because sometimes companies fall in love with one person and end up comparing everyone else to the candidate they can't have," she advised.

While it's against the law to ask a job candidate if they are married or have children, you can ask if they have any family issues affecting a work-related move. At this point, most people will mention that they need a good nursery school or a nursing home for their aging mother. "Elder care is a big issue now and one of the primary reasons people can't leave where they are," said Rainone.

Being aware of spousal issues is also important to a successful relocation. If the trailing spouse will have a tough time finding work or adjusting to life in your town, the relocation could prove to be a disaster, Rainone warns.

Even if you aren't using an executive search firm, consider working with a relocation consultant to collect vital information about schools, real estate prices, and quality-of-life issues in your town. And always look locally and regionally first. You may be able to hire a wonderful person by offering a higher salary, rather than paying all the relocation expenses to hire an out-of-towner.

Remember, you are not just recruiting one person—you may be recruiting an entire family.

GREAT IDEA 139

Work with People You Like

John Chuang, cofounder of Aquent, a talent agency for creative professionals, shared some contrarian advice for entrepreneurs starting a business. "You've heard that two things you never want to do with friends is to lend them money or go into business with them," said Chuang, who founded the company in 1986 with friends when he was an undergrad at Harvard.

"But the reality is that people who go into ventures with people they know and trust are one step ahead of the game." Chuang attributes the success of his high-tech professional temporary agency to the fact that he went into business with friends from college and graduate school. They set out to serve a small base of customers in Boston, but ended up creating a business with offices around the world that places thousands of temporary professionals a month.

Chuang told me that working with people you know helps you work around their strengths and weaknesses. You also communicate better with people you like, and this can be a real advantage over working with strangers, he said. "Hiring trusted friends cuts down on the time spent interviewing and screening," he said. "You know who you trust, and it takes some of the guesswork out of the process."

Sharing the same sense of humor can also help you ride the entrepreneurial roller coaster. "We used humor to weather the tough times," said Chuang.

Best of all, "if you have to work late, you'd rather be with your friends than a room full of strangers."

Hire Talented Seniors

One of the best salespeople I ever met was a tiny woman in her late 70s. One day, my husband, Joe, and I wandered into a suburban Westchester County lighting store, with a long shopping list in hand. Dazzled and baffled by the vast selection of fixtures, we didn't know where to start.

We were met by a pixie. Barely five feet tall and smartly dressed, Ann briskly introduced herself, clipboard in hand. I must admit I was surprised to see a woman of her age still working the sales floor. But we could barely keep up as she trotted us around the showroom.

She answered all our questions about quality, wattage, and installation, often standing on tiptoe to reach the cords to turn on the fixtures.

It turned out Ann was an expert on lighting. She spent more than an hour with us, helping us select what we needed and writing up an order totaling hundreds of dollars.

Dealing with Ann reinforced my belief that experienced older people can be an incredible asset to your business. Most seniors not only have a lifetime of experiences and have seen it all, but are often willing to work flexible hours and forgo a big paycheck.

When I was just starting my business, I had two great seniors working with me: my dearly departed grandparents, Jean and George Coan. One summer, they came to visit us in the sleepy San Fernando Valley suburb where we lived. They were completely bored, and thrilled when I arrived with a huge box of fan mail.

Readers sent in a self-addressed, stamped envelope to receive a free business resource guide. I had about a thousand requests and no time to fill them. My grandparents loved the job.

George got a big kick out of reading my fan mail and questions from readers. Jean was content to slice open the envelopes and stuff the brochures into the return envelopes.

For another wave of requests, I recruited my late aunt, Pearl Weissman. A busy political activist and volunteer tutor well into her 90s, she agreed to stuff a few hundred envelopes every week. The project also gave me a great excuse to visit her and my dear Uncle Sam.

If you aren't lucky enough to have energetic, elderly relatives nearby, recruit some from the neighborhood or contact a local senior center.

GREAT IDEA 141 — Hire Teenagers

Seven out of ten high school students want to start a business, according to a recent Gallup Poll. The primary motivation was to be the boss, not to earn a lot of money.

Although there are no firm statistics on how many of America's teens run small businesses, the numbers are well into the hundreds of thousands and growing, according to those involved in training young entrepreneurs. Teens are selling handmade crafts, moving furniture, detailing cars, and designing clothes, among other ventures. But not all teenagers have a natural entrepreneurial bent.

Despite this strong interest, 86 percent of the teens surveyed said they lacked the skills needed to start even the simplest business. The Gallup study, commissioned by the Center for Entrepreneurial Leadership at the Ewing Marion Kauffman Foundation in Kansas City, Missouri, also found that most of the students were taught little or nothing about running a small business.

Steve Mariotti, founder of the Network for Teaching Entrepreneurship (www.nfte.com) in Manhattan, serves economically disadvantaged teenagers across the country and abroad. The program boasts 15,000 graduates, a multimillion-dollar budget, and more than 200 corporate sponsors.

"Economic illiteracy is an intellectual handicap in a capitalist society," Mariotti said. "It's life threatening for the poor." Mariotti said teens who participate in his organization's classes learn the practical and financial skills needed to make it in the business world.

Many teens get into business because their parents are entrepreneurs. Katy Meyer of Carlisle, Massachusetts, launched her silk scarf business after she won a national business plan competition sponsored by Independent Means.

She now has a company, Meyer Lemon Designs (www.meyerlemondesigns .com). Meyer learned silk painting at an art camp and has been perfecting her technique ever since.

A great way to support aspiring teen business owners is to hire one as an intern or part-time employee. Best of all, a younger person can add a fresh perspective to your team. Thinking about aiming your products at the teen market? Then, ask your teenage employee to set up a Facebook fan page and manage your social media strategy.

GREAT

142

IDEA

Use the BATH System for Hiring

Jay Goltz has been an entrepreneur since he graduated from high school. He knows a lot about hiring, having run several home and garden businesses in the Chicago area.

"Seventy-five percent of good management is hiring the right people in the first place," said Goltz, who has written several books on small business (www.jaygoltz.com).

He said many former employers are reluctant to provide references for fear of repercussions if you don't hire the person. But you can ask them if they would rehire the person. Another way to gauge your current hiring strategy is to consider this hypothetical situation: An employee walks into your office and says they are moving to California. Do you say "yippee!" or would you be sad to see them go?

If you feel relieved they are leaving, they are clearly not the best person for the job. To avoid making bad hires, Goltz said he developed a hiring strategy he calls the BATH test, Here's how it works:

> *"B" is for buy into your concept.* Tell prospective employees what your company is all about. You want to fit square pegs into square holes.
> *"A" is for ability.* Find people who have done this job or something similar.

"T" is for being a team player. Hire people who will tell you what is on their mind. You can spend your whole life playing psychoanalyst with your employees—and it's a waste of time.

"H" is for hungry. "I need people who are hungry and want to work," says Goltz.

After implementing the BATH system, Goltz said his turnover rate dropped to 10 percent. He has another great idea:

Set up a group interview. Bring in several job applicants at once to tell them about your business. Take a coffee break. Don't be surprised if some folks disappear. But it's better to scare off the losers before you hire them.

GREAT 143 IDEA Perform a Personnel Checkup

You get regular medical and dental checkups, right? So how about giving your business a personnel checkup? The reason: Every year, thousands of unhappily terminated employees sue their former employers. Their complaints, justified or not, cost small business owners millions of dollars in legal fees, emotional distress, and lost productivity.

There are so many complex regulations on the books that it's tough to keep up.

As her fast-growing public relations firm approached 50 employees, Ellen LaNicca, former president and cofounder of Patrice Tanaka & Co., felt she needed expert help. Many state and federal employee regulations kick in at the 50-employee level, and she wanted to be sure she was in full compliance.

LaNicca turned to Peter Skeie, an attorney and cofounder of The Personnel Department Inc., to sort through the morass of laws she had to deal with. Skeie and his colleague, Craig Chatfield, left their jobs at Fortune 500 companies to set up their own human resources consulting service in New York City. (They've since closed the company, but Chatfield has a new firm: http://hrinnovations.us.)

How to Evaluate Your Hiring and Firing Policies

- Consult with an experienced labor lawyer. Ask him or her to review your job application to make sure it doesn't violate any state or federal employment laws. (For example, you can't ask a job candidate how old they are or whether they have kids.)
- Ask them to explain the steps and documentation required before you can legally terminate an employee.
- Create an employee handbook and a policy manual. Your policy manual should outline everything from the dress code to employee benefits and vacation days. Be as specific as possible to avoid confusion.
- You can buy software to create these documents or find an online solution.
- Circulate copies to everyone and require employees to acknowledge, in writing, that they have read them.
- Distribute a written policy prohibiting sexual harassment at your company. Make sure all employees read and sign a copy of the memo.
- Encourage your employees to suggest ways to boost morale and improve communication with new policies or changes to existing ones.

"Peter was part diplomat, part human resources legal counsel, and part troubleshooter," said LaNicca. "He helped us through the process of restructuring jobs and creating separation packages for employees being let go."

Skeie helped LaNicca review all the company's personnel practices, including revising the employee policy manual and job applications. "From the beginning, we wanted to have the best working environment possible," said LaNicca. In addition to providing traditional medical benefits and flexible scheduling, the firm has a meditation room to help employees "destress."

Skeie said most small businesses aren't as employee friendly as LaNicca's, but they all face similar people problems. "We realized small companies have the same employment liability as Fortune 500 companies," said Skeie. "Failure to document problems as they occur is at the top of the list," said Skeie. "It's much better to take a half-hour and document (in writing) employee problems because if you don't write them down, it's much harder to defend yourself later in court."

He said too many small business owners tolerate high levels of poor performance from employees because they don't know what to do. "Eventually, a straw breaks the camel's back, and they fire the person," said Skeie. "But then they get sued because this person, who has become accustomed to doing virtually nothing, gets fired and wants revenge."

Remember, not knowing labor law is no defense when an employer gets sued by an irate former employee.

"Another mistake made by business owners is having incomplete policies and procedures," said Skeie. "You can get in trouble if it can be proved there's been a lack of attention to employment-related issues."

Plain management misconduct is another serious problem. "Employers make stupid but innocent mistakes," he said. "They probably don't mean anything discriminatory by asking whether you are going to get married and have children, but it's against the law."

Hire a Welfare Recipient

You can complain about spending your tax dollars on welfare, or you can do something about it by offering an entry-level job to one person on the public dole.

With training programs and support in the form of public transportation vouchers or help with child care, thousands of welfare recipients are joining the working class—some for the first time in their lives. You might think your business is too small to give someone on welfare a chance, but in today's tight job market, you can find untapped talent—as well as do a good deed.

My dad, Marty Weisman, left Max Factor, where he ran the research lab, when Max Factor was acquired by another company and moved its operations to the east coast. As one of the top cosmetic chemists in the country, my dad eventually opened Sher-Mar Corp., a boutique nail products company. Needing help, he hired two brothers; one was a recovering drug addict, and the other was on and off welfare. I was surprised when he hired them, but I respected him, too.

They were so grateful for a chance to work, they turned out to be tremendously loyal employees. Sure, they had their share of personal problems through the years, but most days they worked really hard, mixing flammable chemicals to make nail polish and remover and loading 55-gallon drums on trucks.

My dad became a surrogate father to them, listening to their problems and offering advice. By treating them with respect and expecting them to meet high standards, he helped them get their lives back together. One brother eventually got married and had a son.

Don't rule out hiring people with challenges. Everyone deserves a second chance. If you are open to hiring a disadvantaged worker, there are a variety of state, local, and federal programs available to help business owners hire them. Most welfare recipients are required to work in order to qualify for state benefits. For information, visit www.opm.gov/wtw/.

GREAT 145 IDEA

Hire Ex-Cons

While serving 10 years in prison for burglary, Roy Torres had plenty of time to think about his future. "When I was doing my time, I started reading about everything going green."

In 2009, shortly after his release, he found a flyer advertising a "green career" program sponsored by the Osborne Association in the South Bronx.

"I made the call, took the placement test, and did well," said Torres, who worked as an electrician before he admits falling in "with the wrong crowd."

Funded by $2 million in federal stimulus money distributed by the state of New York, the Green Career Center (www.greencareercenter.org) provides ex-convicts with two weeks of computer and career development skills, followed by four weeks of skills training.

It opened in the spring of 2010. By the fall, 105 people had participated in training programs and 67 graduated, according to John Valverde, director of the center. "Our program gives business owners a chance to hire someone and decide if they want to keep them on a full-time basis," said Valverde. "We feel strongly that our graduates can compete with anyone that's out there looking for a job."

He said many participants learn a trade in prison, but lack the computer and social skills needed to land a good-paying job in the real world.

So far, dozens of small businesses have hired graduates of the program. About 20 percent of the graduates qualify for wage subsidies, which reimburses employers up to $9 an hour for three months. Many states offer wage subsidy programs to encourage companies to hire disadvantaged workers, so check with your state's labor or employment development department.

"I have had great success with Osborne graduates, and I encourage other employers to give them a try," said Frank Cruz, president of Direct Environmental Corporation (DEC), based in the Bronx. The company sells the Big Belly solar-powered trash compactor, designed for residential and commercial buildings.

"Most of the people who have served time are good people who don't want to ever seen the inside of jail cell again, but they can't find a job."

Since being hired by Cruz, Green Center graduate Roy Torres gets up at 4 AM to make a 90-minute commute via subway from Brooklyn to the Bronx to work at DEC.

"The people at Big Belly know about my past," said Torres. "They are courteous and a great bunch of people. It's the first time in 10 years that I've really felt great."

Torres said he's making a living wage and "likes the idea of saving the planet and being connected with something green."

Meanwhile, Cruz admits he was nervous about hiring ex-cons, but was impressed with Osborne's training and screening services. "There was an occasional disappointment but nothing terrible, just a bad attitude," said

Cruz. "It's tough for people who have been incarcerated a long time to open their hearts and trust people enough to let them help you."

Telecommuting as an Option

Telecommuting benefits workers and employers, but only if it's handled right. Telecommuting can boost the productivity of workers who are independent self-starters. Motivated employees who live far from their offices can accomplish more by eliminating a long and stressful commute. But some people just don't have the discipline to work outside of a structured environment.

Here are some tips to consider:

- Determine whether the work can be done well offsite. If the person is responsible for writing proposals or crunching numbers all day, telecommuting may be a viable option. If he or she is managing a team of salespeople making cold calls, it probably won't work.
- Figure out what technology, software, and furniture you'll need to buy for your remote workers and whether it's worth the investment.
- Determine which of your employees are best suited to working at home. In many cases, employees ask to telecommute in order to spend time with their young children, drive the car pool, or to care for a sick relative. Expect them to keep up with their work and meet deadlines in exchange for offering them a flexible work schedule.
- Set up a probationary period to see if telecommuting works. Begin with one or two days a week—this gives you a chance to work out the kinks. Be sure to tell your telecommuters that working at home is conditional and can end at any time.
- Make sure telecommuters keep company files and information confidential and safe.
- Stay home and telecommute at least one day a week yourself. Many busy business owners and managers I know do this to save travel time and focus on important projects.

Tailor Benefits to Employees' Needs

One size definitely does not fit all when it comes to offering employee benefits. Every company has a distinct group of employees with varying personal lives, professional goals, and priorities.

While big companies may offer the same insurance benefits and options to everyone, small companies have an advantage in being able to tailor benefits to their employees' specific needs. In many cases, your employees are covered by their spouses' insurance benefits, and you won't need to duplicate coverage.

If your business is really small, consider giving each employee a fixed amount of money each month that they can use to buy a particular benefit. A single person may want dental insurance, but a young mother might prefer that you help pay for child care. Another employee might want legal insurance if they have legal problems relating to property or investments.

There is a wide array of insurance benefits and programs available to employers. One option is to hire a benefits consultant to help create a "cafeteria" program of benefits to fit your employees' needs. You'll also need professional help to figure out whether to pay for employee benefits with pretax or after-tax dollars.

Basically, as long as you spend the same amount of money on each employee, you'll stay out of trouble. Even $150 a month can help pay for a single person's coverage in a health maintenance organization (HMO) or other group insurance program.

Remember, some of the best benefits you can offer employees may not cost you much money at all. Flexible scheduling is one of the ways small business owners can retain good workers and boost morale. It doesn't cost you any more money to stagger work hours to fit your employees' needs.

If a valuable employee needs to be home when their children get home from school, why not let them work from 6 AM to 2 PM? This works especially well if you are a West Coast company dealing with East Coast clients. Job sharing is another perk to consider. Often, two working mothers or fathers will ask to split a job and split the benefits that go with that job.

148

Offer Classes in English as a Second Language

Many successful entrepreneurs offer free, onsite English as a second language (ESL) classes to employees. When David Giuliani was president of the Optiva Corporation, he faced a major challenge at his fast-growing toothbrush company: his employees spoke 15 different languages.

That's why he decided to offer English as a second language classes at work. "Taking good care of employees is required for good business," Giuliani told me. (He's now CEO and cofounder of Pacific Bioscience Laboratories.)

Through the years, scores of employees took advantage of the free classes. Their improved English skills led to improved productivity and better communication throughout the company.

Marsha Serlin, CEO of United Scrap Metal in Chicago, also provided onsite ESL classes to the mostly Spanish-speaking workers at her recycling business.

"Many of my workers, who started here with nothing a few years ago, are now able to buy their own homes," she said.

If you think your multilingual workforce would benefit from ESL classes, call your local community college or continuing education program to find out how much it will cost. You can hire a private teacher to teach classes at the office, too.

149

Find Out How Disney Does It

No one is surprised when an entrepreneur heads to Harvard, New York University, or the University of Southern California (USC) for a management training program, but eyebrows raise when they sign up for a course at the Disney Institute in Orlando, Florida.

More than 60,000 people a year attend these classes, which offer a behind-the-scenes look at the Disney management philosophy. In recent years, small business owners with fewer than 50 employees represented 44 percent of attendees, say Disney officials.

"Walt Disney was probably one of the premier entrepreneurs of all time," said Valerie Oberle, former vice president of Disney University Professional Development Programs. In fact, Disney started the company in a garage, with next to no cash.

Oberle, who now runs her own firm, the Oberle Group, said Disney began sharing its management philosophy after the company was profiled in Tom Peters's best-selling book, *In Search of Excellence* (Warner Books, 1988). From that point on, she said, business owners and managers were eager to find out how Disney managed the 40,000 people in its Florida parks alone.

The courses on leadership, management, orientation, and quality service feature Disney characters. Lamar Berry, chairman of New Orleans–based International Marketing Systems, said he's sent hundreds of clients a year to Disney University. "There is a tremendous benefit to going to an icon and seeing how that culture is maintained," said Berry.

To learn more about the Disney Institute, visit their web site: www.disneyinstitute.com.

Other entrepreneurial management programs to consider:

- *Harvard Business School's Owner/President Management Program.* This nine-week full-time residential program consists of 3 three-week segments. Participants take one session a year for three years. For information, contact the Harvard Business School at 800-HBS-5577 or visit www.exed.hbs.edu/.
- *New York University, Stern School of Business: Executive Development Programs.* Web site: www.stern.nyu.edu/Executive/index.htm.
- *University of Southern California Marshall School of Business, Executive Development.* For information, check out www.marshall.usc.edu/execdev.
- *University of California, Los Angeles.* For more information about the Executive MBA (EMBA) Program at UCLA Anderson School of Management, visit www.anderson.ucla.edu/x24273.xml.

Ask Your Best Clients to Meet Key Job Candidates

Before hiring a key employee, such as a new sales or account manager, marketing chief, graphic designer, or even an executive assistant, consider introducing your top candidates to your best clients or customers.

This serves several important purposes. First of all, it gives the prospective employee an opportunity to meet your most important clients. It emphasizes the client relationship by involving them in the hiring process. It also gives you the benefit of another expert opinion on your candidate. Keep it informal. Don't make a big deal about the meeting. If you can, leave them alone for a few minutes, so they can speak privately. Give them enough time to form an impression of each other.

There are some risks involved with this courtesy call. If your client feels negative about the person, and you end up hiring him or her, the new employee will have to work extra hard to build the relationship. On the flip side, if your client is very impressed, you might risk losing that person to the client at some point. But I believe the risks are worth it.

If you are looking for a high-level executive for your company, here are some tips from Gregory Winfield, president, Greater Richmond Partnership:

- *Make certain the executive is not a dyed-in-the-wool corporate player.* Those spoiled by the trappings of a huge support staff and a battalion of secretaries may resent having to roll up their sleeves and write a marketing plan.
- *Look for decisive individuals capable of making choices without the support of committees.* The bureaucratic gamesmanship that goes with the turf in a giant corporation cannot be tolerated in smaller firms where speed and agility are vital.
- *Seek executives with an entrepreneurial flair.* Managers who have worked for other small companies are more likely to have the right skills. An ideal candidate will relish the opportunity to net a large bonus, but accept the risk of no bonus at all.

- *Don't hire an entrepreneur on the rebound from a failed venture.* Why would you take that risk?
- *Look for someone who is not looking for a job.* Offer a salary and benefits package attractive enough to lure someone away from a successful company.
- *Be wary of the "small business is a family affair" syndrome.* Although hiring relatives may be a kind gesture, only do it if they are really the most qualified person for the job.
- *Look for those who lead by example rather than by force.* Check references to make sure the person has been successful at a company your size.
- *Ask business associates for referrals.* Use all of your contacts to find good candidates.

GREAT IDEA 151

Hire an Experienced Labor Attorney

"You will be assaulted, abused, or sued by an employee; it's only a question of when and how," declared Robert Millman, a feisty labor attorney who now serves as chairman of the board of Littler Mendelson in Los Angeles.

"Small business owners, in particular, are being hit very hard by employment laws, even if they only have five employees," said Millman, who has been defending and protecting companies from their angry, derisive employees for more than 30 years.

Business owners eagerly buy liability insurance to protect themselves from fires and floods, yet they don't spend time or money getting up to speed on employment laws. "The most dangerous thing you face in your small business is not a fire or your truck driver wiping out a family of six," he said. "The most dangerous thing is one of your employees suing you."

Although an employment liability insurance policy can prevent a lengthy legal battle from bankrupting your firm, you usually don't get to choose your own lawyers to represent you. And the policy may not cover all costs. (See Great Idea #47 about working with an independent insurance broker.)

Millman said far too many small business owners get terrible legal advice and end up spending $500,000 on a case that should have settled for $10,000. Most of the time the bad advice comes from attorneys who want to run up their bills.

His firm, with about 750 attorneys across the country, was a pioneer in training and education for employers. He said the scariest issue is workplace violence because you are liable if someone hurts or kills someone else at your business.

"There are so many telltale signs," said Millman, adding that good employees rarely show up one day for work and go berserk. There is always a pattern of negative behavior and clear signals that employers must learn to spot. "A company is going to face severe liability if someone is sending out signals, and they don't do something about it," warned Millman.

Contact Littler Mendelson at www.littler.com, (888) LITTLER [(888) 548-8537], or e-mail them at info@littler.com.

GREAT

152

IDEA

Hire an Interim Executive

Small companies are hiring more temporary executives with specific skills. In fact, professionals represent about 25 percent of the total interim workforce.

"With temporary staffing, you get a level of executive you may not be able to afford long term," said a spokesman for the American Staffing Association in Alexandria, Virginia.

Temporary staffing companies can find you a secretary or find a skilled executive to meet any business challenge. Another benefit: the staffing company handles all the employee-related paperwork, benefits, and payroll taxes.

With thousands of skilled executives tossed into the labor pool by downsizing during the Great Recession, executive temps often have between 15 and 30 years' experience in their industry.

"Small businesses may need a professional with very specific skills or experience—a financial strategist, a marketing consultant, or someone who has taken a company public," said Marilou Myrick, former president and CEO of Pro Resource Inc., a staffing company in Cleveland. Myrick, who now works as an executive coach, said you should be prepared to pay thousands of dollars a week for a temporary executive.

Hiring someone on a temporary basis is a good way to see how they fit into the mix.

Is Hiring an Interim Executive Right for You?

Interim executives work best for companies in transition. If your business is growing or shrinking, relocating, or launching a new product line, you may want to hire a high-level executive on a short-term basis.

- What specific duties and responsibilities can I turn over to a hired gun?
- Will hiring a temporary executive make my life easier and free me to do more important work?
- What specific skills should the interim executive have?
- Can I find an agency that specializes in finding interim executives for my industry?
- What is my budget for hiring an interim executive?
- How will I check the candidate's references?
- Does the work need doing have a beginning, middle, and end?
- What kind of a contract will I have to sign to hire this person?

One caution: Be sure to prepare your permanent staff before the arrival of a new temporary manager or director. Explain exactly what the new person will be doing and how long you expect them to be on board.

GREAT 153 IDEA

Train Your Employees

Investing in training and education pays off big for you and your employees. For a modest sum, your employees can learn new skills, build confidence, and boost productivity. Subsequently, you and your business benefit from happier, healthier, and more energetic workers.

First, determine what skills they need to improve. If you are doing business overseas, maybe key employees should study a foreign language.

Would signing up for a weekly yoga or tai chi class relieve stress? Would learning a new design or financial spreadsheet program might make their work life easier?

An easy way to get started is to assign someone on your staff to go online and do the research. Review class schedules from local community colleges, extension programs, the Learning Annex, Learning Tree University, and other adult education programs in your area.

Figure out how much you want to spend on a quarterly, semiannual, and annual basis. If money is tight, you might provide a one-time $100 bonus to pay for books and materials. If you can afford it, reward your key managers with a daylong seminar of their choice.

Remember, if you decide to offer training as a perk, be fair, and don't play favorites. You can establish a policy that makes these educational options available after six months or a year of employment. Keep track of who is taking which classes and encourage people to share their experiences and knowledge with coworkers.

An alternative to sending workers offsite for educational programs is to hire your own trainers. Another option is to hire a trainer and split the cost with other small business owners whose employees also need training.

Offer Employees the Right Incentives

If you think glitzy trips to Atlantic City or Las Vegas are great motivators for your employees, think again. When offered the choice between a trip or money, 44 percent of the employees polled preferred the financial reward, while 39 percent said they would take a trip by themselves or with a family member.

Only 5 percent would choose to take a trip with coworkers, according to a survey commissioned by American Express Gift Cheques, Amex's gift certificate division.

A $50 gift certificate was preferred by a four-to-one margin over any other type of monetary appreciation, the survey also found. Only 14 percent of respondents preferred $50 worth of tickets to a concert, show, or sporting event, and fewer than 1 in 10 wanted to be treated to a lunch worth $50. But cash rewards, in the long run, may not be enough to keep employees satisfied.

"Money is a powerful incentive, but it has its limitations if it's the only incentive," said Dr. Barrie Greiff, a psychiatrist and consultant at Harvard University Health Services in Cambridge, Massachusetts.

Greiff said if you prefer to give a monetary reward, try a gift certificate, because cash is "just spent at the supermarket." Greiff said taking time to express your appreciation for a job well done means a lot more than money to many employees.

He said many employers are reluctant to express their feelings to employees, whether they are positive or negative. "It takes a certain degree of skill and candidness—and people are uncomfortable being candid," said Greiff.

"You want to create a profile of incentives," said Greiff. "You want to give employees an interesting work environment, a talented team, opportunities to stretch and grow, and adequate vacation time."

He said it's important to take time to improve communication with employees. "You have to take the pulse of the organization," he advises, recalling that one of his clients was in shock after losing four key employees at his 12-person firm.

They left with most of the clients because they felt they could do a better job serving clients themselves. The owner was disheartened, but decided not to take legal action and, instead, just pick up the pieces and move on.

He favors what he calls "360-degree communication." Twice a year, you should evaluate employees and let them evaluate you as the boss (see Great Idea #21). "If the ultimate goal is to improve the performance of the company, then feedback is a valuable tool," Greiff said.

How to Deal with Domestic Violence

What would you do if your sales manager walked into work one morning with a black eye? What do you say when your secretary shows up with a split lip and puffy, swollen eyes? Do you ask what happened? Do you pretend nothing is wrong?

A battered employee is impossible to ignore. No one likes to invade an employee's privacy, but too often domestic violence adversely affects you and your business. Smaller businesses, which usually operate more like a close-knit family, are profoundly affected when an employee is in trouble.

Chances are that at some point, you will experience the devastating effects of domestic violence. Every year, about one million women are attacked by someone they know. And according to a report by the U.S. Department of Labor's Women's Bureau, battered women can't help bringing their problems with them to the office.

A recent study of women who are victims of domestic violence found that 96 percent experienced some problems at work. More than 60 percent were late for work; 70 percent reported having a tough time concentrating on their tasks. A distracted or unmotivated employee poses a personnel problem, but a battered and emotionally overwrought employee can turn into an emotional and financial disaster.

While corporations have formal employee assistance programs, small business owners, who can't even afford basic insurance benefits, rarely have such programs in place. In fact, only 15 percent of small businesses offer some sort of employee assistance program, according to the Bureau of Labor Statistics. But you obviously have to do something when an injured or emotionally upset employee appears at your office door.

The first step may be to provide basic medical care at a local clinic. Referring the employee to a social service agency that provides counseling on a sliding-scale basis may also be a short-term solution. As an employer, you have to be careful not to cross the line and demand the details, but being truly compassionate rarely gets anyone in trouble. In many cases, a battered spouse feels safe only at work, so your place of business becomes her only haven.

Troubled employees rarely leave their problems at home. You may have to deal with coworkers' fear and be forced to increase security. If coworkers are afraid of the batterer, it can turn into a sensitive company-wide problem, especially if people know the husband or boyfriend. (Most domestic violence cases involve men battering women, but there are definitely women who physically abuse their husbands—and lovers.)

In many states, including California, employers can seek a temporary restraining order on behalf of an employee if the person has been threatened with violence that could take place at work. This provision, in a piece of pioneering legislation, is part of the Workplace Violence Safety Act. Look into the laws that apply in your state.

If domestic violence is affecting your business, don't be an ostrich—deal with it.

Here are some available resources:

- You can contact the Family Violence Prevention Fund at 383 Rhode Island St., Suite 304, San Francisco, CA 94103-5133; (415) 252-8900; www.endabuse.org.
- The U.S. Department of Justice has a special office set up to deal with violence against women: Office on Violence Against Women, 145 N Street NE, Washington, DC 20530; www.ovw.usdoj.gov.
- The Occupational Safety and Health Administration (OSHA) also deals with workplace violence of all kinds: 200 Constitution Ave., NW, Washington, DC 20210; (800) 321-OSHA (6742); www.osha.gov.
- Legal Momentum: The Women's Legal Defense and Education Fund, 395 Hudson Street, New York, NY 10014; (212) 925-6635; www.legalmomentum.org.
- The National Domestic Violence Hotline operates a 24-hour, toll-free national domestic violence hotline [(800) 799-SAFE], providing counseling and referrals to a variety of services including medical care and shelters; www.thehotline.org.

Coping with Mental Illness at Work

Depression affects one in four American adults, so it is not unlikely that you will have to deal with a depressed worker. The indirect cost of dealing with depression and other mental illness is about $79 billion a year, according to the National Institute of Mental Health.

The Americans with Disabilities Act prohibits employers from discriminating against employees with psychiatric problems if they have the skills to perform the essential functions of the job. If they can do the job, but still need "reasonable accommodations," as specified by the ADA, what can you do?

Some reasonable accommodations include restructuring the job, modifying schedules, revising training materials, or providing assistance. If an employee needs to see a counselor during business hours, you should let them take time off. If you don't have a formal employee assistance program, you, as the business owner, will have to figure out what makes sense.

The good news is that between 70 and 90 percent of people with a mental illness can function with medication, talk therapy, and other support, according to the National Alliance on Mental Illness.

GREAT
156
IDEA

Be Serious about Your Sexual Harassment Policy

Sexual harassment is serious business. That's why even the smallest company should have a written policy in place. According to federal regulations, a company is responsible for sexual harassment in the workplace "where the employer (or its agents or supervisory employees) knows or should have known of the conduct."

If you think telling sexual jokes or touching employees is funny, it's not. Of all working women, 40 to 60 percent have reported being subjected to some sort of sexual harassment on the job, according to the American Psychological Association.

Complaints from employees should never be taken lightly or dismissed. The last thing you need is an expensive and time-consuming lawsuit.

Here are some tips to avoid problems:

- Draft and distribute a clear policy prohibiting sexual harassment at your company. Ask employees to acknowledge in writing that they have read it and understand the ramifications of violating it.
- Document all sexual harassment complaints in writing. Create a paper trail that contains details of the alleged event and how you handled it.
- Question any witnesses to the alleged event and document their account.
- Consult an experienced attorney before your employee threatens to file a formal complaint.
- Remember, under federal law, an employer is automatically liable for an employee's behavior in the workplace, unless you can prove that you created and distributed a policy prohibiting sexual harassment.

GREAT
157
IDEA

Rely on Temps and Freelancers

Talented people, especially in the high-tech arena, are fielding multiple job offers. In a seller's market, top people demand high salaries, incredible benefits, and perks. Big companies can afford to woo them, but what can you do to compete for talent?

Don't despair. There are millions of terrific people who, for one reason or another, prefer to work for a variety of firms. So they register with temporary agencies or employee leasing firms. Temping also has a strong appeal to people who are between jobs or people who just need a fresh start after a bad work experience, maternity leave, or a move across country.

Unlike the strictly clerical or secretarial agencies of the past, modern temp agencies attract top talent and frequently specialize in specific industries. There are agencies that place accountants, chief financial officers (CFOs), software engineers, marketing executives, construction managers, graphic designers, and medical doctors. No matter what kind of work you require, you can find a temporary worker to fit the bill (see Great Idea #158).

In fact, temporary workers in the labor force have increased to 10 percent from 8 percent five years ago.

Christopher Dwyer of Aberdeen Group believes such workers will increase to 25 percent by 2011.

As of October 2010, the Bureau of Labor Statistics reported the number of workers placed by temporary-staffing agencies rose to 404,000, making up 68 percent of the 593,000 jobs added by private employers.

The Department of Health and Human Services estimates the average manager spends about 15 percent of his or her time on employee-related administrative tasks.

"Hiring an agency is a cost-effective way to manage a workforce," said Kim Shoemaker, CEO of Aclouché Inc. in Columbus, Ohio. "The staffing company ensures that all government mandates are met."

Temps are on the agency's payroll. Best of all, if they aren't working out, just call the agency and they will be quickly replaced—usually on the same day.

If you hire dozens of workers, most employment agencies will set up an office onsite, according to Shoemaker. She said having a clear job description to present to the temporary staffing agency is critical. You also need to specify the hours of employment, the duration, and whether you want the applicant to be tested for any skills.

"Since we are the employer of record, we handle everything from verifying the hours worked to running the payroll," said Shoemaker.

If you need more short-term or project-oriented help, consider working with a company like Elance.com.

GREAT

158

IDEA

Work with a Virtual Talent Agency

Every week, Grover Righter, CEO of Aftertising.com, works with two or three people he's never met. "It's the modernization of work," said Righter, founder of the small San Francisco-based firm, which enhances the impact of online advertising.

He relies on Elance.com, a leading virtual talent agency, to find freelance programmers and market researchers to hire by the hour or the project. He monitors their work online and pays them through an escrow account using a credit card.

"We could never hire all the skills we need without Elance.com," said Righter, who has spent about $60,000 in the past two years on talent he's found through the site. He said Elance's systems and procedures to track work flow are so good, his full-time staff has adopted them for in-house projects.

That's great news for Elance.com founder, Fabio Rosati. In 2000, Rosati was working for a big consulting firm when he was recruited by venture capitalists funding an online talent agency. When he took the helm in 2001, the tech bubble had burst and the company was floundering.

Under his leadership, Elance.com built enterprise software to help big companies like GE and American Express manage $10 billion worth of vendor relationships.

"When the company was sold in 2006, we didn't sell a tiny web site with a very loyal following of small business users," said Rosati. "I tried to understand what they liked about it and came away convinced that small businesses needed flexibility and access to talent. The Internet was an amazing way for an entrepreneur in the Midwest or a worker in Minnesota to overcome geographic disadvantages."

Elance.com relaunched in 2007 with a focus on helping small business owners find great talent. In the past two years, more than 400,000 projects have been posted. About 70 percent of jobs are related to information technology or marketing.

The company has about one million profiles, with about 295,000 active users, who are either performing or contracting for work.

"Just like cloud computing, there is something called the 'human cloud,'" said CEO Fabio Rosati. "It means a business can tap into a whole network of people."

He said employers are attracted to the concept because everyone on Elance has to pass a verification test and, if necessary, a variety of skills tests. The company provides about 400 skills tests and can publish scores for potential employers to view.

Here's how Elance.com works: Once a freelancer registers and passes the online verification test, the system asks them to specify their skills and the rate they want to be paid for work. The software automatically marks it up by 8.75 percent before posting the information. That 8.75 fee includes 2 percent paid to the credit card company for processing and 6 percent paid to Elance.com.

Having a payment process in place is great for freelancers, especially since 40 percent of freelance jobs go unpaid, according to a Freelancer Union survey.

"If you do hourly work, we collect on a weekly basis," said Rosati. Funds are wired into the provider's account. The company also issues 1099 independent contractor forms required by the IRS. The company is now looking into handling W2 forms for part-timers who are considered employees. (Elance limits access to the site to U.S. residents who file a W9 form.)

Practicing what he preaches, Rosati said Elance.com follows a 30/70 model, which means 30 percent of the staff is full time and 70 percent are "elancers."

He said brick-and-mortar clients are also finding talent on Elance.com. "One of my favorite is a restaurant, Elevation Burger, based in Arlington, Virginia. They supplement their local team with freelance marketing resources," said Rosati. "They also found a thermal engineer to design a new type of grill and a patent attorney."

Meanwhile, Rosati is happy with the way things are going. "Our future looks very, very bright," he said. "We are finally making money and growing."

GREAT 159 IDEA

Send Gifts to an Employee's Spouse

Dr. Allan Weis, president and managing director of Advanced Network & Services, Inc., is recognized as one of the developers of the technical backbone of the Internet. Over the years, he's founded several small, high-tech companies, which demand a lot of their employees.

I met Dr. Allan Weis a few years ago when we were part of a traveling faculty hired by IBM to speak at entrepreneurial events around the country. He shared a great idea to keep employees happy, especially when they are working long hours on complex, technical projects.

One of his morale boosters is to send a bouquet of fresh flowers to the spouses of busy employees as a special thank-you gesture. "I never send roses," said Weis. "That's too emotional." He said the flowers serve several purposes: They cheer up the upset spouse and show his appreciation for the extra effort put in by his staff.

Sending pizza or a meal to a busy employee's home is also a great idea. Show your appreciation for the sacrifices they are making.

Time and Personal Management Ideas

7

· ·

Successful entrepreneurs work incredibly long hours, so it's important to make the most of every minute.

Achieving a balance between work and life isn't as difficult as you think. The secret is to be organized, set priorities, and relentlessly delegate mundane tasks.

You must set boundaries to protect your time and space. If you have to meet a deadline, shut your door. Don't be so accessible. In fact, some of the most successful people in the world, including Warren Buffett, *don't* carry a mobile phone. Think about that.

The phone is an electronic tether. But you can prevent it from strangling you. One way to reduce phone tag is to schedule important calls. A scheduled call has another advantage: it gives you time to prepare for the conversation.

Unless you are under 18, avoid using text messages to conduct business. Text an address or contact information, but don't send confidential information.

I'm convinced e-mail hampers, rather than boosts productivity. I promise if you try checking e-mail on a schedule rather than throughout the day, you will have more time to work.

Unless you are an emergency room physician, brain surgeon, or national security adviser, there is no reason to be online all the time. Not too long ago, business was conducted via letters and memos. The fax machine speeded things up. If something was extremely urgent, we sent documents via an overnight service. So when did people start expecting a response within seconds?

I believe we make really bad decisions because we don't think before responding to e-mail.

If you really want to improve personal productivity, set daily priorities. Focus on the tasks that only *you* can perform. We all can fill up a day with nonessential tasks, but why?

In the past, every boss had a secretary or an assistant. With cost cutting and the advent personal computers and e-mail, business owners started doing everything themselves. No wonder productivity plummeted and blood pressure spiked.

If it's possible to hire an assistant, even for a few hours a week, do it. My incredible research assistant is virtual. Mavis lives in Virginia and I live in Vermont, but through the magic of e-mail and phone, we communicate well.

She managed my interview schedule and conducted much of the research for this book. I couldn't have done it without her help.

If your assistant works in your office, empower him or her to keep the space around you clear. You need to be protected from interruptions so you can concentrate on your work.

Delegating is tough. Business owners tend to be control freaks and have a tough time letting go. I admit, it took me years to stop micromanaging projects I assigned to freelance consultants or employees. I wasted everyone's time by peering over shoulders and second-guessing their work. I finally learned that asking for periodic progress reports builds trust as long as you set reasonable deadlines and hold people accountable.

In addition to practical time management strategies, this chapter features some great ideas for managing your life and time. We have to deal with issues affecting both work and home because when you own a company, you *are* the business.

GREAT

160

IDEA

Get Organized—Right Now

The best way to maximize every minute is to be well-organized. If you are one of those people who insist you work better surrounded by chaos, stop fooling yourself.

To prove my point, try tracking the minutes you spend hunting around for misplaced files or documents, either physical or digital. You'll be shocked at how much time and money your messy office is costing you. Hiring a professional organizer is one option, but prepare to pay between $50 and $150 an hour.

Okay, stop feeling guilty and try these tips for digging out:

- *Schedule a weekend or two to clean up your office.* If necessary, pay employees overtime or hire temporary workers and a cleaning crew to tackle the mess. Put yourself in a good mood by playing your favorite rock 'n roll or dance music. Buy plenty of healthy snacks, junk food, soft drinks, cleaning supplies, and lots of big trash bags.
- *Take everything off your desk and put things on the floor for sorting and tossing.* With a trash can nearby, tackle the piles. Toss what you don't need, and store or distribute everything else. If you can't decide what to do with something, throw it away.
- *Assign someone to review saved magazines and newspapers.* Ask them to tear out articles of interest. Recycle the rest. (See Great Idea #161 on appointing a personal information officer.)
- *It's a big job, but try to toss out old files in your filing cabinets.* Ask your employees to do the same. Be ruthless. You don't need paper copies of digital files as long as you back everything up on a USB drive or store critical data offsite.
- *Remember, your desk is a workspace, not an exhibit area.* Clear off all the plants, family pictures, toys, and gadgets. If you want to have a few photos, buy a digital picture frame, pin them to a cork board or hang them on the wall.
- *Once you've dumped the trash, figure out what nifty supplies will help you stay organized.* Everyone has a different style of organization. Wander around a big office-supply store. (Don't shop online.) Do you want to hang project files on the wall? Would colored files help you keep better track of projects? (I use green folders for contracts and invoices since green means money.) Keep active files in a stand-up rack near or on your desk.
- *Sort through your piles of business cards.* Throw out ones from people you don't plan to contact again. Depending on your work style, put the cards into a business card album or Rolodex in alphabetical order or scan them into a business card database.

- *Find a calendar that works for you.* I keep a big monthly calendar on my desk and carry a smaller, spiral-bound calendar when I travel. I note scheduled calls and meetings in both the calendar and in my phone. Figure out what works best for you.
- *Here's a great idea:* Even if you rely completely on an electronic calendar, every morning list important appointments and phone numbers on a small index card. Index cards are cheap and easy organizing tools. They are easy to carry and don't crash like a computer. Save the cards if you want to keep a record of what you did on a particular day.
- *Now that you've cleaned up your office, try to keep it neat.* Ask your assistant or an intern to sort the mail into categories: bills, personal letters, marketing materials, and so on. Stand over a trash can and toss out the junk mail so it never makes it into the house or office. Try online banking to expedite bill paying. Store paper invoices in a file and note when to pay them.
- *Set aside an hour or two every day to make and return calls.* Scheduled phone calls save time and reduce stress. If you are busy working, let calls go to voice mail. If you are on a deadline to finish a project, turn off the ringer and put your mobile phone in another room. Then, get to work.
- *Promise to stay organized for at least a month.* Then take it one day at a time.

Mobile Phone Apps to Keep Track of Your Time

If you need to keep track of billable hours, here are some cool apps for your smartphone:

Timewerks (sorth.com/timeworks) is a $9.99 app for iPhone, iPod Touch, and iPad that lets you track time and generate invoices. It can also integrate with an app to process credit cards.

Minute 7 (minute7.com) works on all major platforms and costs about $4 per user, per month. It is a cloud-based software-as-service app for QuickBooks users.

TimeDroid (appoxy.com) is a free Android app that works with FreshBooks.

GREAT **161** IDEA

Appoint a Personal Information Officer

Many business owners suffer from information overload. With so much to do, it's difficult to keep up with all the blogs, books, magazines, and professional journals you know you should be reading or at least skimming. One solution is to ask your assistant or another staff person or freelancer to serve as your "personal information officer," or PIO.

Your PIO benefits by being well informed, while you save time by reading only the most pertinent material. Before a trip, I print out articles to read on the bus, train, or plane.

First, decide which magazines, newspapers, and web sites provide valuable information and insights for your particular business. I read the *Christian Science Monitor*'s weekly edition to keep up with global news. Subscribe to your industry's top trade journal or e-newsletter. Bookmark favorite web sites for easy access.

Set up Google Alerts to track news affecting your industry (and your own company). Urge your PIO to be selective. While your PIO's job is to update your "To Read" file frequently, your job is to go through it at least once a week. Every night, I try to read a few business magazines (*Bloomberg Businessweek* and *Entrepreneur*) before relaxing with *O Magazine, Country Living,* or *Self.*

It's easy to keep up with the news via podcasts from Bloomberg Radio or National Public Radio. The *New York Times* daily e-news roundup is also invaluable, even if you just scan the headlines.

I truly believe that a lack of information, not a lack of money, leads to business failure.

GREAT **162** IDEA

Plan "In" Days and "Out" Days

As my business flourished and life became more demanding, I really needed a way to structure my weekly schedule.

I came up with this great idea when I was working out of my home office in Sun Valley, California, a suburb of Los Angeles. Because L.A.

traffic is such a nightmare, trying to make it to one meeting across the city meant I would be out most of the day.

About five years ago, we moved to Sharon, Vermont, from New York. We live in a former summer camp on 440 acres located about 15 to 20 miles from civilization, if you consider Hanover, New Hampshire, civilization. Similar to Los Angeles, you need several hours to get to and from an appointment.

To maximize productivity, I schedule "in" days and "out" days. Here's how it works: on my "in" days, I don't leave the office, except perhaps to mail a letter at the post office or pick up milk at the Sharon Trading Post—a six-mile round-trip. I spend "in" days writing my various columns, marketing materials, or proposals, returning calls, handling financial matters and paperwork.

On my "out" days, I stay out from morning until night. I schedule back-to-back appointments, often ending the day by joining a friend for dinner and a movie in town. During the day, I check e-mail wherever I am, thanks to free public wi-fi, or on my smartphone.

Try this system and let me know if it works for you.

Beat Your Deadlines

I collected this great idea during a brainstorming session with a group of business owners. After setting a deadline to complete a project or proposal, move the deadline up a few days in your mind. Meeting an earlier-than-promised deadline is guaranteed to impress your clients.

This strategy sets you apart from most people, who routinely miss deadlines and beg for extensions. Setting earlier deadlines also helps avert last-minute disasters. If a computer crashes, the printer freaks out, or someone calls in sick, you won't fall behind.

I have never missed a deadline. I once produced a project via phone while suffering from the flu. In fact, I used Zazzle.com, a very cool site that offers all kinds of premiums and personalized products, to create an apron that says, "Make a Promise: Keep a Promise."

Holding yourself and your team accountable when it comes to meeting deadlines is critical to success. As a journalist, missing deadlines is just not an option. I don't recommend working while you are seriously ill, but sometimes work has to take priority.

Do the work. Then get into bed and sleep for a few days.

GREAT IDEA 164 — Spend an Hour a Day Thinking

Too many entrepreneurs lose track of what's important because they are mired in the muck of mundane tasks and to-do's. At the end of the day, you feel like you have been pecked to death by chickens and wonder what you accomplished.

No matter how busy you are, please give yourself permission to spend one hour each day *thinking*, not *doing*. I promise you will make better decisions and avoid making serious mistakes.

Devoting one hour a day to thinking or meditating can improve the quality of your life. If you can't sit still, take a walk. Try dividing your thinking time into three 20-minute segments.

Start with a walk in the morning, with or without a dog. I start my day with a series of stretches and think about what I need to accomplish. At lunchtime, eat lightly, then take a walk around the neighborhood or the mall; or, if you prefer, find a private place to take a nap. Great ideas will float around your mind before you fall asleep. At the end of your busy day, try to take another brisk walk, a jog, or a swim.

People joke about having brainstorms in the shower, but it is the perfect place to think big thoughts. When I'm soaking in the tub, I let random thoughts float through my mind.

I do my best thinking while hiking around our property. We live in a former summer camp located on several hundred acres in rural Vermont. I'm fortunate to have access to miles of scenic gravel roads and trails. Walking to and from the mailbox down the road gives me 20 minutes away from the phone and the computer.

By the time I collect the mail and inspect my garden in the spring or animal tracks in the winter snow, I'm feeling refreshed (especially in the winter, when it can be 10 degrees during January and February).

So, please move away from the phone and computer. Fresh air revives the spirit.

GREAT

165

IDEA

Five Quick Time Management Tips

Time management expert, Peter Gordon, offered me five tips to share with you.

1. *Start with the big picture.* Ask yourself what you want to accomplish, where you are trying to go, and what the most important things are for you to do. "This type of clear thinking will give you a solid foundation for goal setting, prioritizing, and establishing a clear sense of direction," said Gordon.
2. *Use one planning and organizing system.* "Consolidate your various calendars, schedules, and to-do lists into a single electronic or paper organizing system. Eliminate those floating notes and scraps of paper," said Gordon. "Add phone numbers to your contact list for quick access."
3. *Invest the time to plan each day.* "Review and prioritize your to-do list, blocking out time for the most important tasks," said Gordon.
4. *Make appointments with yourself.* Schedule time to do certain mundane tasks, especially ones you don't like to do. Gordon says this is a great way to avoid procrastination.
5. *Batch the little things.* "For maximum efficiency, batch tasks together and handle them all at once, whenever possible."

GREAT

166

IDEA

Work Hard and Play Harder

The most successful entrepreneurs I know work hard and play harder. One friend, who built a $60 million metal recycling company by working seven days a week for nine years, now jets around the world to spend long weekends in fabulous, far off places with her boyfriend.

Another friend thinks nothing of flying to Paris to do some shopping, eating, and drinking for a few days each month. "I've worked hard to build up my company for 18 years, and I deserve to play," she told me.

This work hard/play hard strategy fits the entrepreneurial lifestyle. In the start-up years, you rarely get a weekend off—and taking a real vacation is totally unthinkable. There are many personal sacrifices involved in running a business. So, when things finally do take off, it's time for you to take off.

Getting away from the office, even for a few days, is rejuvenating. Sleeping in a comfortable bed with 500-count cotton sheets, renting a red convertible, or sun-bathing on a silky beach are the perfect antidotes to entrepreneurial exhaustion. We need time to recharge our batteries.

So, cash in your frequent flyer miles for free tickets or buy a coach-class seat and upgrade to business or first class. Bring plenty of mad money and stay in a great hotel.

One weekend, I headed to Las Vegas with my friend Linda. We were treated like VIPs at the Mandalay Bay resort because she was planning to hold a conference for 2,500 people there. We were invited to a fabulous Italian dinner and attended the backstage, VIP party before the Jimmy Buffett concert. We enjoyed amazing spa treatments before heading out to see Cher perform.

Oh, did I mention we were chauffeured everywhere in a bronze-colored limousine? We definitely felt refreshed and rejuvenated after that wonderful weekend!

Don't feel guilty about having fun. Consider your playtime as an investment in your mental health. It beats going to a psychiatrist. If you're thinking that only the really rich can afford to play hard, forget it. Anyone can sneak off to the golf course, tennis court, or bowling alley for an afternoon.

Please make a habit of rewarding yourself well for all you've accomplished.

Tell the Truth

"Lies have short legs," my late mother-in-law, Jean Applegate, would often say. "They will always come back to bite you in the butt."

I loved the wisdom she imparted in her colorful, earthy, Texas twang. Telling the truth is critical to personal and business success. While you may be tempted to hype sales figures or inflate projections, don't. These little untruths will come back to bite you.

Convincing yourself that things are great when they are really bad *always* backfires. Stand up to your problems and face them head-on.

Successful businesspeople readily admit they need help. They acknowledge their mistakes and change direction, no matter how embarrassed or upset they may be. They base decisions on fact, not fiction, and take responsibility for their actions.

Telling your employees the truth shows you care enough about them to share both the good and bad news. Don't keep bad news a secret. Your employees will eventually learn the truth and will feel betrayed by your silence. If you are facing a cash flow crunch or major crisis, rally the troops around you and work together to turn things around.

Being honest with customers and suppliers is critical to building trust. If you screw up, be quick to admit it and remedy the situation. Making excuses, pointing fingers, and shifting blame gets you nowhere. Customers appreciate dealing with a company that admits it's not perfect and quickly solves problems.

Deal with your vendors in an open and honest manner. If sales are slow and you know you won't need as many cardboard boxes, plastic bags, or fabric, give your suppliers a heads-up. They will appreciate your candor and, in some cases, may extend payment terms.

Our clients appreciate my straightforward approach. There have been times when, after signing a contract, I realize that it was a mistake. Depending on the contract, you can usually negotiate a graceful exit. You'll gain points by suggesting a replacement and making an introduction.

GREAT

168

IDEA

Overcome a Fear of Public Speaking—Join Toastmasters

Most entrepreneurs are the company spokesperson, whether they like it or not. While public speaking can be terrifying, knowing how to make a clear, concise presentation can mean the difference between financial success and failure for many small firms.

If the thought of speaking in public makes you ill (it is considered the number-one fear by most people), consider joining a group that has helped more than three million people around the world overcome their fear of speaking during the past 75 years.

Toastmasters International was founded in 1924 by Ralph C. Smedley in the basement of the YMCA in Santa Ana, California. This respected organization teaches people to overcome a fear of public speaking. There are about 8,100 chapters around the world.

In recent years, Toastmasters, with more than 250,000 members worldwide, has helped many business owners learn to feel at ease in front of a crowd by using its positive, peer-counseling approach. Annual dues are $54; there is a one-time $20 membership fee, and chapters usually charge another few dollars a year for materials. Visit www.toastmasters.org for more information.

If you can't get to Toastmasters or afford to hire a speaking coach, there are some excellent books on the topic. Check out books and consulting services offered by a leading presentation coach, Diane DiResta. Her web site is www.diresta.com.

GREAT 169 IDEA

Find a Mentor and Be a Mentor

Finding a mentor is a great idea. A mentor can steer you around the potholes and buoy you up when you are drowning in confusion.

I have been fortunate to have several mentors, who played a significant role in my life.

My first mentor was the late Dr. James Julian, a respected and feared professor who taught media law at San Diego State University. He was tough, demanding, and grouchy. I was afraid of him, especially when he peppered us with complicated legal concepts and rattled us with eye-crossing exams.

One day, he abruptly stopped lecturing to reprimand me for whispering to a friend. I was mortified. He told me to meet him in his office immediately after class. I was shaking when I sat down across from him.

Instead of yelling at me for disrupting the class, he dug through the piles of papers on his desk. He handed me an application for a national student journalism contest.

"Fill this out," he barked. So I did.

A few months later, on the plane to Buffalo, New York, to accept my first award for writing, I realized that I had a mentor. For years, he critiqued my work and pushed me to write better stories and work harder. He also praised my accomplishments and was my biggest fan. We kept in touch long after I graduated and I miss him.

Over the years, I've sought out a variety of mentors to help me overcome all sorts of professional and personal obstacles. I seek out people whose accomplishments inspire me—people who lead lives of purpose and fulfillment.

Sometimes, the best mentor works in a different profession than yours. One of my current mentors, an extremely respected and successful businessperson, is involved in national politics and education.

Once, when I was embroiled in an internal battle around our biggest corporate consulting project, I called him. He listened to my story and asked pointed questions about the key players involved. Then, he gave me some great ideas to help calm the waters and resolve the crisis. His advice was critical to the eventual success of the project.

You're probably reading this and thinking, well, perhaps it's easy for Jane Applegate to find mentors—but what about me? Everyone can find a mentor. There are mentors in every corner of America. No matter how small your town is, there is someone there whom you admire, someone who is living the kind of life you would like to lead.

Writing a simple note, sending an e-mail, or making a telephone call is the first step. Ask a mutual friend or acquaintance to make an introduction. Explain that you admire what they have accomplished and ask if you can meet with them for a few minutes. Don't frighten them by saying, "I want you to be my mentor."

Busy, successful people rarely have time for a long lunch, but they might have time for a chat on the phone or a cup of coffee near their office. If the person you choose turns you down, try someone else. It's easy to find a mentor through the SCORE program. Retired executives volunteer their time to help business owners like you. Visit www.score.org.

Here's another great idea: check out a mentoring program run by Mercy Corps, a nonprofit agency. MicroMentor.org provides free online matches aimed at connecting business owners with volunteer mentors. The site has registered more than 3,500 entrepreneurs and 2,600 mentors and made more than 2,000 matches, according to a spokeswoman for the group.

She said business owners who worked with mentors actually experienced a 75 percent increase in annual sales.

Finally, be a mentor. I enjoy mentoring young women working in the entertainment business. I've introduced them to my contacts and helped them find jobs in New York City. I like to think my advice is helping them pursue their celluloid dreams.

Do Something to Reduce Stress

The entrepreneurial lifestyle is stressful, so you need to manage your stress. Maintaining your psychological health is critical to your business.

Dr. Mark Goulston, a top adviser to decision makers, author, blogger, and one of my favorite psychiatrists, shared this quiz to help you gauge your stress level.

Circle all the items that apply to you. Add up the number of items circled and check your score at the end.

1. I find myself less eager to go back to work after the weekend.
2. I feel less and less patient and/or sympathetic listening to other people's problems.
3. I ask more "closed" questions to discourage dialogue with coworkers than "open" questions to encourage it.
4. I try to get people out of my office as rapidly as possible.
5. I don't think other people take enough personal responsibility for their problems.
6. I am getting tired of taking responsibility for other people's problems.
7. My work ethic is getting worse.
8. I am falling further behind in many of the responsibilities in my life.
9. I am losing my sense of humor.
10. I find it more and more difficult to see people socially.
11. I feel tired most of the time.

12. I don't seem to have much fun at work anymore.
13. I don't have much fun outside of work, either.
14. I feel trapped.
15. I know what will make me feel better, but I just can't push myself to do it.

SCORING

0–4 More exhausted than stressed out
5–8 Beginning to stress out
9–12 Possibly stressed out
13–16 Stressed out

So what's your score? The best thing about stress is that you have the power to cope with it. If you don't do something, stress can take a terrible toll on your health.

I know, having suffered several bouts of "nervous exhaustion," which completely wiped me out. In 2000, after launching SBTV.com (Small Business Television), I headed to Tuscany, Italy on a vacation. Unfortunately, as soon as I arrived at the lovely villa rented by my sister, Andrea, and her husband, Jeff, I collapsed. I don't remember spending five days in bed, unable to move. Lucky for me, my brother-in-law is a physician; he monitored my vital signs and kept me hydrated with Gatorade.

I recovered and was well enough to take the train to Venice for one day before flying home, but never lived down being the houseguest from hell.

So here's my advice: please take care of yourself. If you need help, see a therapist, learn biofeedback techniques, or try acupuncture. Too many people need you to be healthy and strong.

GREAT
171
IDEA

Put on a Happy Face

My dear friend Ivan Rosenberg is a respected consultant on managing change. He's also one of the best readers of people. I think that's why he is so successful when it comes to helping his clients manifest big changes in an organization.

His firm, Frontier Associates, based in Valley Village, California, helps all kinds of companies and federal agencies improve their operations.

Ivan shared this great idea: before you walk into your office in the morning, monitor your facial expression. Your employees look to you to set the tone for the day.

"Maybe you had a bad cup of coffee or a fight with your spouse, but your team may think something bad is going on with the business," said Rosenberg.

So put on a happy face and paste on a smile, so your colleagues won't worry. At least, until you get to your desk.

Customer Service

8

We all know that an unhappy customer is more likely to blab or tweet about how awful you or your staff has treated them. So your mission is to encourage your happy customers to spread good news and create a positive buzz.

But providing excellent customer service takes time, money, and extraordinary patience. It means taking personal responsibility for making sure no complaint goes unresolved.

I've learned a lot about customer service from my husband, Joe. He refuses to put up with poor service or shoddy products. Once, a clerk at Staples told him he couldn't return a cordless phone because he'd thrown the box away. Joe asked to speak with the manager, who gave him a full refund. "I had the receipt, so he had to give me my money back," Joe explained.

A few days after returning the phone, he sent a broken plastic dimmer knob back to the manufacturer. A few days later, a nicer brass one arrived in the mail. We told everyone about that pleasant experience.

Being a squeaky wheel works—most of the time. It didn't work when we took the kids to Disneyland years ago on a blistering hot Sunday. The concession stands ran out of soft drinks, and hordes of unhappy visitors started shouting at the frustrated workers. That day, Disneyland definitely was not "the happiest place on Earth."

Joe wrote a letter explaining our horrible experience at the theme park. Disney's marketing department sent us four free passes, which Joe returned with another note. He hasn't visited Disneyland since, although I recently spent three very pleasant hours at Disneyland with my parents,

Marty and Sherrie; my sister, Amy; my brother-in-law, John; and my niece, Zoe. (I'm hoping Joe will eventually visit a theme park with our future grandchildren . . . hint, hint.)

In this chapter, you'll learn how to conduct a customer survey, how to train your employees to answer the telephone with enthusiasm, and why "mystery shoppers" can alert you to serious problems. I also explain why taking your product to your customer's home or making high-end apparel to order is a great idea.

As tough as it is to be pleasant and patient some days, remember that if you put people first, the money will follow.

Customer Service the Zappos Way

Maura Sullivan, senior manager of Zappos' customer loyalty team, frequently does cartwheels around the office. During the holidays, she wears a Santa hat.

Sullivan sets an upbeat and positive tone for the 500-person customer service team answering phones at the super-successful Las Vegas–based company.

In 2009, Zappos (a word play on *zapatos*, the Spanish word for shoes) was acquired by Amazon for more than $1 billion in a cash and stock deal. The company expected to post $1.2 billion in revenues in 2010, so they must be doing something right. Providing incredible customer service is a core value.

Everyone told founder and CEO, Tony Hsieh, he was crazy to sell shoes online. They were wrong. Zappos' devotion to customer service is legendary. Customers order shoes online or on the phone, try them on at home, and have a year to return them. Zappos asks only that you don't wear the shoes outside. "We're not a shoe rental company," said Sullivan.

She said customer service is such a high priority that every employee is required to pass a four-week call center training course. No exceptions.

"Our new COO just went through it (the training)," said Sullivan. "If you can't pass the training, you won't go on to your new position."

If you call to place an order in November or December, don't be surprised if a guy named Tony answers your call. Hsieh answers phones in the call center for about eight hours—along with every other executive during the busy holiday season. "We call them our holiday helpers," said Sullivan. "It brings back that family spirit."

Zappos now sells much more than shoes. Company warehouses are stocked with footwear, housewares, and accessories. The company also offers free shipping on most purchases, making it easy to buy and return products. She reminds her team to "stay positive and have fun." Most importantly, "just focus on helping the customer that you are on the phone with."

Although only 5 percent of sales are made over the phone, Zappos relies on 500 full-time customer service reps and no seasonal workers. Although they deal with such a small percentage of customers on the phone, "we have the opportunity to wow the socks off them."

"Our number one thing is providing the best service and being helpful," said Sullivan. "If someone doesn't have an answer, their job is to get one."

She said product-related questions are often relayed to members of a special "resource staff." If Zappos doesn't stock whatever you want, the rep is instructed to tell you where you can buy the product from another company. Pretty cool.

Here's the big Zappos secret for providing great customer service: "It's really about hiring the right people," said Sullivan, who previously worked for Nordstrom. "It seems like such an easy thing to do—just hire friendly and helpful people."

Sullivan said customers buy from Zappos even when its prices are higher than competitors. "The customers end up doing the marketing for you because they share the good experience with their friends."

She admits she never imagined herself in the shoe business. She has a degree in anthropology and was living in San Francisco and working part time at an Asian art museum. Looking to earn more money, she took a job answering phones at Zappos seven years ago and never looked back.

When we spoke, she told me she was planning to do most of her holiday shopping at Zappos. "We get a pretty good discount," she joked.

My last question: how many pairs of shoes does she own? She paused: "Around 100 pairs."

Quick Customer Service Quiz

Take this customer service quiz to find out whether you are treating your customers the way you, yourself, want to be treated.

1. *Do you really know who your customers are?* If you are unsure, get busy collecting information on their purchasing habits and preferences.
2. *When customers return a product, do you treat them the same way as when they purchased the product?* Treat returns and complaints as a way to improve your operations and generate goodwill.
3. *Do you respond to e-mails and telephone calls immediately?* With so many options, customers expect a prompt response. Voice mail is great, but it should never replace a human at the other end of the line when a caller presses "0."
4. *If your product is guaranteed, do you honor that guarantee?* If a customer buys a product with a guarantee, but you refuse to provide a replacement or refund, you are not providing good service. Honor all product guarantees, even if the conditions are not fully met. Nordstrom takes back any item, usually with no questions asked.
5. *Does your staff have all the information they need to provide excellent service?* Everyone needs to know everything about the products or services you sell. Review their performance and reward employees for providing great customer service. Consider hiring a mystery shopper (see next idea).

Hire a Mystery Shopper

Carol Cherry makes her living from shopping, but you won't catch her wandering around a store.

"I hate shopping," she told me when we spoke a few years ago. "I can't remember the last time I've been to a mall."

Cherry is the owner and president of Atlanta-based Shop'n Chek Inc., one of the nation's largest mystery shopping companies. Business owners and managers hire her shoppers to determine whether employees are providing good customer service.

Founded in 1974, the company has about 50,000 freelance shoppers working in the United States and abroad. They visit restaurants, department stores, gas stations, bowling alleys, and anywhere else people shop, eat, or play.

"This industry can really help a small business, especially one with two locations when the owner can't be in two places at once," said Cherry. Although her client list reads like a Who's Who of American business, a promise of confidentiality precludes her from sharing their names.

The mystery shopping industry began more than 35 years ago as a way for big retailers to figure out why certain appliances weren't selling. Mystery shoppers now work undercover in retail stores, hotels, and the travel industry.

The cool thing is mystery shoppers are regular folks who are observant and comfortable dealing with people. They are usually paid per assignment, which involves filling out a detailed questionnaire right after a visit. Mystery shoppers set their own hours and do the work more for fun than money. A shopper might earn $10 to $20 for reviewing service at a local bowling alley.

They note how they are greeted by salespeople. They examine the way merchandise is displayed and how salespeople handle their questions, complaints, and returns.

Mystery shoppers will also check to see if employees offer information about special promotions or clearly explain company services. A good mystery shopping service spends time learning about your business.

Some mystery shopping services specialize in certain industries. For example, Melinda Brody & Associates in Orlando, Florida, focuses on tourism, travel, and home building. Brody, who worked as an apartment leasing agent and sales trainer prior to starting her business, knows the real estate business well.

One of their company's specialties is checking on what real estate salespeople say to potential buyers. Home builders obtain permission to tape record what their salespeople say to customers. The salesperson never knows whether that nice older couple looking to buy a condo are real customers or one of Brody's mystery shopping teams.

If you think hiring a mystery shopper would improve your customer service, do it. Companies are usually listed in the Yellow Pages under "shopping services" or look online.

Listen to the Telephone Doctor

Nancy Friedman, known as the "Telephone Doctor," is passionate about teaching people how to make the most of their most valuable business tool: the telephone.

Friedman is in demand as a speaker and consultant because too many employees take the telephone for granted. They don't make a fuss when a customer calls. They answer calls without enthusiasm, half-listen to what's being said, and take confusing, incomplete messages.

We may carry smartphones around and answer them day and night, but Friedman believes people rarely tap into the telephone's real power. Here are her best tips:

- Teaching your employees to answer the phone properly and make calls in a professional manner, will boost sales as well as morale. When we spoke, Friedman offered more great ideas: *Teach your employees to smile before they answer the phone.* Even if it's forced, smiling brightens your voice and boosts your energy.
- *Keep important numbers handy.* In all print and online correspondence, note the addressee's phone number. This makes it easy for you to call the person to follow up.
- *When you are out of the office, call your staff at random times.* When you check in, ask them to tell you what's happening. No business owner ever wants to hear "nothing's going on" when they call their office.
- *Learn to love voice mail.* Voice mail is your friend. Leave clear and specific messages. If you don't want to leave a message, follow the prompts to reach a live person to leave a message.

To find out more about the company's products, including customer service courses, presentations, and DVDs to improve telephone skills, visit Friedman's web site: www.telephonedoctor.com.

Don't Make Your Customers Angry

George Coan, my beloved, late grandfather, was one of the smartest businesspeople I knew.

Coan began his retail career as a boy, selling clothes from a pushcart on the Lower East Side of New York City. He worked for pennies a day, sleeping on couches and making his own way after his family drifted apart.

Movie-star handsome and always sharply dressed, he was about 17 when he landed his first job as a salesman at a men's clothing store. He eventually worked his way up to be a vice president at Howard Clothes. (A funny aside: When he was offered a job managing a store in a predominantly Irish neighborhood, he changed the spelling of his surname from Cohen to Coan. He never changed it back.)

Although he did not finish high school, Coan was a respected executive, responsible for all union negotiations before he retired. He loved selling clothes and opened a tiny shop in his North Miami condo to sell men's shirts. He also loved to take my husband, Joe, shopping for clothes, offering excellent advice on fit and fabric.

A modest man, he rarely talked about his professional accomplishments. But, when I pressed him, he finally shared some insights on customer service and marketing. One of his greatest marketing ideas was selling winter coats on layaway in the middle of a summer heat wave. The mannequins in the window attracted so much attention and so many customers, competing stores copied the promotion.

He also takes credit for being one of the first retailers to display ties, handkerchiefs, and cuff links in glass cases adjacent to the cash register. That made it easy for customers to buy accessories to complement a new suit, increasing the total sales ticket.

He urged his staff to always provide excellent customer service and he shared this great idea based on years of waiting on thousands of customers: "Whatever you do, don't make your customer angry."

It sounds simple, but so many things can go wrong in a retail store. For example, customers can get upset if you take too long to find their size or can't find the item they need. If your salespeople are rude, bored, or careless, you risk alienating customers.

Nothing is worse than waiting while a salesclerk chats with a colleague or makes a personal phone call. If an angry customer leaves the store, they may never return. So, strive to make every sales experience a dream, not a nightmare.

Make House Calls or Have a Trunk Sale

In this high-tech, impersonal world, a little personal service goes a long way. Why not set yourself apart from the competition by visiting your clients at their home or inviting them to a trunk show at a nearby hotel?

Dog groomers and car detailers make house calls. So does Nadya, a charming fashion designer with an international following. Once or twice a year, Nadya (known just as Nadya) leaves her colorful home in Bali to travel across America, meeting with devoted clients in private homes or in hotel suites. The sales process feels like a party—including plenty of food and wine.

"I love getting to meet the people who buy my clothes because it's a very personal business," said Nadya. "Getting their feedback is a very important part of my whole design process."

Originally from Chicago, Nadya fell in love with Bali while vacationing there in 1978. Inspired by the gorgeous colors and vibrant local fabrics, she started making clothing for herself. No matter where she was, women stopped her to ask where they could buy her one-of-a-kind designs. (We met on an airplane when I asked her where she bought her clothes.) Most of her signature jackets are reversible and often embellished with unusual beads and amazing embroidery.

In 1980, she started hiring artists and seamstresses to create a line of batik or hand-painted cotton and rayon clothing. She now employs about 45 seamstresses and skilled craftspeople at her home in Bali.

Nadya spends about six months a year supervising production in Bali. Then, she packs everything up and heads back to America, setting up shop in hotel suites in Los Angeles; Washington, DC; Boston; New York City; Chicago; Seattle; San Francisco, and Atlanta.

"When she's in town, it's a party," said Margy Boyd, a long-time friend who wears Nadya's clothes most of the time, but especially while taking clients on art-oriented trips around the world.

"I have a big house, and when Nadya is in town, we can have hundreds of shoppers stopping by," said Boyd. Before starting her own art tour business, Boyd worked for the San Francisco Museum of Modern Art. "Her clothes are absolutely beautiful."

For more information about where to find Nadya's colorful apparel and a schedule of trunk shows, visit www.Nadya.com.

Make Apparel to Order

As a young woman, Nina McLemore's career goal "was to be a fashion buyer and earn $25,000 a year."

She's done much better than that. McLemore worked her way up to be the executive in charge of accessories for Liz Claiborne. In 1993, after 13 years at Claiborne, she surprised everyone by enrolling at Columbia University to complete her MBA. After graduation, she leveraged her new financial skills to work as a venture capitalist, helping to raise and invest $25 million. Although she was often invited to sit on the board of directors of the firms she funded, she yearned to start her own business.

"Friends always called me and asked if I could help them shop for clothes," said McLemore, a tall, attractive, silver-haired woman. "I walked into stores and asked to see suits that would work for an investment banker at Goldman Sachs. I was surprised to find there were so few options. That's when I realized there was a huge opportunity to create clothes for Baby Boomer women who had moved up the career ladder."

In 2003, she started her own apparel business, which relies on independent sales reps and some specialty stores to sell made-to-order career and evening wear.

"The reps show customers our samples and then write an order," she said. "Most items are delivered within a month."

In 2010, the company had about 100 reps and six Nina McLemore stores, mostly on the East Coast. The company also has stores in Cleveland, San Francisco, and Dallas and sells the line in 30 specialty stores.

Like most entrepreneurs, McLemore said she started the business with her own money. She later raised additional capital from angels and venture capitalists. (She declined to reveal any financial information about the privately held company.)

Today, Nina McLemore and her team are busy meeting demand for elegant, professional clothes, priced somewhere between high-end department stores and designer apparel. A Nina McLemore suit retails for about $1,200. The pieces are designed to be mixed and matched and worn for several seasons. McLemore says she designs about four new lines a year.

The recent recession actually boosted sales. She said many professional women stopped buying designer labels, even if they could afford to buy them.

On the positive side, layoffs during the recession sent many professional women back into the workforce to look for new jobs. Dressing for success is essential for professional women, contends McLemore.

"How you dress affects your life and success," she told me. "Men don't buy suits off the rack because they understand the importance of quality and fit. If a woman doesn't dress like a serious player, it can hurt her career."

McLemore's designs are sewn in the United States and made from mostly imported fabrics. She imports silk from India and fine woolens from Scotland and Italy. (I'm planning to wear her wonderful designs while speaking on my book promotion tour, so keep an eye out.)

"Production is not a problem, but a big problem is finding pattern makers," said McLemore. "It's a dying art."

Luckily, she can still find pattern makers overseas, and "a lot can be done on the computer."

Another company relies on personal service to sell custom-made apparel. J. Hilburn deploys 650 sales reps, called "style advisers," to customers' homes or offices. There, they take measurements and send the details off to a factory near Macau, China. The company's shirts are made from Italian fabrics.

The venture-backed company, founded in 2007 by two former financial executives, expects to post sales of about $9 million in 2010. Veeral Rathod, one of the founders, told *Bloomberg Businessweek* that no one seemed to be focusing on serving male shoppers.

Advisers, many of whom work part time, earn commissions of up to 25 percent after paying $399 for training, fabric samples, and sales materials.

The business model seems to be working. Brian O'Malley, a board member and investor, said the company benefits financially by not making a shirt until it's sold.

Demand Great Service from Vendors

David Gumpert, an author, journalist, and consultant shared this idea when we met a few years ago in Washington, DC.

He doesn't niggle on price when he's negotiating with new suppliers or vendors. Instead, he tells people: "I will pay you top dollar, if you promise to always give me excellent service."

That means they will return his phone calls promptly, deliver his order on time, and resolve problems quickly. He said his strategy works. Vendors appreciate not being beaten up over price and provide excellent service in exchange for being paid fairly and promptly.

It often makes sense to pay more for good service. For example, when you need technical support, you may have the option of waiting on hold for hours, or paying to be helped immediately.

Remember, your time is valuable.

Get to Know Your Customers Personally

Soon after landing a job as a financial reporter at the *Los Angeles Times* Orange County, California, bureau, I was sent to interview David Tappan, then chairman of Fluor Corporation.

Fluor is a giant, a global engineering and construction firm. Anxious about meeting with such a high-profile executive, I did my homework.

I read his biography, scoured the annual report, and prepared a list of intelligent questions.

I arrived early and checked in with the security guard. At the exact moment of my appointment, his well-dressed secretary ushered me into his enormous office. My heels sunk into the deep carpet. Tappan, a handsome, silver-haired man, stood up gracefully, smiled, and extended his hand.

"Welcome to Fluor," he said, making me feel at ease. "Before we get started, Jane, tell me, how is Joe adjusting to life in Costa Mesa?"

I was puzzled. How did he know my husband's name? How did he know where we lived? Then, he asked if our daughters were enjoying their new nursery school.

Flustered, I asked him if he hired private investigators to collect information on every reporter who requested an interview. He laughed and pointed to his Rolodex, as big as a compact car tire, sitting on the credenza behind his desk.

"I like to know who I'm doing business with," he said. "So I ask my staff to do the research before I meet with someone I haven't met before. Then, I write the details on these cards."

I will never forget that meeting and how comfortable he made me feel. Although he was running a giant multinational company, he acted like a small business owner who wanted to know everything about me.

You don't have to be a bigwig to find out something about the person you are about to meet. It's incredibly easy today, with all the information posted on LinkedIn, Facebook, Google, and company web sites.

After doing your online research, call mutual friends or acquaintances. When you meet someone new, don't be shy about asking for basic details about their spouse, significant other, children, or pets. Most people like to talk about themselves.

We all like to do business with people who are genuinely interested in who we are and what we do when we aren't working. With e-mail, it's easy to keep in touch. But, please, send a paper card for birthdays.

Speaking of cards, I started sending Thanksgiving cards and gifts to clients to beat the Christmas rush. I also scheduled holiday presents to be delivered during the first week in December.

It sounds old school, but nothing makes a positive impression like a handwritten note. The most successful, important people I know still write notes.

One of my friends—a person who once advised President Clinton and was later appointed by President Obama to head a high-profile, bipartisan commission—still sends me handwritten notes. And, of course, I send him a handwritten note in response.

If you really can't bear to write personal notes, check out Send Out Cards. The company makes it easy to go online and keep in touch with customers, friends, and family members. (Read my exclusive interview with founder Kody Bateman at the end of Great Idea #99.)

Wrap It Up

One of the nicest things you can do for your customers is send them out the door with their merchandise beautifully gift wrapped. It saves time and money, and great packaging is one of the smartest and most cost-effective advertisements for your retail business.

Think of Tiffany's signature turquoise box and how much excitement that creates.

Before it closed during the Great Recession, I loved shopping at Takashimaya, an elegant Japanese-owned department store on Fifth Avenue in Manhattan. In addition to selling unique clothes, jewelry, and housewares, the store was known for its amazing gift wrapping.

Gift items were nestled in layers of tissue paper and tucked into a triangular paper box. No matter what you purchased, whether it was a $15 scented candle or $1,500 earrings, the gift was made more special because of the elaborate gift wrapping and triangular bag.

As an avid shopper, I'm always surprised when a merchant hands me my purchase in a generic paper or plastic bag. If you can't gift wrap merchandise, at least invest in colorful paper bags and customize it with a sticker featuring your company logo, address, and phone number. Turn every customer into a walking billboard for your business.

One last note on gifts: it doesn't matter how much you spend as long as you really think about what the person would enjoy and not necessarily need. I wanted to thank Tony Bolton, the terrific Bloomberg TV sales rep who books most of my speaking engagements through the company's Idea Exchange program. So, I logged on to Zazzle.com to design a T-shirt featuring one of Tony's many mottos:

Why Be Late When You Can Be on Time?

He loved the shirt.

GREAT IDEA 182

Customer Service at Its Best

Maybe I'm lucky to live in a civilized place where most shopkeepers are happy to see you, but I want to acknowledge some people and companies that provide exceptional customer service.

When I need something printed, I head to Gnomon Press on South Main Street in Hanover, New Hampshire. Every person who works there, especially Meliss and Andy, is pleasant, professional, and friendly. When I e-mail a document for printing, they always check it for accuracy and often suggest ways to improve the design. They offer discounts for customers willing to wait a few extra days to pick up an order. They also admire my son Evan's design work. He's my go-to guy for posters and other projects. I always look forward to visiting Gnomon and am happy to sing their praises.

Kim Souza and her retail team at Revolution, a vintage and designer boutique in downtown White River Junction, Vermont, offer customers a fresh cup of coffee or cappuccino when they walk through the door.

It puts you in the mood to take your time looking at the great merchandise. If you need a break, there is a comfy sofa and chairs.

Revolution is also a community cultural and arts center. Kim produces funky fashion shows, with customers serving as models, as well as a glittery Oscar® Night party every February.

Cole, a young salesclerk at Kohl's in West Lebanon, New Hampshire, stands out. He provided excellent service when I arrived to pick up a heated mattress pad a few months ago. I had called the store to ask that it be set aside because it's a 22-mile trek from my house to the store.

When I arrived, Cole couldn't find the mattress pad in the hold area, but quickly led me into the bedding department, assuring me I would find the item. (These heated mattress pads are amazing—there is nothing better than climbing into a toasty bed on a frosty night.)

With the mattress pad safely in my shopping cart, I sought him out to verify the price of a set of pots and pans. He not only checked the price, but carried the heavy box to the checkout counter. A few minutes later, he carried the box out to my car. That guy has a bright future in retail!

One other compliment goes out to the team at Bob's Service Center in White River Junction. When you make an appointment for service, they actually honor it! I take my Subaru there for oil changes and to change the tires between winter and summer (a New England ritual). The coffee in the waiting room is fresh, and the wait is never too long.

A few online merchants also deserve praise. Duluth Trading has an easy-to-use web site and offers excellent service. I love their catalogs, too. So far, every Amazon.com vendor I've dealt with has been great. I recently ordered a digital camera from a vendor, but it didn't work. I fretted about returning it. But the seller responded quickly to my e-mail. She called me and told me to ship it back. Within days, she sent a replacement. Those customer reviews really keep the quality high.

It doesn't take much to make customers happy—you just have to make an effort.

One final note: My favorite nail salon deserves a mention for great customer service. J. J.'s Fine Nails on 55th Street in New York City is the first place I visit when I arrive in Manhattan. They are always happy to see me and you can't beat the Monday to Wednesday $20 special deal on a first-class manicure and pedicure.

Going Global

9

I f your business is ailing, going global won't save it. But if your business is poised for growth and offers a product or service with universal appeal, read on.

Entering the international marketplace has never been easier. The Department of Commerce, Export-Import Bank, and the U.S. Small Business Administration (SBA) all offer excellent programs and resources to encourage export.

The White House has been on the export bandwagon since President Obama took office. In 2010, the Department of Commerce's Advocacy Center assisted hundreds of American companies competing for export opportunities, supporting $11.8 billion in U.S. exports and an estimated 70,000 jobs.

Halfway through 2010, the Commerce Department had coordinated 20 trade missions with over 250 U.S. companies to 25 countries. By the end of 2010, the number was closer to 40 trade missions.

So how do you explore the possibilities? The first step is doing your homework, starting with the Commerce Department, which has offices in 126 countries with commercial experts available to help you make local contacts.

"Every company should look at having an export strategy," said Karen Zens, deputy assistant secretary for international trade, Commercial Service, International Trade Administration (ITA). "Seventy percent of the world's purchasing power and 90 percent of the population is outside of the United States."

Zens, who manages the agency's overseas operations, has spent the past 25 years with the department. She's worked in several countries, including Spain.

When she was posted in Spain, she met with a U.S. textile maker who was very excited about selling bed linens to Spanish retailers. Unfortunately, he had to rethink his plan when she told him European beds are different sizes than U.S. beds.

Once you determine there is demand for your product abroad, focus on a few countries to start.

"We contracted to a conduct a study which showed the most successful companies export to four or five markets," said Zens. "The more you export, the better you get at it. Exporting also makes your product more competitive in the United States."

When you are ready to get going, contact the ITA at www.trade.gov.

"We start with counseling, which is totally free," said Zens. "We have more than 100 U.S. Export Assistance Centers in all the major markets in the United States."

The next step would be meeting with potential customers. One strategy is to sign up for a trade mission. The ITA puts together companies in similar sectors and sets up meetings, often taking business owners to visit several countries on one trip.

"We often take a senior executive from the government along to impress the people in the market," said Zens.

Her department also has Gold Key service that is tailored to meet an individual company's needs.

"We can set up a whole day's worth of appointments with six weeks' notice," said Zens. "For a very modest fee, you get off the plane and have tailored appointments."

The Gold Key fee for a small company is about $700.

"The fee covers the additional cost of setting up appointments, but all the rest of our counseling is free," said Zens, who recommends total novices start by taking some basic exporting workshops offered by the SBA.

It's no surprise that Canada and Mexico are the top importers of U.S. products. Japan, Germany, the United Kingdom, South Korea, Brazil, and the Netherlands also buy U.S. products and services. India is the 15th largest market, and the Chinese buy a lot from us. The European Union is easy to work with because it's all one market now.

You'll need to have the right financing in place before shipping your first order. "The Export-Import Bank has a variety of financing products for small companies, including loan programs and guarantees," said Zens, adding that you should start slowly and not "take on the whole world at once."

And it's critical to find the right people to deal with overseas. "We offer background checks to verify the people you want to deal with are legitimate," she said.

Cultural differences are also challenging. Many foreign businesspeople don't like to say "no" during a meeting, which creates misunderstandings.

"Until a year ago I was working in Mexico," said Zens. "They are lovely people who don't like to say 'no' to your face. Many business owners were upset because they would have a positive meeting, but never got an order."

You should work with a local lawyer who speaks the language fluently and make sure your contracts and payment terms meet local regulations. "Every market is different," said Zens. "We found in Italy, they were the worst payers and would drag out payments for a long time."

One last tip: start labeling your products in English, French, and Spanish. Printing labels in multiple languages doesn't cost a lot. Best of all, you will be ready to export, even if it is to just French-speaking regions of Canada.

GREAT IDEA 183

Return to Your Homeland to Export Products

Kesang Tashi, known as Tashi, was the first Tibetan to attend Dartmouth College. That's just one astonishing fact about this amazing man. He's traveled a long road from Tibet to India to Hanover, New Hampshire. When he about 10, he and his family escaped from political oppression in Tibet and fled to India. His mother ended up working at a school run by the Dalai Lama.

Tashi graduated from Dartmouth and headed to New York City to begin a career in banking. He was working in New York City for financial mogul Edward Safra, but after a few years, Tashi realized he had no passion for banking.

"My entrepreneurial spirit was calling me . . . I come from a long line of merchants," he said. "I wanted to do something more meaningful and fun and make an impact on my homeland."

When he finally visited Tibet in 1986, he was appalled to see local weavers making hideous rugs out of cheap synthetic fibers. "Instead of wool, the rugs were polyester and brightly colored with terrible dyes," said Tashi.

It was especially shocking because Tibetan weavers have been making beautiful wool rugs since the 11th century. "The arts and crafts of Tibet suffered immensely during the Chinese cultural revolution," said Tashi. "Mao Tse Tung wanted to uproot the past and create a new society and new values."

While visiting villages in Tibet, Tashi vowed to revitalize traditional rug making. "My goal was to work with old masters and turn their work into a viable product."

The warmest and toughest wool fiber comes from the highland sheep of Tibet because they live at 14,000 feet.

"When you walk on the rugs, you feel like your feet are getting a massage."

In addition to rugs, Tashi started importing jewelry, scarves, and other items indigenous to Tibet and the Himalayan region.

Today, his company, Khawachen/Inner Asia, designs and produces authentic Tibetan rugs that cost up to $25,000. Some are designed by U.S. artists, including Vermont artist Lizi Boyd. Designers and consumers have embraced his products.

Doing business in Tibet is not easy. More than 25 years after he returned to Tibet, he still faces a tough time traveling in and out of the country. He is careful to keep a low profile and remain apolitical.

"It was a matter of convincing the Chinese officials to let me work there," he said. "At first, we were communicating via telex. I would send an urgent telex and wait for a week to get a reply."

Today, e-mail makes it easier to manage his foreign operations. "We have special software so you can walk in with fabric swatches from your home, and within 24 to 48 hours we'll come up with a design for your rug."

With the click of a mouse, his designers can change the colors or scale of the pattern and send it to the weavers in Tibet.

"We take a deposit and deliver your custom rug in five months."

In addition to a retail store in Hanover, New Hampshire, Tashi opened a second atelier in Gyalthang, which means land of limitless bounty. He also opened a store in Bejing during the Olympics, but it was challenging to get customers into the store due to limits on travel imposed by Chinese officials during the event.

When we met in 2010, Tashi had already expanded production and importation of other arts and crafts such as Tibetan miniature paintings and religious scrolls. "I'm a collector of Indian miniatures, which depict stories through calligraphy and artwork."

Meanwhile, he travels to Tibet three or four times a year to supervise operations. "I hope to fulfill my vision of a big arts and craft production center. I still have a lot of work to do."

GREAT 184 IDEA
Move Your Manufacturing to Mexico

Japanese giants Sony, Sanyo Electric, and Hitachi paved the way by investing hundreds of millions of dollars in Mexican border factories called *maquiladoras*. Now, scores of U.S. businesses are taking advantage of Mexico's affordable skilled labor force.

Shared production plants offer big and small businesses a cost-effective way to make products. There are about 3,000 maquiladoras employing more than one million workers in Mexico. The biggest attraction is paying workers very low wages compared to U.S. wages—about $2.50 an hour.

The majority of border plant workers are assembling electronic equipment and automotive parts. They also make medical devices, textiles, and furniture.

While it's easy for mega-corporations to deal with government permits, customs regulations, and cultural and language problems, working in a foreign country is daunting for most entrepreneurs.

In the late 1990s, Jeff Paul, formerly the owner of Sierra Pacific Apparel, had about 1,000 Mexican workers making blue jeans for U.S. retailers, but labor and financial problems made it an unpleasant experience.

He tried again a few years later and had 400 workers in California and about 100 in Mexicali, Mexico. Although sewing jeans in Mexico saved Paul about 75 cents per garment, it wasn't easy.

"Our employee turnover in central California was 5 percent a year," said Paul. "In Mexico, we lost 5 percent a week."

The second time he ventured into Mexico, Paul set up his Mexican operation in partnership with North American Production Sharing Inc. (NAPS), a small Del Mar, California–based company that helps U.S. companies set up shop over the border (www.napsmexico.com).

NAPS, founded by Bill Lew and Richard Jaime in 1991, works with U.S. companies doing everything from refurbishing telephones to making computer cables. NAPS screens applicants and hires workers, manages the payroll, helps train workers, and even rents buses to collect workers for one client's second shift. Best of all, they handle all the permits, payroll-related paperwork, taxes, and customs requirements.

But before they'll help a company move across the border, they spend quite a bit of time evaluating the company's needs and goals.

"We start by helping them understand if it makes sense to be in Mexico," said Lew, NAPS vice president and a former loan officer for Wells Fargo Bank. "We make sure the client is right for Mexico."

Tips to Consider before Moving Production to Mexico

- Carefully calculate and compare your current labor costs to wages in Mexico.
- Determine whether unskilled or semiskilled workers can be trained to make your product.
- Determine whether you have time to wait for finished products to be shipped back to the United States or abroad from Mexico.
- Budget extra funds for start-up costs.
- Find a partner who knows how things work in Mexico.
- Learn about the Mexican culture and how business deals are done there.
- Be patient.

The low labor cost is what attracts most U.S. businesses to Mexico. But contrary to popular belief, Lew said his clients are not firing U.S. workers and fleeing to Mexico. They head to Mexico to expand production.

"It's not a zero-sum game. Our clients are not closing down U.S. factories," he said. In fact, he cautions, "Mexico won't save a company—Mexico will help a growing company."

GREAT 185 IDEA
Forge an International Alliance

Forging an international alliance is a quick way to expand your business without spending a lot of money. The secret is to find a partner who can share his or her contacts and also understand your vision and integrity. Entrepreneurs in the service sector often have the easiest time striking informal agreements to work together because they are selling time and talent.

A few years ago, a mutual friend introduced Manhattan architect William Leeds to Indian architect Bobby Mukherji. Mukherji, founder of a five-person firm in Mumbai, was interested in entering the U.S. market. Leeds was eager to tap into India's thriving economy, which is growing rapidly.

For several years, the two architects designed a variety of projects, including a fabric showroom, a trendy Chicago restaurant, and a major Indian government office in New York City. Although they are no longer working together, Leeds said they benefited from sharing their clients, contacts, and talents.

"To be working with somebody from a place as far away as India gives us a new perspective on architecture and a new approach to planning," said Leeds. "Bobby brought in new ideas that we wouldn't necessarily have at our fingertips."

Besides new ideas, Mukherji provided access to unique Indian building materials and a team of 25 Indian craftsmen and artisans on his payroll in Mumbai. Many Mukherji projects, especially nightclubs, feature original artwork and hand-carved details. Although they lived thousands of miles apart, Leeds and Mukherji kept in touch, communicating frequently via phone and e-mail.

The firms worked together for years on a project-by-project basis based on a handshake, not a written agreement. They split the expenses and profits depending on who did what. Joint projects with Mukherji comprised about 10 percent to 15 percent of Leeds's total billings.

One of the benefits of the relationship was acting as each other's marketing representatives in the United States and India. "We looked out for his interests and helped him to grow," said Leeds. "In India, Bobby helped us because he could determine who was real and who was not."

GREAT IDEA 186

Do Business in India

President Obama was warmly received when he and First Lady Michelle Obama visited India in November 2010.

"I'm here because I believe that in our interconnected world, increased commerce between the United States and India can be and will be a win-win proposition for both countries," Obama told the U.S.-India Business Council.

The president pointed to $10 billion worth of export contracts that support 54,000 jobs in the United States.

India, with 1.2 billion people, is an attractive market for big and small U.S. companies. The Indian economy is projected to grow 8 percent in 2011, and a growing middle class is eager to buy American goods ranging from computers to clothing. More than 60 percent of the population is under 35, making it even more attractive for U.S. exporters.

Business expansion is rampant in Mumbai, New Delhi, and Bangalore, where there is a vast pool of cheap, skilled labor.

There are security issues and political instability, so you need to be aware of those issues.

Firsthand information is always best, so when I met Bobby Mukherji, an Indian architect, he agreed to share some tips for Americans interested in working on projects in India.

More Thoughts on Doing Business in India

- Learn how India's Foreign Exchange Regulation Act affects financial transactions.
- Find an accountant who is familiar with Indian accounting rules and regulations.
- Cultivate personal relationships. Bring American-made gifts that are not widely available in India.
- Make sure your Indian business partner has a good reputation, as well as good contacts.
- Learn as much as you can about the culture and what to expect before making travel plans.
- Book hotel rooms in advance. Many, especially in major cities, are filled with foreign businesspeople.
- Be on the lookout for torn or damaged bills. Many merchants won't accept money with holes. (Banks staple the notes, and the staples often rip up the bills.)

Offshoring and Outsourcing in India

Even if you don't plan to sell products to India, you might consider hiring people there to conduct all sorts of operations. The outsourcing industry actually started in India and has grown to about $47 billion a year, capturing more than half of all offshore outsourcing.

The United States and Europe are the largest customers for the Indian outsourcing industry. The United States accounts for 60 percent, and Europe 31 percent. Financial services companies represent 41 percent; high-tech/telecom, 20 percent; manufacturing, 17 percent; and retail, 8 percent, according to federal government reports and Financial Express.com. In 2009, offshoring companies employed about 2.2 million people in India.

India's outsourcing industry is expected to surge nearly fivefold to $50 billion by 2012.

Be prepared to encounter gut-wrenching poverty in the midst of great wealth. "An American who has never been exposed to the Indian culture will find the conditions extremely different from anywhere else in the world," said Mukherji.

He recommends hiring a driver to get around, but you won't need to hire an interpreter because most Indians speak English. The business infrastructure is getting better, but you will probably experience power outages and telecommunications issues, although mobile phones are prevalent.

"India is an extremely friendly, social place," said Mukherji. "Personal relationships are very important. There is a lot of weight given to word-of-mouth agreements, and people respect that."

GREAT

187

IDEA

Explore Opportunities in Russia

If you want to understand the challenges of doing business in Russia, consider this: Although automated teller machines (ATMs) adorn major boulevards in Moscow, most people are still reluctant to use them. Fear of being robbed is one reason, but that's not all.

Until 1997 it was legal to drive your car on the sidewalk. In light of that, what Muscovite in their right mind would line up on the sidewalk in front of an ATM?

In addition to impossible traffic jams and crime, Russia's allegedly corrupt politicians, a confusing business infrastructure, and crippling bureaucracy pose real challenges to foreign investors.

No matter how tough it is, doing business in Russia still has tremendous appeal to brave Western entrepreneurs. Since 1993 the Russian Federation, especially modern Russia, has welcomed Westerners and their cash. But wanting to do a deal in Russia and actually doing it are two different stories.

Mary Heslin, an American business consultant, opened her Limpopo drop-in day care center in a suburban Moscow community center in the late 1990s to protect herself and her employees from the Mafia. Unlike American day care centers, her facility has a highly educated staff, including a doctor and an engineer, tending kids and hosting birthday parties.

It took $4,000 and nearly a year to obtain the permits she needed to open the center, but things are going well. She hopes to open more around Moscow.

If you have a product or service that you think will appeal to Russians, start doing your homework now. You can call the U.S. Commerce Department and ask to speak to a trade specialist. The U.S. Agency for International Development also has assistance programs for people wanting to do business in Russia.

The Russia House Ltd. (www.therussiahouse.co.uk/visas-russian.html) has been involved with procuring Russian visas since 1970. Requirements often change. The Russia House was set up in 1970 by Barry Martin, who is still the managing director of the company. His goal is to foster Russo-British trade. People from other countries also rely on his services.

GREAT 188 IDEA · Do Business in China

For some great ideas about doing business in China, I turned to Edie Tolchin, known as "The Sourcing Lady." She's an author and columnist for *Inventors Digest* magazine. Although she's an expert in doing business in China, I was surprised to learn she's never been there.

Here are some highlights of our interview:

- *What's the best way to find out what products or services might appeal to the Chinese consumer?* One way is to try posting "goods for sale" on www.alibaba.com and see if there's any interest or demand specifically from China. Another way is to establish contacts with businesses in China to establish a demand. A third way is to plan a trip there, first as a tourist, to see what the Chinese people are buying over there.
- *Do you recommend going on a trade mission to China?* They *can* be good, but they're mostly "fluff." Some tour companies will take you to the typical tourist areas and then arrange visits to factories and businesses that pay the agency to bring travelers there. So then you

basically visit only the factories that the tour guides arrange to visit. The problem is this: you are often spending a few thousand dollars for a controlled itinerary without much flexibility to accomplish what you might want to (i.e., visiting with your own, previously established contacts).

- *Is there a lot of red tape and paperwork involved in doing business in China?* Yes, tons—there are import licenses and permits involved (importing into China), duties, and taxes, as well as customs issues. Documentation (shipping documents) must be "perfect" or shipments can get stuck for a long period of time, missing windows of opportunity.
- *How do you find a company or broker to help you navigate the waters?* You will need a freight forwarder. (Just to clarify: freight forwarders *export* and arrange shipments from one country *into* another. Customs brokers *import* shipments from a country that is *exporting* into the country that the customs broker is *importing* products to.)

Tolchin said to locate a reputable freight forwarder to assist you with arranging your shipments to China, contact the National Customs Brokers and Forwarders Association of America, Inc. at www.ncbfaa.org. You can contact Tolchin at EGT@warwick.net. Her web site is www.egtglobaltrading.com; office number: (845) 651-3107; mobile: (845) 321-2362.

GREAT
189
IDEA

Meet U.S. Safety Rules for Products Made Abroad

If you are ready to manufacture a product in China, be prepared for many challenges, including meeting stringent U.S. safety standards for consumer products.

In 2008, the Consumer Products Safety Commission supported the passage of the "Consumer Products Safety Improvement Act."

The act was drafted in response to scores of unsafe products flooding the United States. The government was overwhelmed by efforts to recall products that were dangerous, toxic, or posed a choking hazard to children.

"The number one mistake small business owners make is not getting their products evaluated for safety issues," said Edie Tolchin, an expert on manufacturing products in China. "Your product must be safe before you go into manufacturing."

Tolchin, who charges about $200 an hour, works with many small companies making consumer products in China, including Dipe-N-Go and Stretch Towel.

The first step is to familiarize yourself with the safety regulations, which are posted on the Consumer Products Safety Commission web site: www.cpsc.gov.

Then, look on the site for a list of accredited safety testing labs. You can send your prototype to the lab for a "product design evaluation." Based on the feedback, be prepared to make changes.

Tolchin said making sure your product is safe before you mass-produce it is critical to overseas manufacturing success.

GREAT
190
IDEA

Learn about a Culture before Going Abroad

Sometimes an international deal that makes perfect sense falls apart for no apparent reason. The numbers look good, but personalities clash or someone says something that sends the deal spinning out of control.

The problem may be caused by a breach of business etiquette, according to experts in protocol and negotiation.

"About 80 percent of all business owners going abroad fail to complete a deal because they don't do their homework," said Syndi Seid, founder of Advanced Etiquette, a training and consulting firm based in San Francisco.

Frank Acuff, author of several books on global business, agrees. "American culture focuses on the logical part of the deal, but in other cultures the relationship comes first," said Acuff.

Knowing how to act in a foreign business situation is critical to your success, he said, especially since many entrepreneurs are thinking globally for the first time.

Acuff said Americans are considered too open and direct by most foreigners. "We are not widely regarded for our business savvy in other parts of the world."

For example, Americans often complain that Japanese businesspeople do not look them in the eye. But the Japanese consider looking directly at someone to be a sign of disrespect, according to Acuff.

"Some countries, like China, have a strong need for harmony," he said. "So although a person may agree to do something, they may not comply with the terms of the agreement."

He said Americans are often frustrated when foreigners have a totally different concept of time. Americans, Germans, Swiss, and Australians tend to be prompt and expect meetings to begin on time. But Latin Americans, for instance, usually begin meetings a half-hour after the appointed time and can't understand why their American guests are so agitated.

Another common problem: Americans prefer to have about three feet of space around them. Yet Latin Americans and Middle Easterners often embrace their business associates, which can seem weird to many American men.

Learn as much as you can about a country before you book your plane ticket. You'll save money and time by being a savvy traveler.

Here are some tips:

- Before visiting a foreign country, talk to people who have done business there. Listen to their experiences and learn from them.
- Meet with people from the country you plan to visit. Ask them what they like and don't like about doing business with Americans.
- Do your homework. Learn as much as you can about the culture and customs of the country you are planning to visit.

GREAT
191 Translate Your Marketing Materials
IDEA

In the 1970s, Chevrolet made a legendary cultural faux pas when it decided to market the Chevy Nova in Mexico. The family car was a big hit in the United States, but the Mexican advertising campaign was a joke. "No va" in Spanish means "no go." Who wants to buy a car that doesn't go anywhere?

Another famous goof involved a soft drink company that used a photograph of a Japanese family dressed in white clothes enjoying a picnic. The ads were beautiful, but the campaign backfired. White is the color of mourning in Japan, so a happy family drinking soda was offensive.

If you are going to spend thousands on marketing materials, spend some more up front to make sure you are saying just the right thing. You should avoid using slang at any cost.

It's easier than you think to find people who are fluent speakers in whatever language you need. You can hire university graduate students or professional translators. Most translators charge by the project, and their fees are negotiable.

Contact the consulate of that country and ask if they can recommend a native speaker who does freelance work. Advertising agencies and marketing consultants who specialize in target marketing rely on a stable of skilled linguists on call.

Above all, be sure to do your homework and learn everything possible about the culture; you don't want to end up offending the people you are trying to attract.

GREAT
192
IDEA

Abide by the Etiquette of International Trade

Advanced Etiquette founder, Syndi Seid, teaches people how to work abroad without embarrassing themselves. One of her greatest ideas is to get to know foreign visitors to the United States by contacting the U.S. Agency for International Development and signing up to host visitors to your city.

Here are some other great ideas from Seid:

- *Avoid calendar confusion.* One of the most confusing things about dealing with foreign businesspeople is the way they note the date. In many foreign countries, the norm is to put the day, month, and year, rather than follow the U.S. custom of writing the month, day, and year. One good way to avoid confusion is to write a date like this: 5 February 2012. This can save you the grief of a missed appointment or conference session.

- *Always bring gifts.* Many foreigners will expect you to present them with a gift before any real business can be done. "Consider the person's heritage, religion, and culture before choosing a gift," advises Seid. For instance, items made of cowhide are verboten in India because cows are considered sacred. Never give a Chinese person a clock, because if it stops, it's considered bad luck. Mexicans are offended by letter openers or sharp objects. So what is the best universal gift? Chocolate! If it's too hot to bring chocolate, try a well-crafted business accessory such as a business card case.

- *Don't wrap your gifts.* You will probably be asked to open them by customs officials. "Take paper and simple ribbon along to wrap it after you arrive," Seid advises.

- *Treat shopkeepers with respect.* Always acknowledge the person standing behind the counter when you visit a shop. "Americans have often been criticized for being rude because we don't say anything to the clerk or cashier," said Seid. "Most small stores throughout the world are owned by husbands and wives and often staffed by family members. It is customary for visitors to greet the shopkeeper when entering the store and say goodbye, even if you don't buy anything." Visit AdvancedEtiquette.com for more information and to register for Seid's workshops and seminars.

Great Ideas and Insights from VIPs

10

Herb Kelleher—Be a Maverick

Herb Kelleher, his friend Rollin King, and banker John Parker, sketched out the concept for Southwest Airlines on a cocktail napkin while sitting in a bar.

The notion was simple: transport passengers to destinations on time, charge the lowest possible fares, and make darn sure they have a good time. If you've ever flown Southwest, you know that's what it's all about.

When I met Kelleher, he told me he always admired the way the now-defunct Pacific Southwest Airlines pioneered cheap, short-haul service throughout California. But trying to start a similar airline in Texas generated a firestorm of industry opposition and a tangle of red tape.

Undeterred, they kept pushing. Finally, after much wrangling, the Texas Aeronautics Commission approved Southwest's plan to fly between three cities in 1968. The next day, competing airlines went to court and obtained a temporary restraining order against Southwest. It took three years to clear up the legal mess, but Southwest finally took off.

Service began June 18, 1971, and in 2010, the airline known for having fun-loving flight attendants, continued expanding by announcing the pending acquisition of AirTran.

"Our people were perfectly aware that our company could cease to exist at any given time," Kelleher told me when we met for an interview at Bloomberg TV. "In that kind of environment, you come together as a band of warriors."

Customers still rave about the magic formula based on frequent, cheap, no-frills service. Southwest Airlines flies over 100 million passengers a year to 66 cities across the country, taking to the air more than 3,200 times a day. Southwest also has one of the youngest fleets in the nation, with 500 jets. To reduce maintenance costs, it only buys 737s.

Not all the planes are khaki and orange. The fleet features three flying killer whales, known as the "Shamu" aircraft. *Lone Star One,* painted like the Texas flag, marks Southwest's 20th anniversary. Southwest also flies *Arizona One, California One,* and *Silver One,* the 25th anniversary plane. The company's *Triple Crown One* celebrated winning five consecutive Triple Crown travel industry awards.

Since 1987, when the Department of Transportation began tracking customer satisfaction statistics, Southwest has consistently led the entire airline industry with the lowest ratio of complaints per passengers boarded. (I was impressed when after a harrowing, post-blizzard trip across the country, Southwest offered to FedEx our daughter's lost suitcase to her next stop. Unfortunately, that wasn't an option since her bag contained all our holiday gifts. Jeanne spoke with a supervisor who agreed to send a courier to deliver the bag from Boston's Logan Airport to our home in rural Vermont.)

In a cyclical and often depressed industry, Southwest has been profitable more than 30 years in a row. By having passengers line up in groups to board, but not assigning seats, ground crews can turn around a flight in 20 minutes or less. Southwest now offers early boarding for an additional fee. Whenever possible, the crew opens both the front and back doors to get people on and off faster. They also save money by serving peanuts or pretzels and a limited selection of beverages.

Today, Southwest Airlines is still considered to be one of the best companies to work for in America. It pays to be a maverick.

Lynn Tilton—Be a Modern Industrialist

Lynn Tilton describes herself as a modern industrialist. She's dedicated to reviving American manufacturing companies that have fallen on hard times. She also claims to be a mystic who believes she has been called on to change the world.

"When I started this business, I wanted to prove making money and making the world a better place were not mutually exclusive," said Tilton, a striking woman with platinum blonde hair and a penchant for wearing short skirts and stiletto heels.

In the past five years, Tilton's Manhattan-based Patriarch Partners has acquired about 75 companies, including Stila Cosmetics, an Arizona helicopter company, Rand McNally, Snelling Staffing, and Natura Water.

Tilton told me she believes "joblessness is a plague" upon America.

"My mandate is to make the companies I buy competitive again," she said. "I believe with every cell of my being that we must be an industrial economy. We have to look in the mirror and realize that outsourcing all our manufacturing will leave us permanently unemployed."

A graduate of Yale and Columbia, she started her career in high-stakes banking, developing proprietary methods to package and resell jumbo loans. "At one point, I ended up with $2.5 billion worth of loans made to small, distressed companies," she explained. Instead of repackaging and reselling the loans, she decided to "raise private equity to buy out the other investors."

Tilton is outspoken and passionate about reviving "beaten-down American brands." One of her biggest success stories involves the revival of Old Town Fuel and Fiber in Old Town, Maine. The company makes jet fuel from wood and now employs 250.

Unlike many investors, Tilton prefers to be hands-on. She said she evaluates the management team as soon as she closes the deal. It takes her about 90 days to determine who will stay and who will go. In most cases the CEO is let go. "The current management tends to hold on too tight to what was done in the past," she said.

So that means she replaces the CEOs and assigns someone on her team to supervise daily operations during the turnaround. The secret of her success relies on new strategies. "The biggest driver of success is talent," said Tilton. "You are only as good as the people around you."

She also believes "you absolutely cannot fix what you cannot face."

"When you buy a broken company, you are in the abyss, in the darkness," Tilton explained. "You need to create the force that levitates you from the dark abyss into the light."

As you can imagine, it takes an enormous amount of work to turn about troubled companies. Her schedule is so demanding, her assistants have to work in shifts. Most days, she begins with a workout in one of her four homes. Tilton owns homes in southern New Jersey, South Florida, Arizona, and Lake Como, Italy. She has a home in Italy to be close to her Italian company, a 156-year-old maker of large industrial motors and equipment. It has about 1,500 employees in Italy, France, and Germany.

When she's working to improve operations, she studies mystical teachings. "I come from a long line of mystics and scholars," said Tilton, who has studied with Mayan Indians, among other spiritual leaders.

So what is her personal recipe for entrepreneurial success?

"It's a confluence of cash and creativity," she told me. "Companies die because they lack innovation."

GREAT IDEA 195 Mike Bloomberg—Keep It Simple

Michael Bloomberg is a plain-spoken genius whose success inspires all entrepreneurs. He personifies the American dream. He grew up in a middle-class family in Massachusetts. He is very close to his mother and a devoted father to two grown daughters.

Bloomberg left a Wall Street job to start a technology business, and became a billionaire. Oh, did I forget to mention he's also served three terms as mayor of New York City, making big improvements in education and the quality of life in the city?

A very smart man, Bloomberg developed pioneering back-office systems for a Wall Street brokerage. In 1981, Bloomberg left Salomon Brothers with about $10 million in hand. He used that money to start his own company, Bloomberg LP.

A few years later, Merrill Lynch invested millions to help Bloomberg develop what remains the premiere, proprietary information system for traders and serious investors. (Bloomberg bought back Merrill's stake a few years ago.) The Bloomberg terminal provides real-time and historical data on thousands of companies and subjects that matter most to professional traders, brokers, analysts, and investors.

It's also a cash machine: clients lease about 300,000 terminals for about $1,975 a month. (You can't buy a Bloomberg terminal.) Clients can also access Bloomberg data online.

I was working for Mike Bloomberg when he scoffed at predictions that all the free information available on the Internet would make the terminal obsolete. He was right and all those self-important analysts were *so* wrong.

Once focused exclusively on providing the most accurate and current financial and stock market data, the Bloomberg empire now boasts a global news service, radio and television networks, and the newest ventures, B-Law and B-Gov. Those services track and aggregate legal and government news.

Bloomberg also publishes glossy, high-profile magazines, including *Bloomberg Businessweek*, which it acquired from McGraw-Hill. (My talented son, Evan, is a graphic designer for *Bloomberg Businessweek*.)

I was disappointed when Mayor Bloomberg's media relations person said he was too busy to speak with me to update this chapter, but here's what he told me when we spoke a few years ago:

"Do something simple that you can really define," he said, twirling his reading glasses. "Sitting in your office, pondering momentous, abstract ideas doesn't always work."

I was lucky to have worked with Bloomberg during the start-up years of Bloomberg Television. Bloomberg was still very hands-on when I was hired as a producer and correspondent for Bloomberg's new small business TV program, *Bloomberg Small Business,* in 1996.

His desk was tucked into a corner of the newsroom. He had a tiny glass office, but preferred to sit at his desk. You could find him in the lobby, greeting guests before or after their interviews with reporters. His accessibility freaked people out. A very successful investment banker who stopped by to say hello to me almost choked on the carrot stick he was munching when Mike walked over and asked me to introduce him to my guest.

During our interview a few years ago, Bloomberg said it is important to share your dreams and "your game plan."

"I went out and said to someone, 'I'm going to do it,'" he told me. "Then, I did it."

I owe much of my success to Bloomberg. I had no experience in television when he hired me in a very crazy way. I was working with Avon on some small business marketing projects when I decided to write and produce a talk show, *The Power of Women in Business.* Avon agreed to pay the expenses to produce a pilot. We shot it at KPBS-TV, the public TV station in San Diego. Ron Stein, my wonderful ex-husband, directed and edited the show. Apart from my bouffant hairdo and dramatic makeup, the show looked pretty good.

The problem was I had no clue about how to sell a TV show. I made 100 VHS copies and sent Brooke, my marketing consultant, off to Las Vegas to attend a major TV programming convention. The problem was that he didn't know anyone at the convention. His plan was simple; he stopped at every booth, dropping off a copy. I was not happy to hear what he did, having paid for the trip to Vegas. I was sure nothing would happen.

A few weeks later, my phone rang. An assistant said Mike Bloomberg wanted to speak with me. Known for being direct, he said my show was terrible. So, I asked, why was he calling me? He said he needed a small business expert for a new small business show he had just sold to USA Networks. Was I interested in moving to New York City?

I had been hosting an advice segment called the "Mail Bag" for CNBC and been a guest on many shows, but I was not a trained broadcaster. Turns out my lack of experience didn't matter. In fact, it was an advantage. Always a contrarian, Bloomberg believed anyone with a brain could do television. In fact, in the early years, Bloomberg was known for hiring super-smart, but not especially glamorous or handsome reporters. Now, Bloomberg TV's on-air personalities are very attractive.

Being part of a scrappy new cable network was a kick. No one believed he could make it work. Everyone hated the original screen, which had all kinds of data in boxes around the talking head of the reporter. Uncertain about the future, I was reluctant to move my family from Los Angeles to New York.

Not a problem. The first year, I spent two weeks a month in New York City, producing four shows. Life was very sweet. I worked long hours but stayed in the swanky Regency Hotel on Park Avenue. Sixteen blizzards buried New York that first winter I worked at Bloomberg. Many weekends, I was happily stranded. (My colleagues were shocked that I relied on a 17-year-old nanny to keep an eye on my kids while I worked 3,000 miles away. But Joline was the most responsible babysitter we ever had and the kids turned out great.)

In 1996, Bloomberg was hiring so many people so fast, I sat on the floor and shared a desk and phone with my producer, Carla Ceasar for several months. When our friends stopped by, they thought we were crazy.

Today, Bloomberg is a global multimedia empire with about 12,000 employees. Need a Diet Coke? An espresso? Just hang out in the Bloomberg lobby and enjoy the hustle and bustle in the two well-stocked pantries. You never know who you'll meet or bump into. (Vanessa Redgrave was here the day I was in the office reviewing this manuscript.) The open structure is deliberate.

"Walls and titles act as barriers," said Bloomberg. No one at Bloomberg has a title. Open space is the rule. Conference rooms are glass-walled and employees work at long counters, elbow to elbow. There is no privacy or personal space.

Although it appears that the company took off like a rocket on day one, Bloomberg said it took years to build the business because "we didn't try to do everything at once."

Bloomberg is the most generous person I've ever met. In the 1990s, he gave $55 million to Johns Hopkins University to set up a school of public health. Bloomberg recently announced that he will join Bill Gates, Warren Buffett, and a bunch of other billionaires who have pledged to donate half of their fortunes to charity.

He always encouraged employees to donate to charity. He was always ready with a check to match his employees' charitable contributions. In addition to being a thrilling place to work, Bloomberg LP treats employees well. In exchange for working extremely long hours, the company provides extremely competitive salaries and amazing benefits.

When Bloomberg Press published the first edition of this book, the company hosted a lavish party. I still have a great photo of me with Mike at that party. He's wearing a tuxedo because he was on his way to another engagement. (John Wiley & Sons purchased the Bloomberg Press imprint in 2009.)

Here is Bloomberg's final bit of advice for you:

"You've got to sit back and do things carefully," advised Bloomberg. "You can't jump to the endgame."

GREAT

196

IDEA

Tom Peters—Forget Credentials

Tom Peters is a best-selling author, high-level consultant, entrepreneur, keynote speaker, and fellow Vermonter. His wife, Susan Sargent, owns a textile and bedding company based in Pawlett, Vermont.

Before starting the Tom Peters Group, which he sold in 1997, Peters worked for McKinsey & Company, a management consulting firm, where he eventually became a partner.

Peters admired Japanese companies and adopted many management strategies from many them. A popular keynote speaker, he shared two great ideas for small business owners with me.

1. *Focus on a creative brand design.* "Produce first-class marketing materials for your company," he said. "Find an innovative, young design team on day one to create a Starbucks/Nike kind of feel for the enterprise."

   Peters said you should then add your cool logo to "everything from the web site to your business cards." Although graphics and printing are costly, "spend the money whether you are running a 12-table restaurant, a 3-person company, or anything in between."

2. *Look beyond credentials.* "Great businesspeople love hanging around great people," said Peters. "When you are building your team, my advice is, 'forget the certificates.'"

   When he and Susan wanted to hire their first administrator for the textile company, Peters said he took advice from Apple Computer founder Steve Jobs. "Jobs said, 'this is a company that from day one intends on being insanely great. So, if you're not insanely great—don't even think about applying.'"

   "Well," Peters said with a smile, "that approach may attract some flakes you wouldn't touch with a 20-meter pole—on the other hand, it was great to see the responses from all over the map."

Peters shared one last thought: "You gotta be damn good at something. Your 'it' has to be fabulously special."

Kay Koplovitz—Leverage a New Technology

Kay Koplovitz is the first woman to start a cable television network. She's also a venture capitalist who cofounded Springboard Enterprises, an organization devoted to preparing women business owners to raise venture capital. She also serves as chairman of the board of Liz Claiborne Inc.

Koplovitz told me her greatest idea came to her during a lecture at the London School of Economics. "I went to a lecture on geo-synchronous orbiting satellites," recalled Koplovitz. "I learned that satellites provided a way of communicating anywhere on earth. No one could jam or stop those signals. This information was so moving and so powerful I decided to do something with it."

In 1968, she wrote a master's thesis on how satellites were changing the communications culture. That thesis formed the foundation for the business plan for USA Networks. She had to wait until 1975, when the federal government approved the use of satellites for commercial broadcast, to start raising money.

In 1977, USA Networks finally launched, pioneering a new model based on two income streams—advertising revenues and licensing fees paid by cable operators and viewers.

"Cable television generates enormous fees, but now there are major challenges since consumers are accessing so much content via broadband," said Koplovitz. "Cable networks are trying to maintain their revenue streams . . . but (the Internet) is posing a real threat to their business."

Her second great idea was founding Springboard Enterprises. "It's still necessary to make an effort to get women into the marketplace," said Koplovitz. "Ninety-five percent of venture capitalists are men. Their networks are still skewed toward their buddies, the people they play sports or golf with."

Although raising venture capital "is still a testosterone-laden business," Koplovitz said there are still some "very bright and successful women venture capitalists, including Ann Winblad."

Springboard is a nonprofit group that provides coaching and organizes "boot camps" aimed at helping businesswomen polish their business plans and prepare their pitches before meeting with potential investors. "This is not a social experiment," she said. "Their goal is to raise and make money."

Koplovitz has been advocating for women in business for many years. During his tenure, President Clinton appointed her to chair the National Women's Business Council. "When President Clinton asked me to do it, I said I would if I had the freedom to help women get access to significant amounts of venture capital. At the time, only 1.7 percent of venture money was going to women." (It's still less than 5 percent.)

"Springboard's track record is really quite spectacular," said Koplovitz. "So far, 450 companies have raised more than $5 billion. A third of those companies have positive liquidity. This is remarkable for anybody—not just for women."

Koplovitz is busy with her board positions, investments, and Springboard. I asked what she did to relax.

"I'm an altitude hiker," said Koplovitz. "I'm also into whitewater rafting. We've spent many years visiting cities and museums. Now, if I want to get away, I like to get out in the wilderness. The idea is not to be connected. It's good for the soul."

GREAT
198
IDEA

Wally Amos—Reinvent Yourself

On March 10, 1975, at a storefront located at 7181 Sunset Boulevard in Hollywood, Wally Amos, show-biz talent manager, became Famous Amos, the "Cookie Man."

Using his Aunt Della's chocolate chip cookie recipe, Amos began baking and selling deluxe cookies for the unheard-of price of $3 a pound. Celebrities and locals alike lined up to buy Famous Amos cookies. Sales skyrocketed. Media attention drove sales as he increased production to keep up with demand.

But the initial success wasn't enough to keep the company in Amos's hands. Looking back, Amos sees clearly why, 10 years later, he lost control of the company.

"I was irresponsible about the management," he said. "I really wasn't focused on the core business. I was doing audiocassette tapes, television shows, and I was focused on getting into a movie," he admitted.

After four management changes between 1985 and 1988, his original cookie venture was eventually acquired by an investor-backed conglomerate. The *Famous Amos* brand is still around. In fact, the hunky, romantic lead in *Burlesque*, starring Cher and Christina Aguilera, holds a box of *Famous Amos* cookies in front of his private parts during a funny seduction scene.

After Amos sold the company, the new owners filed suit to keep him out of the cookie business. He fought back in court, eventually winning the right to use his name for other ventures, including a line of dolls named "Chip" and "Cookie." In 1993, he started Uncle No Name's bakery.

Amos and his partner, Lou Avignone, now bake "Uncle Wally's" muffins. The company, based in Shirley, New York, sells small-portioned, fat-free and sugar-free muffins.

"Now, I'm the muffin man," Amos told me. "I didn't plan it. Circumstances created it. And you have to go with what works.... I believe if you have an idea and focus on achieving your goal, your whole energy is focused on doing it, and ideas just come to you."

He told me his management team runs the business while he focuses on marketing and promotion.

"You never know what the hell is going to happen. Life is unpredictable, yet we spend much of our time trying to predict it. I have no regrets. I'm still feeling good. And, for Uncle Wally's, the future looks fantastic."

GREAT 199 IDEA Lillian Vernon—Advice from the Mail-Order Queen

When I interviewed Lillian Vernon about 15 years ago, I thought, "I hope I have as much energy and look as great as she does when I'm older!"

Like many small business owners, Vernon started her business on her kitchen table. It was in the early 1950s. She was pregnant and needed to earn money, but working outside the home was frowned upon. Since her father was in the leather business, she thought she might make money by selling fashion accessories.

Using some money she received as a wedding gift, Vernon placed a $495 ad in the September 1951 issue of *Seventeen* magazine: "Be the first to sport that personalized look on your bag and belt," read the copy, touting a $2.99 leather purse and $1.99 belt. That ad attracted $32,000 worth of orders—an enormous amount of money at the time.

"I make quick decisions based on my golden gut," said Vernon, who named her firm after Mount Vernon, the New York City suburb where she lived. Later in life, she legally changed her from Lillian Hochberg to Lillian Vernon.

In several interviews, the feisty entrepreneur told me how, despite a lack of formal business training, she turned $2,000 in wedding money into a successful mail-order business serving more than 20 million customers. "To this day, I don't know how to read a financial statement," she admits. "I still need help with the numbers."

When mail order companies went online, Vernon's sales company suffered and the company filed for bankruptcy. A group of investors eventually rescued the company and the Vernon brand remains strong. The company's sweet spot is still kids' clothes, toys, and all sorts of kid-friendly merchandise that can be personalized.

Vendors submit thousands of products for consideration every year, but Vernon's biggest hits have been the things she dreams up.

One year, for instance, Vernon received 120,000 orders for the Battenburg lace Christmas tree angel she designed. Not bad for a Jewish woman whose family fled their comfortable life in Leipzig, Germany, after the Nazis chased them out of their home in 1933. Vernon's amazing rags-to-riches story is detailed in her autobiography, *An Eye for Winners* (Harper Business, 1997). Vernon's book mixes intimate and painful details of her life story with practical business advice.

Known for her sharp wit and strong support of Democratic politics, Vernon, now in her 80s, told me she always tried to hire professional managers to complement her entrepreneurial style. "At one point, I surrounded myself with experienced veterans of large corporate cultures," she said. "Unfortunately, they almost killed us—they took analysis to the point of paralysis."

Vernon shared this advice: "Risk your own money, trust your creative instincts, and find someone who can execute your vision."

Charles Shackleton—Follow Your Passion

Charles Shackleton attended a prestigious art school in England and was happy to land a job as a glassblower with Simon Pearce. Pearce is a well-known glass artist who runs an iconic studio, showroom, and restaurant on a river in Quechee, Vermont.

"I was making 120 wine glasses a day and I was bored," said Shackleton. Not sure what to do next, he started making furniture, using hardwoods and traditional woodworking techniques.

He realized that his passion was for working in wood, not glass. But in 1998, he was reluctant to tell Pearce, his friend and mentor, that he didn't want to make glass objects anymore. "He thought I was crazy," recalled Shackleton. "In fact, his wife took me out to lunch and encouraged me to stay on."

Undeterred, Shackleton decided to take the leap. Pearce ended up commissioning the second bed Shackleton made and they remain friends.

"The trickiest thing was redefining ourselves after we went away from Simon Pearce," said Shackleton. His wife, Miranda Thomas, is a renowned potter, hence the company name: Shackleton Thomas.

It hasn't been easy, but following his passion paid off. Today, Shackleton Thomas, produces high-end, handmade furniture and pottery. Shackleton's 20 employees start with simple projects like bowls and spoons and work their way up to making bed frames, bureaus, and dining room sets. Clients are invited to visit the workshop, which is located in an old mill in Bridgewater, Vermont. Watching the woodworkers work encourages clients to order a $30,000 dining room or bedroom set and pay $8,000 for a dining room table.

Demand for high-end furniture slumped during the recession. When sales were soft, Shackleton said he had to lay off a few employees and reduce everyone's hours to 30 a week. Sales were about $1.5 million in 2010.

His biggest challenge is spending so much time on each piece, while keeping it somewhat affordable. "We are artists and businesspeople at the same time."

Set Your Ego Aside and Ask for Help

People often ask me to pick one favorite great idea. I guess if I had to pick just one, it would be this: set your ego aside and ask for help. The smartest businesspeople I've met through the years are very good about admitting they don't know everything.

They surround themselves with people who complement their strengths. They acknowledge their weaknesses and focus on doing what they do best.

Entrepreneurs need a strong ego and the confidence to push forward through adversity. But the most successful business owners never let their ego get in the way of achieving their goals.

Admit you don't know everything and reach out for answers. I believe more businesses fail due to a lack of information than a lack of money. There's no excuse not to get the information you need to succeed.

Conclusion

I f you've read all the way to the end of my book, thanks so much. I hope you found some great ideas to solve problems or just to cheer you up when you are having a bad day. Perhaps some of these ideas inspired you to come up with a few great ideas of your own.

Revising the book was an adventure. I was asked to update about 60 of the 201 ideas, but once I got going, I realized every idea needed to be refreshed or updated. That's why there are dozens of new ideas related to technology. Twitter, Facebook, LinkedIn, Bing, and Groupon.com weren't around when I last updated this book.

In exchange for all these great ideas, I'd like to ask you a favor. If you have a great idea that has helped you boost profits or solve a problem, please send it to me! I'll do my best to share it on the 201GreatIdeas.com web site and in my other columns and blogs.

I want to thank all the business owners and experts who graciously agreed to be interviewed for this third edition. I truly appreciate your time and your candor. I also want to thank my husband, Joe, for being so supportive and patient. It's not easy living with a busy writer, especially one who does quite a bit of reporting over the phone. Thanks, too, to Mavis Carr, my wonderful research assistant.

During the past few weeks as my deadline approached, I thought I should have written a book titled *Two Great Ideas for Your Small Business*. Marry a rich person and use their money to do what you love.

Of course, I'm kidding. I'm heading back on the road, and looking forward to meeting and interviewing more wonderful entrepreneurs just like you. We'll also be shooting video interviews with business owners at many of my speaking events, so comb your hair, put on your lipstick, and be ready to share a great idea or two with me and my crew.

Please keep in touch. I welcome your comments.

My e-mail is jane@theapplegategroup.com.

I'm also reachable via LinkedIn, on my Facebook fan page, and @janewapplegate on Twitter.

Resources

● ●

U.S. Government Help

Note: This resource list is current as of February, 2011.

The U.S. Small Business Administration (SBA) is the agency designated to help business owners. The site offers detailed information about applying for an SBA-backed loan, free counseling services (online and in person), low-cost seminars and workshops, and so on.

www.sba.gov

Look for a nearby Small Business Development Center (SBDC). The centers coordinate all sorts of federal, state, local, university, and private resources for small business owners. There is an SBDC in every major city in the United States. You can find the telephone number of the SBDC nearest you by visiting the SBA site or calling the SBA's toll-free number (800) U-ASK-SBA.

Service Corps of Retired Executives (SCORE)

National SCORE Office
409 3rd Street SW, 6th floor
Washington, DC 20024
(800) 634-0245
www.score.org

In addition to free one-on-one counseling by retired business executives, SCORE offers a variety of free publications, low-cost seminars, and workbooks.

● ●

Regional Government Agencies

Every state has a primary agency or office devoted to helping business owners at the state level. Check your state's web site for the details. Following are listings for some of the biggest states.

California Trade and Commerce Agency

980 9th Street, Suite 2450
Sacramento, California 95814
Phone: (916) 323-5400
Fax: (916) 323-5440

New York Department of Economic Development
Business Assistance Hotline

633 3rd Street
New York, NY 10017
(800) 782-8369

Office of the Governor, Economic Development and Tourism

1700 North Congress Avenue
Austin, TX 78711
(512) 936-0100

Federal Government Resources

Information about the Americans with Disabilities Act

www.ada.gov

U.S. Business Advisor program

www.business.gov

Web site with links to government business resources.

E-Verify

(888) 464-4218
www.dhs.gov/E-Verify

Online way to verify citizenship for new employees.

Federal Marketplace

www.fedmarket.com

This site provides information for companies interested in selling products and services to the U.S. government.

U.S. Copyright Office

U.S. Library of Congress
101 Independence Avenue SE
Washington, DC 20559-6000
(202) 707-3000 (information)
www.copyright.gov

The U.S. Patent and Trademark Office

P.O. Box 1450
Alexandria, VA 22313-1450
(800) 786-9199
www.uspto.gov

Internal Revenue Service

File form SS-4 to obtain an employer identification number (EIN) when you form a new business. For information, call (800) 829-1040. The IRS has audio and video clips on a variety of small business topics at www.irs.gov/businesses.

Social Security Administration

For information about payroll taxes:
(800) 772-1213
www.ssa.gov

Department of Commerce

1401 Constitution Avenue NW
Washington, DC 20230
(202) 482-2000
www.commerce.gov

National Institute of Standards and Technology (NIST)

100 Bureau Drive
Gaithersburg, MD 20899
(301) 975-2000
www.nist.gov

U.S. Export Assistance Center (USEAC)

A partnership between the SBA, Department of Commerce, and U.S. Export-Import Bank aimed at helping small companies serve the global market.

www.sba.gov/aboutsba/sbaprograms/internationaltrade/useac/index
.html

The SBA has several loan programs to help companies that import and export. The SBA also offers surety bonds for companies needing a bond to compete for government contracts. For information on the Surety Bond Guarantee Program, visit www.sba.gov/osg.

U.S. Department of Agriculture

1400 Independence Avenue SW
Washington, DC 20250
(202) 720-2791

U.S. Chamber of Commerce

1615 H Street NW
Washington, DC 20062
(202) 659-6000
www.uschamber.org

The national headquarters provides materials geared specifically for small business.

Equal Opportunity Employment Commission (EEOC)

1400 L Street NW, Suite 200
Washington, DC 20507
(800) 669-EEOC (Publications)

Export/Trade Resources

OIT (Office of International Trade)

www.sba.gov/oit

The agency offers export-related guaranteed loans.

International Trade Administration (ITA)

(800) 872-8723

Speak to a trade specialist to discuss export opportunities and get advice; they also publish industry reports, distributor lists, country market reports, and more.

Export/Import Bank (EXIMBANK)

811 Vermont Avenue NW
Washington, DC 20571
(202) 565-3200

This agency provides export financing to large and small businesses and exporters who have had difficulty obtaining loans from commercial lenders.

Family Business

The Family Firm Institute, Inc.

200 Lincoln Street, #201
Boston, MA 02111
(617) 482-3045
www.ffi.org

Offers a variety of resources including a directory of professionals who offer services to family businesses.

The Family Business Institute

4700 Homewood Court, Suite 340
Raleigh, NC 27609
(877) 326-2493
www.familybusinessinstitute.com

A for-profit organization specializing in family business issues.

Franchising

International Franchise Association

1501 K Street NW, Suite 350
Washington, DC 20005
202-628-8000
ifa@franchise.org

www.franchise.org

News and resources for members who own or sell franchises.

Financing Information and Resources

Small Business Investment Companies (SBICs)

SBICs are privately capitalized, owned, and managed investment firms licensed by the SBA that provide equity capital, long-term financing, and management assistance to small business. Contact your nearest SBA office.

National Association of Small Business Investment Companies

Brett Palmer, President
1100 H Street NW, Suite 610
Washington, DC 20005
bpalmer@nasbic.org
(202) 628-5055
www.nasbic.org

National Venture Capital Association

1655 North Fort Myer Drive, Suite 850
Arlington, VA 22209
(703) 524-2549
www.nvca.org

A membership organization for venture capital firms. NVCA.org provides information about the industry and how to find a member.

Minority Business Resources

Office of Minority Enterprise Development (MED) SBA

409 3rd Street SW, Suite 8000
Washington, DC 20416
(202) 205-6410

Helps foster business ownership by individuals who are socially and economically disadvantaged. The SBA has combined its efforts with those of private industry, banks, local communities, and other government agencies to meet that goal.

Minority Business Development Agency (MBDA)

U.S. Department of Commerce
1401 Constitution Avenue, N.W.
Washington, DC 20230
(888) 324-1551

Management and technical assistance provided to businesses primarily through a network of local Minority Business Development Centers.

National Minority Supplier Development Council (NMSDC)

1359 Broadway, 10th floor
New York, NY 10018
(212) 944-2430

Organization provides information about how to become certified as a minority contractor. NMSDC has matched more than 15,000 minority-owned businesses with member corporations that seek to purchase their goods and services.

National Association of Minority Contractors (NAMC)

The Ronald Reagan House Office Building
Suite 700
1300 Pennsylvania Avenue, N.W.
Washington, DC 20004
(202) 204-3093

A trade association formed in 1969 to address the needs of minority contractors worldwide.

U.S. Hispanic Chamber of Commerce

1019 19th Street NW, Suite 200
Washington, DC 20036
(800) USHCC86

Represents the interests of more than 400,000 Hispanic-owned businesses. Its annual convention combines a trade fair, business sections, and workshops designed to promote business opportunities.

Advocacy Groups

National Federation of Independent Businesses (NFIB)

1201 F Street NW, Suite 200
Washington, DC 20004
(800) 634-2669
www.nfib.com

Nation's largest small business advocacy group; represents more than 650,000 small and independent businesses before legislatures and government agencies at the federal and state level.

National Retail Federation

325 7th Street NW, Suite 1000
Washington, DC 20004
(202) 783-7971

Direct Marketing Association

1120 Avenue of the Americas
New York, NY
(212) 768-7277

Retail Industry Leaders Association

1700 North Moore Street, Suite 2250
Arlington, VA 22209
(703) 841-2300
www.rila.org

National Association of Wholesaler-Distributors

1325 G Street NW, Suite 1000
Washington, DC 20005
www.nawpubs.org

National Business Incubation Association

20 E. Circle Drive, Suite 37198
Athens, OH 45701
(740) 593-4331
www.nbia.org

Provides a comprehensive listing of incubator programs.

National Restaurant Association

1200 17th Street NW
Washington, DC 20036
(202) 331-5900
www.restaurant.org

Promotional Products Association International (PPAI)

3125 Skyway Circle North
Irving, TX 75038
(888) I-AM-PPAI (888-426-7724)
www.ppa.org

Women's Business Organizations

SBA Women's Office

www.sbaonline.sba.gov/womeninbusiness

An office of the SBA that advocates the ownership and success of women-owned businesses. Provides information and special assistance programs.

Ladies Who Launch

www.ladieswholaunch.com

A national membership organization for more than 100,000 women entrepreneurs, from start-ups to veterans. Offers networking, resources, local chapters, and special events. LWL is a national sponsor of my *201 Great Ideas* book promotion tour.

National Association of Women Business Owners (NAWBO)

601 Pennsylvania Avenue NW
South Building, Suite 900
Washington, DC 20004
(800) 55-NAWBO (800-556-2926)
www.nawbo.org

Membership-based federation with local chapters. NAWBO helps women-owned businesses to expand operations and represents women's business interests to federal and state governments.

Women Presidents' Organization

155 E. 55th Street, Suite 4H
New York, NY 10022
(212) 688-4114
www.womenpresidentsorg.com

International membership organization for women with annual revenues in excess of $1 million. Chapters in the United States, Canada, and abroad.

Women Impacting Public Policy (WIPP)

1714 Stockton St. #200
San Francisco, CA 94133
(415) 434-4314
www.wipp.org

National membership organization for women interested in politics and policy making.

Center for Women's Business Research

1760 Old Meadow Road, Suite 500
McLean, VA 22102
(703) 556-7162
info@womensbusinessresearch.org
www.womensbusinessresearch.org

Women's Business Enterprise National Council

1120 Connecticut Avenue NW, Suite 1000
Washington, DC 20036
(202) 872-5515
www.wbenc.org

Organization offering third-party certification for women business owners who want to do business with 240 major corporations that have supplier diversity programs.

U.S. Department of Labor

Women's Bureau
200 Constitution Avenue NW, Room S-3002
Washington, DC 20210
(800) 827-5335
www.dol.gov/wb

The bureau researches and promotes policies to improve working conditions for women. A good source of information about issues relating to sexual harassment, medical/family leave, pregnancy, and discrimination.

Other Associations

National Association for the Self-Employed

P.O. Box 241
Annapolis Junction, MD 20701-0241
(800) 649-6273
www.nase.org

Offers health plans and business resources and information for members.

Network for Teaching Entrepreneurship (NFTE)

www.nfte.com

Provides training for low-income students.

Other Resources

Entrepreneur

www.entrepreneurmag.com

Inc. magazine

www.inc.com

Black Enterprise magazine

www.blackenterprise.com

Bloomberg Businessweek

www.businessweek.com

201 Great Ideas web site

www.201greatideas.com

Small Biz Daily

www.SmallBizDaily.com

Blogs

Check out blogs written by Seth Godin, Guy Kawasaki, and Mari Smith.

For fitness tips, subscribe to the *Morning Stretch,* a daily e-newsletter by Denise Austin, my favorite fitness guru.

Recommended Reading List

Here are some of my favorite books in no particular order:

Cliff Ennico, *The eBay Sellers Tax and Legal Answer Book* (Amacom, 2007). Ennico has written a series of eBay books that are all great.

Seth Godin, *Purple Cow* (Portfolio, 2003), or any other marketing book by Godin.

Guy Kawasaki, *Enchanted, The Art of Changing Hearts, Minds and Actions* (Portfolio, 2011).

Jason Fried and David Hansson, *Rework* (Crown Business, 2010).

John Townsend, *Handling Difficult People* (Integrity House, 2006)

Larry Selden and Geoffrey Colvin, *Angel Customers & Demon Customers* (Portfolio, 2003).

Geshe Michael Roach and Lama Christie McNally, *The Diamond Cutter: The Buddha on Managing Your Business and Your Life* (Doubleday, 2009).

Tony Hsieh, *Delivering Happiness, A Path to Profits, Passion and Purpose* (Business Plus, 2010).

Sam Horn, *Pop!: Create the Perfect Pitch, Title and Tagline for Anything,* (Penguin, 2009).

Danny Meyer, *Setting the Table: The Transforming Power of Hospitality in Business* (Harper, 2008).

Bruce Alan Johnson and R. William Ayres, *Carry a Chicken in Your Lap or Whatever It Takes to Globalize Your Business* (St. Martin's Press, 2009).

About the Author

Jane Applegate is one of America's most respected business journalists. She is an award-winning writer and producer. Her previous books are: *Succeeding in Small Business: The 101 Toughest Problems and How to Solve Them, Jane Applegate's Strategies for Small Business Success,* and *The Entrepreneur's Desk Reference.*

Applegate is the leading small-business speaker for Bloomberg Television's Idea Exchange speakers' program. The Applegate Group Inc., founded in 1991, is a multimedia communications and production company. TAG produces independent films, documentaries, and promotional videos. In 2009, she produced *Much Ado in Mostar,* a documentary about a summer theater program for teenagers affected by war. In 2010, she served as the line producer on *Brief Reunion,* a psychological thriller written and directed by John Daschbach.

A former syndicated columnist for the *Los Angeles Times,* Applegate also consults with a select group of corporations dedicated to providing better products and services to business owners. Clients include Cox Communications, Bloomberg LP, and Montecito Bank & Trust.

Applegate is happily married to Joe Applegate, an editor who repairs and installs news articles at the *Valley News* in West Lebanon, New Hampshire. He also contributes to the feature section and has had three short plays produced. They have two wonderful and talented kids, Jeanne and Evan, who do not live with them in Sharon, Vermont.

Index